IS THE
CEMETERY
DEAD?

IS THE CEMETERY DEAD?

——

David Charles Sloane

The University of Chicago Press
Chicago and London

The University of Chicago Press, Chicago 60637
The University of Chicago Press, Ltd., London
© 2018 by The University of Chicago
All rights reserved. No part of this book may be used or reproduced in
any manner whatsoever without written permission, except in the case
of brief quotations in critical articles and reviews. For more information,
contact the University of Chicago Press, 1427 E. 60th St., Chicago, IL
60637.
Published 2018
Printed in the United States of America

27 26 25 24 23 22 21 20 19 18   1 2 3 4 5

ISBN-13: 978-0-226-53944-7 (cloth)
ISBN-13: 978-0-226-53958-4 (e-book)
DOI: https://doi.org/10.7208/chicago/9780226539584.001.0001

Library of Congress Cataloging-in-Publication Data
Names: Sloane, David Charles, author.
Title: Is the cemetery dead? / David Charles Sloane.
Description: Chicago ; London : The University of Chicago Press, 2018. |
Includes bibliographical references and index.
Identifiers: LCCN 2017037680 | ISBN 9780226539447 (cloth : alk. paper) |
ISBN 9780226539584 (e-book)
Subjects: LCSH: Cemeteries—United States. | Funeral rites and
ceremonies—United States.
Classification: LCC GT3203 .S56 2018 | DDC 393.0975—dc23
LC record available at https://lccn.loc.gov/2017037680

♾ This paper meets the requirements of ANSI/NISO Z39.48–1992
(Permanence of Paper).

To Beverlie Conant Sloane
Sweet dreams, Love always

To Anne Bray
Thanks for going walking

Sloane family on Easter morning, Syracuse, NY, spring 1959 (photograph by Greg Sloane). Most people would never consider taking a holiday photograph in front of a cemetery gate. Not my family. My dad was the cemetery superintendent. I am standing in front of my mom, with brother Larry to my father's left, while oldest brother, Greg, is behind the camera.

CONTENTS

Illustration note: All photographs not credited
to a source are by the author.

DECISIONS

Death is always with us. Yet for most of us, death became a distant presence during the twentieth century. People lived longer on average. Many fewer infants died.[1] The dead were isolated from the living. We professionalized the care of the dying in hospitals and of the dead in funeral homes and cemeteries. Not surprisingly, perhaps, we developed an aversion to discussing death. We carefully managed our emotions about death, and our ways of speaking about it. We developed a "death taboo."[2] We said less about death in public, and in private we shielded family and friends from it, to the extent we ever could.

Today, that taboo is weakening, as we undergo a revival of death.[3] A person is more likely to die at home, families are preparing the body for burial, and they are burying the body themselves. Other people are embracing cremation, scattering remains out at sea, in the backyard, or in any number of public places. People are personalizing their mourning and commemoration, whether in person or via the Internet. Young people pour out their grief on social media and rush into public spaces to erect roadside shrines and place ghost bikes. Others are experimenting with social, environmental, technological, and cultural innovations that are transforming our beliefs and altering our practices.

But questions arise, disruptive ones. And families are often deeply conflicted about them — do we cremate or bury, embalm or conduct a "natural burial," erect a headstone or just plant a tree, memorialize or scatter the ashes? Do we buy a traditional monument or choose a "living" memorial? Each of these decisions requires taking a stand: choosing traditions that have shaped burial practices for two millennia—and that millions still practice—or embracing something new. This choice is not easy. How a loved one will be handled after their death, and whether or not they will be commemorated, is a decision that can wrench an already-grieving family.

Though fewer people die young now, death is always hard on us, the survivors. It brutally transforms our lives, shakes our faith, and undermines our reality. News of a friend's death can literally take our breath away, leave us dazed and unfocused, even unbalanced. And that pain is magnified many times when the person is a spouse or a child. For many people, the reality of death is unimaginable; for others, the loss is all they can think about. Death always has been the reality that defines humanity; that has not made it any easier to live with.

In Western society today, we have come to believe that everyone deserves to be remembered, no matter how famous or obscure, young or old, rich or poor. The question is *how* best to memorialize someone. Sometimes the cost of a traditional funeral and burial is a factor, and many people believe we have invented cheaper alternatives as a result, but I don't think economics is the main issue.[4] People have complained that American funerals are too expensive since at least the 1930s.[5] And they are right: a funeral, not including cemetery charges, today often costs over $7,000.[6] Yet if concerns about cost were propelling us to reconsider commemoration and burial customs, changes would have happened long ago and would have resulted in dramatically lowered costs. Instead, the death taboo means we rarely talk about what others have spent on funerals or even feel comfortable thinking about the cost. Moreover, while cremation can be less expensive, many nontraditional dispositions are not cheaper than traditional burial.

No, changes in mourning and memory reflect a broader shift of the cultural boundaries that have traditionally separated the sacred from the profane and the cultural from the commercial. We recognize such changes in other spheres—such as how medicine has moved to the mall, education online, and art to the street—so it should not surprise us to see death transformed, too. The personal has become public, and immortality is not distant but something within reach, in different ways, of every individual.[7] Call them what you will—post-structural, postindustrial, postmodern, or liquid modern—these fundamental fissures in culture and society have changed how we die and mourn, just as they have changed how we live.

The real disruption is not that change is happening. Change is always happening. But this change challenges traditions deeply embedded in society and undermines the foundations of their associated institutions. We can see the trends in methods of disposition, funeral rites, and memorialization, but the biggest trend is the increasing prevalence of the abstract notion of cultural hybridity—whereby all practices coexist in time and space. The practices discussed in this book sometimes replace traditional rituals, other times they complement them, and at even other times they are integrated into those traditions.

Death as Personal Experience

I grew up in a family where the right of everyone to be remembered was a bedrock principle. Oakwood Morningside Cemetery in Syracuse, New York, was my backyard, and my father's job. We lived in two houses, first on the western edge and then on the eastern edge of the cemetery, where my dad was the superintendent. When I was thirteen, I began working there, watching families cry while I helped fill the graves of the people they loved. By the time I was sixteen, I was driving (without a license) around the grounds, filling in sunken graves, raking leaves, and burying little white baby caskets. Death was a constant presence, a somber reality, but not a menacing one. As I joked, the Sloane kids had many friends, but not many sleepovers.

I was so comfortable with death and the cemetery that in graduate school I chose it as a dissertation topic at a time when historians largely ignored it.[8] I gave public lectures on it, wrote articles and books about it, and consulted with companies on cemetery develop-

FIGURE I.1. Roadside shrine, Sunset Boulevard, Los Angeles, CA, 2016.

ment. Even the deaths of my father and mother, while emotionally wrenching, still remained somehow within the frame of what was acceptable. Both my parents died at an "appropriate" age, even if it was far too early for me. My mom bore the brunt of my dad's death, while my brother Steven and his wife Beth took upon themselves the care and the funeral of my mom. I had a mature, almost abstract conception of death.

That is, until the horrible afternoon of December 10, 2007, when death finally became real for me. I came home and found my beloved wife of twenty-seven years, Beverlie Conant Sloane, dead from a massive stroke. By the end of the evening I had experienced three of Elisabeth Kübler-Ross's five stages of grief: denial, anger, and acceptance; bargaining and depression came later.[9] Upon finding Beverlie, I immediately entered a state of denial—*asking* her to sit up. Then I was angry, *demanding* she get up. I felt those waves "that weaken the knees and blind the eyes and obliterate the dailiness of life."[10] Eventually, four hours later, after the paramedics, police, and funeral home representatives had come through, I sat with a friend and *realized* Beverlie was dead.

The cruel realities of death had become shatteringly clear. I had to make a series of decisions: home or funeral home, cremation or burial/entombment, autopsy or no autopsy. In the days that followed, more choices arose: church funeral or secular memorial service, a niche in a cemetery or scattering her ashes. Then what music, who would speak, how would we format it? Did I have old photos, videos, other material I wanted to use? Each choice was relatively easy, but I worried. Am I doing the right thing? Is it what she would want? How will people judge my choices?

I was fortunate. Colleagues, friends, and family guided me along a familiar path, one my dad would have recognized and approved. Calls to Beverlie's relatives led to talks with her students and old friends. Meetings with funeral directors were followed by plans. A lovely memorial service was followed by a very personal committal service.

Yet even as I followed this path, I repeatedly collided with the death taboo—the one that rejects public grief and mourning. Yes, friends said, a memorial service is good. No, they seemed to suggest, continuing to emote about the death was not. No one stopped me from talking about Beverlie, but I could feel the discomfort in many people. Some people said objectionable things—"I am sure you have many things you wish you would have said to Beverlie"; others were incredibly sweet and reassuring. Still, nearly everyone quickly nudged me toward acceptance and that most awful of phrases, "moving on." A couple even asked when I would begin dating, which seemed unthinkable.

The impossible situation that death places us in became increasingly obvious. On one side was Philippe Ariès's reflection that under the death taboo, public mourning had become "shameful and forbidden."[11] Indeed, society urged families to affirm the "authenticity of their grief" by removing themselves from society.[12] As a result, the dying and the dead themselves had to be moved out of the house to the hospital, funeral home, and cemetery. Modern society marginalized death, separated it from routine life.

At the same time, society wants one to "get over it."[13] Mourning was okay, as long as it was private, didn't disturb society, and didn't go on too long. I tried. I taught a class four weeks after Beverlie died, while trying to show as little grief as possible. Then I went home and cried every night at even the slightest memory of her.

Even as I was balancing these contrary demands, I was introduced to a different perspective. Other, often younger, friends and family rejected such restraints, arguing that I should accept grief's presence and that I should celebrate Beverlie's life in multiple ways. They sent e-mails with images and messages. The death came just a little too early (for me) to memorialize her on Facebook or other social media, but several friends suggested creating a website. I didn't know yet about virtual cemeteries (see chapter 8), but at least one person pointed me toward a site. Their reactions surprised me, forcing me to wonder why I had immediately fallen into well-trod paths of memorial service and interment.

I was shocked when people asked what seemed an unthinkable question: Why was I interring Beverlie at all? They wondered (indirectly and politely) whether a memorial was really needed. Isn't the cemetery dead, just like the bodies buried there? Some, gently, went further, asking, is the conventional modern cemetery ethical? Can we defend a place founded upon embalming chemicals, hardwood caskets, and large lawns, maintained by the use of pesticides and still more chemicals? Do you really want to stash someone you loved in a niche isolated from the rest of your life?

Eventually, I decided that for me, no, the cemetery is not dead. But it does seem that we have entered a new phase in the cemetery's evolution as an institution. Will the millennial generation continue to embrace the cemetery when they can celebrate an untimely death more immediately and informally? Or when they can publish a memorial web page accessible across the world rather than visit an often-inconvenient gravesite? Or when they find the cemetery and its accompanying rituals environmentally unacceptable? How does this age-old institution adapt, once again, to society's changing attitudes—or can it? Such questions shape and define this book.

The American Way of Death

If you will accept for the moment the establishment of Mount Auburn Cemetery 187 years before 2018 as the origin point of the modern way of death in America, then we can define three overlapping periods

TABLE I.1 Comparison of eighteenth-century burial grounds and nineteenth-century cemeteries

	Eighteenth-century burial grounds	Reform cemeteries
Size	Tiny—less than an acre	Larger—10 to 500 acres
Location	Middle of town, farms	Suburban, urban fringe
Landscape aesthetic	Not designed or ornamented	Well ornamented from master plan
Burial lot size	1–2 graves, family generations separated	10 or more graves; single graves marginalized
Memorial style	Vertical, standing individual memorials, often artistically etched	Elaborate family monuments and mausoleums, some artist designed
Ownership	Family, public, or faith based	Public or nondenominational, nonprofit organizations

that have defined our evolving attitudes toward dying, mourning, and commemoration. In the period of sentimentality, from 1831 to roughly the 1890s, death continued to be very present in families' homes, in the growing cities, and in literature and other cultural products. We remember this period for the black dresses of Queen Victoria, the locks of hair carefully stored after the death of a child, artists embracing the weeping willow as a symbol of tears of mourning, evocative epitaphs on gravestones, and other sentimental, melodramatic, sometimes grotesque representations of the dead.

The birth of the modern cemetery did not transform how we cared for our dead, but the move from the unkempt colonial burial ground to the picturesque "reform" cemeteries reinforced sentimentality about death and the idea that the dead should be separate from us.[14] As table I.1 shows, the new cemeteries differed dramatically from the older graveyards in size, ornamentation, memorial style, focus on families, and ownership.

The new cemeteries embodied the period's fascinating stylistic reaction to death. The grounds were designed to draw visitors into a natural world filled with surprising turns, blooming bushes, towering trees, and winding pathways. Even when the designers mimicked an urban grid, they filled the sides of the streets with trees and bushes, profiling the gravestones with nature's bounty and beauty. Inside these grounds, lesser- and sometimes well-known artists, such as Augustus Saint-Gaudens and Antonio Canova, produced strikingly evocative three-dimensional family monuments that represented the mystery, fear, and glory of death. Families tried to recapture life in photographs of the recently deceased, by writing sentimental poetry about loss, and by finding solace under a canopy of trees.

Mourning was not a singular event like it is so often today. The funeral was part of a long process of events, including wakes and visits to the family after the funeral. Families would regularly visit the cemetery. Then, at some future date—Yahrzeit a year later for Jews, All Saints' Day or Day of the Dead for Catholics, and Qingming for the Chinese—the family would return and mark the death with a new celebration, renewed memories. Throughout, family members would wear black clothes or other items to signify their loss and their sorrow.

The new cemeteries were active participants in public life. These cemeteries were neither aristocratic family plots hidden on vast estates nor churchyards people passed by every day. The cemetery instead was becoming a destination space—a third space, in contemporary terms—which one had to seek out purposively. And thousands of visitors and mourners did.[15] They came to see the sculptures, the flowers, the broader landscape, and even to be seen themselves by the living. The places of the dead were emerging as one element in an increasingly wealthy, more consumption-driven, more image-conscious modern society.

The second era of mourning and commemoration commenced in the aftermath of the Civil War (1870s–1970s), as new institutions began to play increasingly important and culturally specific roles. Professionalization came to dying and death. Separate institutions came to oversee the "care" of the dying and dead in isolated spaces (as with treatment of contagious diseases). The dead were now to be kept away from the living, with only controlled access to them. Jessica Mitford much later cynically called the results of this second era the "American way of death."[16] The change led to the "practical disappearance of the thought of death as an influence directly upon practical life."[17] By the middle of the twentieth century, most Americans died in a hospital or nursing home, and funeral homes were ubiquitous, with almost 19,000 of them opening by 1948, doing over \$500 million of business.[18]

The institutionalization of the rituals surrounding dying, death, and commemoration resulted in the "dying of death."[19] In the United States, the epitome of the period was Forest Lawn Memorial Park, whose owner, Hubert Eaton, spent his professional life trying to rid his burying grounds of any sign of death. Eaton stripped away much of what a new generation found distressing or depressing in nineteenth-century "stoneyards," now crowded with decades of memorials. Eaton and others of his generation put memorials flush to the ground, opened up the grounds, dotted the burial sections with carefully chosen large institutional monuments, and reduced the complex landscape to one that mimicked a suburban lawnscape. By the 1950s, Eaton's "memorial park" form had spread across the country.[20]

Even immigrant and other socially marginalized communities, such as African Americans, who often held tenaciously to older traditions, embraced embalming, funeral homes, and memorial parks (when they were not restricted by race) by later in the twentieth century. Newer immigrant families might have maintained older customs longer, but not forever in the face of the pervasiveness of the industry's institutions.

Even as those institutions took control of death rituals, cemetery managers noted a rising set of concerns, the most important of which was the isolation of the cemetery, not just physically but socially and culturally. Fewer people were visiting cemeteries, and those that did, did so less often. Into the early 1960s, prominent cemeteries held Fourth of July parades and Easter sunrise services, but soon they were downsized, even abandoned. Death had been commoditized, standardized, and marginalized. Many mourners distanced themselves from the cemetery, viewing it as archaic and unnecessary.

Within this fracture, a third era—a "revival of death"—started unfolding in the 1960s and 1980s. The mourning, cemetery, and memorial practices of the second era began to come under considerable criticism, and alternatives started to develop. This new era is "increasingly being shaped by neither the dogmas of religion nor the institutional routines of medicine, but by dying, dead or bereaved individuals themselves."[21]

Certainly death has re-emerged as a cultural topic, as evidenced by the remarkable ways that mourners have responded to such highly publicized deaths as those of Princess Diana, the 9/11 victims, the Korean ferry disaster, Ronald Reagan, Michael Jackson, Prince, and the celebrity and public victims of terrorist incidents. We can talk about death in ways that we couldn't before. This shift makes it easier to talk about the mechanisms of dying and death, and how we might change them. We have seen the emergence of natural burying grounds that reject pesticides and embalming fluids, the development of the World Wide Cemetery and other virtual cemeteries, and the proliferation of everyday memorials for celebrities and ordinary people alike. These new practices retain elements of conventional rituals yet are divorced from traditional sites of mourning, such as churches, funeral homes, and cemeteries. Some more radical practices openly reject conventional rituals and attitudes, while others clearly are intended to complement traditions.

This transformation is being propelled by three trends in American life and death. First, while the vast majority of deaths occur in old age (almost 70 percent of all deaths in 2010 were after age 65), "trauma [is now] the leading cause of death in individuals 46 and younger."[22] So, even as the majority of deaths result from expected natural causes, rising rates of suicide and drug overdoses, along with continuing high rates of homicide and unintentional injuries, mean that traumatic deaths are a reality in American communities. Survivors want to mourn and commemorate traumatic deaths immediately given the shock and tragedy of the death; institutions usually take too much time, and their rules often preclude the type of activities people desire.

Second, cremation has become hugely popular. In 1960, fewer than 5 percent of dead Americans were cremated. Most were buried or entombed in cemeteries after religious services. By 2015, a larger percentage of the dead were cremated (roughly 48 percent) than were

FIGURE 1.2. Christmas decorations in Holy Cross Cemetery, Culver City, CA, 2003.

buried (46 percent). Projections suggest this trend will only escalate, perhaps to 70 percent cremated by 2030.[23] Unlike burial, which necessitates the use of the institutions of the American way of death, after a cremation survivors use those institutions only when they make an affirmative choice. They own the cremated remains, which shifts control of the process to them. Scattering of ashes has become a common practice, and most people who do it don't bother memorializing the death in a cemetery.

Third, as the other trends suggest, the modern institutions that anchored twentieth-century society are under increasing pressure to adapt to twenty-first-century postmodern, postindustrial conditions. We live in a period when the unfailing belief in and approval of the institutions of the death industry are no longer givens. As a result, the institutions constructed to serve the dead have been shaken, and are dissolving. Growing dissatisfaction with the medicalization of death can be seen in the rise of hospices and home deaths; in the emergence of an environmentally conscious preference for a more natural death; and in a renewed belief in public mourning, as evident in the everyday memorials on our streets and in digital media. Together, these changes are creating a seismic shift in our social and cultural attitudes toward dying, death, and commemoration.

Changing Cultural Landscape of Death and Commemoration

As Susan Letzer Cole has written, the "central *shareable* experience of death is the enactment of mourning."[24] The cemetery was long a key site of this shared experience. Yet, today many "probably think of mourning as stereotyped, delimited, often artificially induced."

The changes in mourning and burial that I discuss in this book represent significant cultural shifts. Such shifts are notoriously difficult to measure. Between my move as a baby to Oakwood Cemetery in 1953 and Beverlie's death in 2007, five shifts have been particularly influential: (1) trends in religious faith and secularization, as represented by declining institutional affiliation contrasted with a deepening of religious orthodoxy; (2) changing ideas of dying, as seen in Elisabeth Kübler-Ross's works on death and dying in the 1960s; (3) the rise of an environmental sensibility, culminating in the first Earth Day on April 22, 1970; (4) popular recognition of DIY (Do-It-Yourself) public mourning, signaled by Maya Lin's Vietnam Veterans Memorial (1982) and Cleve Jones's AIDS Memorial Quilt (1985); and, finally, (5) the emergence of digital media, suggested by the almost immediate establishment of one of the first virtual cemeteries, the World Wide Cemetery, in 1995.

Trends in religious attendance and membership send seemingly contradictory messages, yet overall suggest a shrinking core audience will continue to value the cemetery as part of a religious ritual. In the last three-quarters of a century, America has become more secular. Gallup has been surveying religious faith since the 1950s. In 1951, 96 percent of respondents expressed a specific religious preference, with only 1 percent saying they had none.[25] By 2016, the number saying they had none had risen to 18 percent, with another 10 percent stating they were nonspecific Christians. Similarly, in 1992, when Gallup first asked if respondents belonged to a church or synagogue, 70 percent of respondents said yes, a percentage that had dropped to just over half (55 percent) by 2016. This shift reinforces other cultural changes that draw people away from an institution such as a cemetery.

However, even as the society overall has become more secular, a division has been created between secular and faith-based individuals and communities. In the Gallup polls, this difference is clearest in the responses to the question of whether people define themselves as a "'born-again' or evangelical Christian." While the other percentages have declined, the number of Americans answering yes to this question has risen from 36 percent to 41 percent over the past twenty-four years. Deeply held commitment to faith could certainly affect choices people make regarding death, interment, and commemoration, as suggested by the regional differences toward cremation around the United States.

Psychiatrist Elisabeth Kübler-Ross argued that modern society had displaced the dying in this process of secularization. She testified before the US Senate in 1972 that "We live in a very particular death-denying society. We isolate both the dying and the old, and it serves a purpose. They are reminders of our own mortality." Philippe Ariès reinforced her view when he asserted that death, so "omnipresent in the past that it was familiar," had become "shameful and forbidden."[26] While in the past friends and family had helped the dying welcome death, they now moved the dying to the hospital to shield themselves (and society) from the "ugliness of death" and the "unbearable burden" it creates.

Put another way, during the twentieth century, the "ritual of death" had been replaced with the pragmatics of secularized health care.[27] Zygmunt Bauman described this change as reducing death "to an *exit* pure and simple." The focus in this medicalized view is on "making [death] happen or not allowing it to happen," not on celebrating one's life.[28] The modern hospital bed surrounded by machines and professionals had replaced the medieval deathbed where the dying person dispensed wisdom. Instead of communication, we got impersonality. As Tony Walter reported about modern disposition in England, "when

TABLE I.2 Comparison of twentieth-century memorial parks and natural burial grounds

	Twentieth-century memorial parks	Natural burial grounds
Size	Medium to large—10 to 200 acres	Medium to large—10 to 400 acres
Location	Suburban	Suburban, urban fringe
Landscape aesthetic	Suburban lawnscape	Natural, limited design
Burial lot size	Typically 3–4 graves; single graves marginalized	1–2 graves
Memorial style	Flush markers, institutional features	Trees or local stones, limited design
Ownership	Private or nonprofit organizations	Private or nonprofit organizations

the crematorium duty master [essentially their funeral director] does not have a personal touch," they fail the deceased, who "spent his or her life carving out a little bit of individualism," and "those survivors who wish to hang on to some remnant of that individualism."[29]

Kübler-Ross emphatically rejected the existing system. Instead, she, and the myriad scholars and advocates who followed her, aspired to reintegrate life and death. "We can give families more help with home care and visiting nurses, giving the families and the patients the spiritual, emotional, and financial help in order to facilitate the final care at home."[30] Europeans have been pioneers in overthrowing this cultural standard, by establishing organizations, such as the English Natural Death Centre (1994), to promote a more natural approach to dying and disposition.

The natural burial grounds described in table I.2 began as an offshoot of the natural death movement, but they were enhanced by a growing environmental sensibility. Americans may not agree on the scientific basis of climate change, but a remarkable consensus exists around the need to be more environmentally aware and responsive. Such writers as early ecologist Aldo Leopold and science researcher Rachel Carson propelled that emergence through their books.[31] Leopold's "land ethic" represents an accessible, yet profound, reordering of the human relationship to the world. Simply put, Leopold came to believe something was ethical if it "preserved the integrity, stability, and beauty" of nature, and was not if it did not.[32] In story after story, he related how human indifference had cataclysmic consequences for the land.

Carson illustrated the potentially catastrophic consequences of such human arrogance in her incisive critique of the modern pesticide industry, a symbol of modern technology and progress. For Carson, the pervasive acceptance of pesticides in the 1950s, and the resulting desperate plight of the nation's songbirds, revealed our ignorance. In our blind adoption of DDT, we had begun to silence the songbird, leaving our yards less colorful, our neighborhoods duller, and our ecology unbalanced.[33] More broadly, Leopold's ethic and Carson's portrait helped awaken an environmental sensibility that led by the 1980s to a new generation of English activists who argued that the modern cemetery was unnatural and unethical. Instead of preserving environmental values, the cemetery polluted the soil and water and air. Ken West's development of a natural burial alternative reflected this sensibility.

The same environmental sensibility that drove the natural burial movement informed Maya Lin's revolutionary memorial design for the Vietnam Veterans Memorial. Instead of rising up like the Washington Monument, embodying masculine power, her memorial invited visitors to walk into a valley of memories created by the individual names of those who died in the war.[34] The design de-emphasized the physical memorial by placing it at grade with the mall. I cannot overstate the influence of the memorial on commemorative design, nor its popularity even today with Washington visitors. In the decades that followed, public memorials to other wars, the Holocaust, and other events used it as a template.

Perhaps even more remarkably, Lin's wall created a safe space where, unlike any previous national monument, thousands of people could leave medals, letters, photographs, and other objects.[35] By becoming a DIY memorial, the Vietnam Veterans Memorial narrowed the space between the dead and the living, allowing survivors to publicly participate in the celebration of those who had passed by incorporating private memories into a national monument. People were newly encouraged to perform their acts of mourning in public.

Americans began to combine DIY activities with public mourning, creating new types and styles of memorials. In 1985, for instance, San Francisco activist Cleve Jones attended a rally where protestors hung signs from the federal building demanding that the government take action on the AIDS epidemic. Jones noted that the signs looked like a quilt; he soon spearheaded the production of the AIDS Memorial Quilt, which brought together quilt squares created by people who had lost family or friends to AIDS. The quilt demonstrated that DIY thinking could create a powerful symbol of protest and mourning. These joyous artifacts honored individual lives, and evoked LGBTQ culture as well as the politics of marginalization.

After the success of Lin's design and Jones's imaginative protest, performing mourning in public became increasingly common, slipping quietly into everyday life. Roadside shrines appeared more frequently. R.I.P. murals were painted more regularly in urban neighborhoods. In St. Louis, Patrick Van Der Tuin invented a new everyday memorial: the ghost bike, commemorating bicyclists killed in traffic. Memorial tattoos became more prevalent even as vinyl decal makers began producing memorial motifs. All of these memorials were symptomatic of a broader "everyday urbanism" with new forms of public engagement.[36] These everyday memorials suggested that people felt, as at the Vietnam Veterans Memorial "Wall," increasingly comfortable expressing their grief in public, thereby creating a renewed space for grief and mourning.

Such public mourning happens on the streets, but along with seemingly everything else in life, it happens on the Internet now as well. The performance of grief can occur in our own home at a computer yet be viewed by thousands, even millions, through digital connections. As a result, performing mourning has changed as technology progresses. Remarkably, as I write in 2017, the World Wide Web is still just over a quarter of a century old; the first web page was posted on August 6, 1991.[37] Strikingly, only four years later, an imaginative dying Canadian, Michael Kibbee, decided mourning should move to the web.

In 1995, Kibbee established the "World Wide Cemetery" (WWC), which reflected both the newness of the Internet and the ways that

innovations often rely on older traditions—such as the term "cemetery"—as a way to legitimate themselves. The initial page was, like
most sites then, mostly text. The WWC had a rectangular green box
at the top of the page with its name in capital letters. Underneath was
their tag line, "Welcome . . . to a place where Internet users, their
families and friends can erect *permanent* monuments to our dead"
(my emphasis). Along the left side of the page, bunched as if written
on a typewriter, were the various subpages: about, create a memorial,
visit a memorial, view, leave a flower, and a list of notable "real" cemeteries.[38] Kibbee, who was dying of cancer, expected his entry to be the
first memorial on the site, but he went into temporary remission, and
was not memorialized until 1997.

The WWC was emblematic of an emerging DIY performative digital commemorative culture. The web's virtual memorials and the
memorial pages on various social media sites suggest the pervasive
and fundamental nature of the seismic shift we are experiencing.
Many people today reject a world where the dying and dead are voice-
less, isolated, and separated. They embrace changes in the conventions of funerals, burials, and memorials. They question the traditions
and conventions, asking whether they fit with our contemporary concerns about environmentalism, inclusiveness, and our changing relationships with technologies. They adapt older traditions to new
technologies, and develop new technologies to respond to deeply felt
emotional needs. They question the very concept of the conventional
cemetery: Can we adapt the old model or do we dismiss it altogether
in this new age?

Nature, Memorials, and Mourning

In this book, I combine analysis of the latest scholarship on death and
dying with a personal story that connects to the issues that underlie
both the cemetery's value and the reformers' critiques. Three substan-
tive sections examine key values that have shaped the cemetery and
are central to today's critique. The cemetery provides a *natural* place
where people can *mourn* their loss, embodying that loss through

memorials, all within a culturally specific landscape. These values are also key points of dissatisfaction. Reformers and critics wonder if the cemetery is an artificial place where *nature* is manipulated, survivors cannot *mourn* authentically, and *memorials* are less accessible and timely than the everyday places that people can connect to more emotionally.

As a historian, I believe strongly that trying to understand what is happening today is impossible without the context of the past. How did society create and shape a place for the dead in the nineteenth and twentieth centuries? How have changing demographics, technologies, and attitudes toward death and the environment created new concerns that provoke alternative rituals and actions? Specifically, how have natural burials, everyday memorials, and digital graveyards altered the modern practice and discourses around commemoration?

And, indeed, many reform practices are part of an "evolving tradition."[39] Critics and cemetery managers alike are touting the new, even as they repackage the old, and make older practices seem new again. Burying the deceased in a grave in a shroud or simple pine box is both part of the new natural burial movement and an ancient ritual. Reaching forward to change the modern way of death, reformers have actually reached backward to resurrect older practices they view as more environmentally sensitive and culturally appropriate.

However, burials in shrouds and pine boxes often result in sunken graves when the dirt settles or the boxes collapse. I spent many summers filling such graves at Oakwood. Getting up early, I would arrive at work at 8 a.m., drive my pickup to a giant pile of dirt, and fill the pickup bed with my shovel. Then I would start on an older section, filling wheelbarrow after wheelbarrow with dirt and shoveling it into sunken graves. When the grave was level, I would rake in grass seed and move to the next grave. After the truck bed was empty, I went back to the giant pile and started over. While nineteenth-century poets might have liked the uneven landscape the sinking graves created, modern cemetery managers need a level lawn that does not damage larger mowers or create liability when people stumble.

Growing up in the cemetery, I put out flags for Memorial Day,

TABLE 1.3 Sloane family superintendents and their cemeteries

Ambrose H. Collier (1814–1892)
Woodland, Ironton, OH
1876–1886

Nathan P. Sloan (1841–1892)
Woodland, Ironton, OH
1886–1892

Edward Sloan (1868–1968)
Woodland, Ironton, OH
1894–1907
Marion, Marion, OH
1907–1929

Frederick I. Sloane (1876–1963)
Woodland, Ironton, OH
1907–1914
Belmont Park, Youngstown, OH
1914–1922
Tod-Homestead, Youngstown, OH
1922–1957

Jack F. Sloane (1921–2002)
Tod-Homestead, Youngstown, OH
1947–1953
Oakwood, Syracuse, NY
1953–1992

R. Gregory Sloane (1948–)
Oakwood, Syracuse
1992–1996

Lawrence F. Sloane (1951–)
Oakwood, Syracuse
1981–1985
L. F. Sloane Associates
1985–Present

Steven S. Sloane (1966–)
L. F. Sloane Associates
1989–1999
Woodlawn, Bronx, NY
1999–2006
Woodlawn, Syracuse, NY
2007–Present

sledded along the railroad tracks that separated our house from the burial grounds, planted flowers, and watched as the funerals passed our house led by a black Cadillac and somber hearse. It was what our family did. Members of my family have been managing cemeteries since 1876. As shown in table I.3, my siblings and I were raised in a cemetery in Syracuse, New York, and my father was born in one in Youngstown, Ohio. Four generations of Sloane superintendents preceded my generation, as pictured in figure I.3. The family saga started at Woodland Cemetery in Ironton, Ohio, where my great-great-grandfather Ambrose Collier became sexton, and continues 140 years later at Woodlawn Cemetery in Syracuse, where my brother is superintendent. I draw many of the historical examples in this book from the six cemeteries that members of my family have helped manage: Woodland Cemetery in Ironton; Belmont Park Cemetery and Tod-

FIGURE 1.3A–D. First four generations of Sloane superintendents, 1876–1992. *From left*, Ambrose H. Collier (with wife, Matilda), Nathan P. Sloan, Frederick I. Sloane, and Jack F. Sloane.

Homestead Cemetery in Youngstown, Ohio; Oakwood Morning-side Cemetery and Woodlawn Cemetery in Syracuse; and Woodlawn Cemetery in New York City.

Yet the events and ideas I am going to discuss are happening all over the world. Everyday memorials are especially prolific (and pre-date the US embrace of the idea by centuries) in Greece, Ireland, and Mexico. Just as the English placed thousands of flowers around Kensington Palace in honor of Princess Diana, Koreans distributed millions of yellow ribbons throughout their country after the Sewol ferry capsized, killing hundreds of schoolchildren. The quarter mile of shrines for those killed by a terrorist truck driver in Nice mirrored smaller but similar memorials in Istanbul and Baghdad. The Taiwan-ese and the Japanese are now experimenting with woodland burial grounds, as urban space is at a premium in those congested societies. And Internet cemeteries are as popular in Europe as they are in North America. Still, I focus my arguments on the United States, because I know its cultural and social contexts better than the international ones.

Garden View

Near the end of his career, my dad was asked to give a speech on "How I Got in the Cemetery Business."[40] He told a version of the story of how the family entered the business, and gave some basic information on financing and maintenance. He ended by rhetorically asking why we should not just "throw my ashes to the winds." His response was that "we are all here but for a very short time and personally I would like to be remembered at least by my family, so I want my name on something to show that I was here." Like him, that statement is a bit wandering and sentimental. Still, people have felt that emotion for thousands of years—we want to be remembered, and the cemetery is the one place where most of us can have a memorial that marks our presence. Those memorials are physical embodiments of the abstract themes of memory and loss that connect me, my dad, and Beverlie—and ultimately all the other members of our family.

FIGURE I.4. View into Beverlie's niche, Mount Auburn Cemetery, Cambridge, MA, 2011. Beverlie loved nature, especially flowers, which she photographed and with which she made greeting cards. I think she would very much like that her niche faces these bushes.

While I never doubted that I would inter Beverlie in a cemetery—she loved nature so—I struggled with where (a challenge faced by many increasingly mobile urbanites). We have family plots in Maine, Ohio, and New York, but they didn't hold any meaning for her. She and I lived in Los Angeles, but Beverlie never considered it home. I finally decided she should rest in Boston, the place she most fondly remembered from her adolescence; her sister still lives in the area with Beverlie's four beloved nephews. Once the decision was made, the choice of a cemetery was easy; she had to be interred in Mount Auburn Cemetery in Cambridge.

Mount Auburn is an iconic American institution, visited by millions of people since 1831. The cemetery is beautiful, well kept, and financially sound. Its rolling hills and vales hold a variety of plantings that merge in color and fragrance. Its marble and granite memorials amount to a sculpture garden. It is the prototype of the modern American burial place. I first visited in 1978, with Beverlie, just after a devastating snowstorm. The cemetery was closed, but after I told Mount Auburn's executive director, Bill Clendaniel, that I was a superintendent's son, he let us drive around. I have been back numerous times, always finding something new to photograph and contemplate.

Beverlie's ashes rest—as she had always asked, in an urn big enough for two, so we could spend eternity together, in "love forever"—in a columbarium in the basement of the 1930s Story Chapel near Mount Auburn's main entrance. I hope she, given the chance, would have chosen this spot, near her family and with a window view of the flowers and trees she so loved (as shown in figure I.4).

My experience in locating that space, with the generous help of family and the cemetery staff, demonstrates why I, and many other Americans, continue to embrace the cemetery as an institution. She is safe, well cared for, and rests in a place that imbues the love of nature and art that shaped her personal and professional life. As my dad wrote, she has her "name on something to show that [she] was here." This experience affirmed for me that the American cemetery remains an essential component of my American society, a place of memories unlike any other space.

Many other people, though, have questions about the cemetery as a necessity. In 2001, the Veterans Administration conducted a survey that asked questions about whether veterans would be buried or cremated. The results found that 30 percent of veterans wished to be cremated, the same as the nation's cremation rate that year. However, when the survey asked respondents if they wished their cremated remains to be buried or scattered, 65 percent responded that they wished to be scattered. And when they broke it down by age, 84 percent of younger respondents chose scattering over burial or entombment.

These findings generally reflect surveys that find most Americans still hold on to traditions, but a growing number are questioning them.[41] This book reflects their ambivalence and the cultural instability they represent—as did the ways that we remembered and interred Beverlie. We held two memorial services, each emphasizing her life and memory more than religion. At one of them, condolences were read from e-mails, not telegrams or letters. We also showed a video about her life. A digital slide show filled the room with her gorgeous photographs. Yet a minister opened the memorial service in Los Angeles, and we prayed and cried together in what felt like an old-style wake when we interred her at Mount Auburn six months later.

The words of writer and funeral director Thomas Lynch remind us: "The facts of life and death remain the same. We live and die, we love and grieve, we breed and disappear. And between those existential gravities, we search for meaning, save our memories, leave a record for those who will remember us."[42] In this book I ask, how will the coming generations leave a record of their memories? How will they remember the dead? Will the cemetery live on?

PART 1

NATURE

FIGURE P1.1A–C. Evolving concepts of nature. The illustrations are Belmont Hills Cemetery, Youngstown (OH); Forest Lawn Memorial Park, Hollywood Hills (CA); and Prairie Green, Greenwood Cemetery, Milwaukee (WI).

Recently, environmentalists have come to view the modern American cemetery as a site of pollution. Although they praise the grounds as bird sanctuaries, open space, and contributors to a healthy tree canopy, they reject the foundational elements of the modern way of death. They abhor the chemicals used in embalming, the destruction of forests for hardwood caskets, the dumping of concrete and steel into the earth as burial vaults, the spreading of herbicides and pesticides on the lawns, even the mercury and other chemicals exposed during cremation.

Their attitude would surprise the founders of nineteenth-century cemeteries, which embodied their Romantic love for and respect of nature. They located the cemeteries on the fringes of the hustle and bustle of towns and cities so they could be big, bucolic spaces filled with flora and fauna. The cemeteries offered spots of contemplation and education within the spaces for mourning and memory.

In their purest form today, "natural burial grounds" return to this Romantic past. Critics of contemporary cemeteries argue that we should wrap bodies in shrouds, place them gently into the earth, cover them with the original soil, and commemorate them with a native stone or tree. The most restrictive conservation cemeteries intend that each burial be part of a funding process that ensures that the land where people are buried will become a natural asset for the community in perpetuity.

Most green cemetery sections, however, are mere extensions of current cemeteries. Cemetery managers are designing natural burial sections inside their existing cemetery or at new sites under the same institutional umbrella. Is this just another consumer choice or are the managers, like those who embraced cremation a century ago, unwittingly changing the underlying cultural and economic model of the cemetery?

1

NATURAL SANCTUARY

Have you ever walked far inside a large nineteenth-century American cemetery? First, you hear the quiet; then, you are enveloped by nature. One day, walking in Allegheny Cemetery in Pittsburgh, I stumbled upon two small deer. I took photographs as they sat in the grass. They stayed for a few minutes, then got up and sauntered away, perfectly comfortable in this sanctuary for the dead. The wind breezed across the hilltop and the leaves fluttered as they loped away. It was a perfect moment of contemplation, repose, and rest.

The founders of the cemetery where I grew up would have been happy that, as I sat on that hilltop, I felt separated from the rest of Pittsburgh, and I focused on the beauty of the trees, the softness of the wind, and the stillness of the scene. If the founders could have spoken to me as I arrived at the cemetery, they would have advised: "commune with nature in her loveliest forms, and in these secluded retreats . . . forget for an hour the toils and cares of life."[1] They wanted to create a space where nature reminded visitors of the cycle of life and death. By engaging visitors in a bucolic setting, they hoped they could move them spiritually, encourage them to leave behind their commercial concerns, and focus on the eternal values.

Nineteenth-century urban leaders were ambitious in their moral and civic aspirations. They wanted their cities to grow, prosper, become more beautiful, and rival any other city. These aspirations drove them to establish historical societies, libraries, and schools. They printed enormous tomes celebrating their cities' histories, and ended

FIGURE 1.1. Two deer, Allegheny Cemetery, Pittsburgh, PA, 2007.

them with biographical appendices of contemporary leaders like themselves. Their belief that nature was imbued with morality propelled them to plant botanical gardens, pleasure parks, and elaborate private gardens. They promoted campaigns to plant urban trees not only to beautify the streets, but also to reconnect city residents' relationship to nature's lessons. The cemetery was a civic and spiritual project, a part of the improvement campaign to clean up, beautify, uplift, and order the emerging cities.

Moreover, there was a pressing need for new cemeteries. Older burial places not only were inconveniently located in their rapidly expanding downtowns, but they also were laid out according to the precepts of a passing cultural age. The graveyards occupied land that was increasing in value even as their appearances seemed ill-fitting. American burial grounds and churchyards were not quite empty of any nature, nor were they as reliant on mass burial chambers as the European burial grounds. The American burial grounds typically consisted of unrelieved lines of gravestones cluttered together in tiny parcels that were adorned only by a few flowers and erratically planted trees and shrubs.

In response, two variations of reform cemeteries emerged during the first two-thirds of the nineteenth century: grid cemeteries and rural cemeteries. Most city burial places were in the grid style. These cemeteries were incrementally larger than those they replaced, more natural yet still very orderly, and located along the edge of the built-up area of the city. At the same time, like earlier burial grounds, they were usually still owned by the city or the church, rather than by lot holders or nonprofit organizations. And they sold family lots, but usually in small numbers.[2]

Architectural historian Dell Upton has shown that grid cemeteries adopted a kind of "spatial order" that maintained similar social hierarchies among the dead as among the living.[3] They also, he notes, sustained the importance of the individual, as they "sought to alleviate some of the terrors of burial inside the city and to soften the abode of death with plantings and other amenities" even within a design that imitated the city's grid. Thus, especially in small city burial places, the graves are located along "streets" arrayed much like those outside the cemetery gates.[4]

In 1796, for example, fears of urban contagions and of new farm owners not maintaining the previous family's burial grounds pushed New Haven, Connecticut, residents to create a six-acre nonprofit, non-denominational cemetery on the outskirts of town. The new cemetery emulated the town's street plan with thirteen avenues crossed by three streets. The organizers softened the grid by planting Lombardy poplar trees along the avenues and scattered a few of the newly popular weeping willows throughout the sections. Individual and family lot holders were allowed to add smaller plantings to their private burial space, bringing nature that much farther into the human grid. Organized and maintained by the families themselves through a new non-profit institution, the graves promised to be more permanent than the farm and city burial grounds they replaced.

New Haven is an amazingly early example of the English and European revolution in burial ground location and design. The cemetery was founded eight years before the iconic Père Lachaise in Paris and thirty years before the influential work of English author and landscape designer John Claudius Loudon.[5] Loudon argued that the geometric, analytical new grid cemeteries would reinforce order, in contrast to the "confused, useless or dangerous" organization of the jumbled city graveyards.[6] In a well-organized grid cemetery, each grave would have a precise location within a carefully orchestrated space, producing a rationality that would ensure that decomposing bodies did not function as a source of miasmatic vapors contributing to the spread of contagious diseases.

Many other cities throughout the United States, Canada, and other parts of the Western world eventually established similar grid cemeteries. Syracuse, for instance, established Rose Hill Cemetery for much the same reasons and with a similar design. In Montreal, Protestants opened a new cemetery well north of the settled parts of the city in 1799, and doubled its size in 1815.[7] Such cemeteries would continue to be established throughout the century as towns and cities coped with growing populations, an increasing number of dead, and the public's uneasiness as epidemics continued to take horrible tolls.

Splendid Isolation

Despite the prevalence of grid cemeteries, they were not nearly as noteworthy as the second variation of their time, the "rural" cemetery. When Père Lachaise opened in 1804, some parts of the cemetery mimicked traditional formal gardens, while others followed the more organic styles favored by English country estate planners. This hybrid landscape joined city and country, order and nature into a single landscape. By mid-century, rural cemeteries had largely abandoned the formal aspects, and in turn had become a media sensation, overshadowing cemeteries that continued older traditions or adopted only limited reforms. Partially, they were more notable because their design was so different from previous burial grounds, but they also were well promoted through events, brochures, and public relations materials. As a result, the experimental cemetery was written about in all the right journals, was visited by celebrities, and attracted the wealthiest families in the largest cities.

The rural cemeteries rejected standard urban form as the basis of their design. In place of gridded streets, they included curvy roads and pathways. Instead of long vistas, one's vision was mysteriously blocked by a bend in the street, the obstacle of a tree, or a change in elevation. Nature dominated. In 1860, A. D. Gridley argued that a cemetery should be planted with a wealth of trees, flowering shrubs, climbing vines, and flowers.[8] The image evokes a certain wildness we associate with Thoreau and others of the period. In certain places — much like Olmsted and Vaux's Ramble in Central Park—one could imagine a visitor conjuring up Walden Pond.[9] The rural cemeteries were carefully designed to ease visitors' accessibility with roads and paths, but retained the uncertainties of a natural place.

Often situated on hills and incorporating varied topography, these cemeteries sought to meld the dead with their trees, monuments, and buildings. Visitors were educated not only about tree specimens and types of flowers, but also about the profound moral reality of natural cycles. The transition from life to death was softened as the visible symbols of death were integrated with elements of natural beauty, creating the composed stillness that I experienced in Pittsburgh.

Yet I was startled when I first came upon the deer in Pittsburgh, because I had not seen them — nor had they seen me—from afar. I was suddenly stripped of the distance most of us have from large wild animals. And as a result I was momentarily transported to less settled, wilder times. We were reduced to a natural relationship rather than shielded from one another.

But why did the "rural" design arise at all? While health and economic issues certainly played a role in the relocation of both grid and rural cemeteries, I believe the primary reasons for the cultural popularity of the rural cemeteries were the influence of Romanticism on garden design and the founders' ambitions for their cities. The Romantics believed that nature taught morality, and that its power grew, the deeper one insinuated oneself into a natural environment. Further, these new institutions were not just burial places, but part of an emerging urban social and cultural infrastructure. In 1859, civic leader, retired lawyer, former Congressman, amateur horticulturist, and local historian Elias W. Leavenworth celebrated the establishment of Syracuse's Oakwood Cemetery by arguing that "an ample, permanent and attractive resting place for our dead, seems to be the last great necessity of our city."[10] The event was significant enough that over one-third of the city's 15,000 residents spent a beautiful afternoon listening to speakers and poets who gathered in Oakwood's Dedication Valley after a two-hour-long parade of fire companies, politicians, and countless fraternal groups. They imagined Oakwood as one more signal of their maturity as a city.

The Oakwood I grew up in 100 years later had a very different meaning for my family and me. By that time, society's relationship to nature, the way we designed landscapes, and especially our attitudes toward the dead had shifted dramatically. So, my dad, who was born in 1921 inside the superintendent's house at Belmont Park Cemetery in Youngstown, Ohio, and I, born thirty years later in a hospital down the street, had very similar experiences of the cemetery. We moved to Syracuse when I was six weeks old, into a house on the western side of the cemetery, in front of an imposing gate, but so much a part of the cemetery that I viewed it as my backyard.

For my dad and me, the cemetery was a cultural place filled with mourners, birders, lovers, and walkers looking at amazing art and statuary; a natural place, with a remarkable array of birds and myriad animals living amid the thousands of flowers, trees, and bushes. Each cemetery was also a personal space, where an adolescent Jack played with his three sisters and forty years later I set up forts with my toy soldiers or played tag with my siblings. While the personal experience was unusual (to say the least), we were in sync with the intentions of the landscape design: For us, the cemetery was a place of culture and nature that welcomed a diverse group of users.

Designing Oakwood

Between the founding of Mount Auburn Cemetery in 1831 and the dedication of Oakwood in 1859, dozens of landscaped rural cemeteries opened all over the country. Years before the first great urban park, Central Park in New York City, was completed, a pioneering group of cemetery designers developed the basis for the modern profession of landscape architecture. One of them, Howard Daniels, lost out to Frederick Law Olmsted and Calvert Vaux in the competition to design Central Park, yet he was a success from his design of Spring Grove Cemetery in Cincinnati in 1845 until his death in 1863. Active in New England, New York, Pennsylvania, and Ohio, he was laid to rest in Green Lawn in Columbus, Ohio, another of his over a dozen cemetery plans—including Oakwood in Syracuse.

Daniels's original plan for Oakwood has not survived, but we can learn a great deal from early maps and the landscape itself. As H. P. Smith wrote in his 1871 guidebook, Oakwood was "a mile and a half from the business center."[11] For the first forty years, after passing along a treelined entryway and past a simple, Gothic-styled entrance building, a visitor would come to a similar iron gate on the western edge of the cemetery. In 1902, a more elaborate stone entrance bridge was constructed (see the frontispiece). This shielded the railroad tracks that ran above grade here.

As Smith noted, "[g]enerally speaking, the whole cemetery faces the west, rising with a gradual ascent to the eastern boundary on the hill-top, which completely overlooks the valley, City and lake."[12] Immediately after the gate, the main road split, with Pine Ridge Road veering left, rising northward slowly into a broad valley with burial sites on the surrounding hills. Here, in Dedication Valley, was where those thousands of folks had gathered to celebrate the cemetery's opening. A second avenue, Midland Avenue, snakes out eastward from the gate along the bottom of a long valley out of which roads weaved up the hill to the northeast. In the flat portion near the gate, the association built the cemetery's office (1902) and chapel (1879), as well as an elaborate greenhouse (circa 1902).

Under Daniels's direction, "fifty or sixty men" worked for months shifting dirt, shaping hills, laying out roads, and planting a profusion of trees and bushes on a carefully constructed topography.[13] Imagine what a visitor from the bustling, chaotic boomtown of Syracuse would have found at Oakwood. Walking into Dedication Valley, they would have been suddenly cut off from their urban world, having entered the largest garden any of them had ever seen. The winding of the narrow streets created constantly shifting views of the surroundings. Lawns were covered with a wide range of shade trees and an array of bushes clustered to dictate vistas and views. Visitors were especially attracted by the natural elements that seemed to magically appear as they rode or walked through the grounds.[14]

H. P. Smith reported that the original site was "almost an unbroken oak forest, interspersed with a few pine, ash, maple, and many hickory trees, and filled with underbrush, logs and stumps."[15] When I was young, walking through the old sections of the cemetery in the fall, I was almost overwhelmed by the yellows, oranges, and reds of oak and maple leaves. My father's workers raked them into great piles by the streets, creating a rainbow of rusty colors. Sometimes, they "accidentally" caught on fire so the cemetery did not have to dispose of them.

Seeing the landscape today must be a quite different experience. The lots are filled with mismatched monuments whose gray tones and tall spires compete with the natural setting. Angels came to stand guard atop their pedestals, broken columns and stone tree stumps signified shortened lives, and garlands of ivy and laurel were carved into marble and granite to mimic the plants covering nearby graves. The most dramatic monument stood on the hillside overlooking Dedication Valley. Drawing upon the era's fascination with Egypt, Cornelius Longstreet used money he made providing goods to Union soldiers during the Civil War to erect a pyramid where he provided crypts for his family and others, including Comfort Tyler, one of the founders of Syracuse.

In the nineteenth century, the ratio would have favored the trees and shrubs. Even as the mausoleums and monuments appeared on one side of Midland, the founders retained a large wooded section on the other. So, culture dominated on the north, while on the south, nature creates an imposing, contrasting picturesque wildness of dense foliage. As children, my brothers and I spent hours walking through the "woods," feeling very far from the urban civilization that started just a few steps beyond the gate.

FIGURE 1.2. Pastoral scene, Oakwood Cemetery, Syracuse, NY, 2009.

When Oakwood was founded, before almost any bodies were embalmed, no pesticides or other chemicals were used to maintain the plantings, and before lawn mowers, trimmers, backhoes, and other power machinery were present, the cemetery was an environmentally "natural" place. Most cemeteries stood out as spaces with a wide range of native and exotic trees, shrubs, and flowers. They embodied the idea, expressed by American tastemaker Andrew Jackson Downing and others, that the presence of nature was an important part of civilized urban life.[16] They also embodied the social and class inequities we shall discuss later, but from an environmental perspective, they were outstanding examples of an integration of nature and culture.

Beautiful Landscapes of "the Whole"

As the cemetery evolved, the role of nature changed. The sense of wildness in the city evoked by the rural cemeteries gradually gave way to a garden's beauty as urban and especially suburban Americans became less comfortable with wild animals and unruly wilderness as a part of their routine lives. They viewed the older design of the cemetery, where visitors were surrounded by nature, as old-fashioned, inappropriate, and discomforting.

As the nineteenth century progressed, cemetery managers increasingly dictated that the design and maintenance of the cemetery should ensure unity in the surrounding landscape. They attempted to tame what they viewed as the extravagances of lot holders. Forty years after Reverend Gridley rejoiced in the clutter of trees, shrubs, flowers, and vines, landscape architect Julia Rogers dismissed myrtle clambering atop graves and weeping willows bending over them.[17] She termed "barbaric" the use of rowan trees to "keep away evil spirits," and evergreens "clipped into grotesque shapes," all inviting thoughts as "somber as their foliage." She wrote that thankfully the "race has outgrown many of its old superstitions." Her generation had moved away from "the formal, the fantastic and the inharmonious," while embracing "calm meditation" and a spirit that is "to solace rather than to harrow the feelings of the living." A "landscape or garden cemetery" had replaced the overgrown grounds of the past.

The reversal was driven partially by the popularity of the new large urban parks, which were convenient enough to draw casual visitors, not just mourners. Since they were not divided into lots, designers could create unified landscapes. And leading national design firms designed many new parks, providing local landscape gardeners and architects with influential models. In essence, these industry leaders created a new design paradigm.

Fairly quickly, park design principles began to influence, if not dictate, cemetery designs. In 1896, Massachusetts gardener Fanny Copley Seavey argued at the annual national superintendents' conference that "a cemetery needs to be treated as a whole."[18] A symbol of the discord that designers and managers wished to unify were the stone enclosures and iron fences that had bedeviled them since the founding of Mount Auburn. A key reason, influential landscape gardener Ossian Cole Simonds wrote, that cemetery superintendents fought for the "abolition of fences, coping, and other lot inclosures" [sic] was that they believed the focus should be on the "beauty of trees, shrubs, lawns, and flowers," all coordinated to create a consistent setting. Clearing such interferences allowed the visitor's eye to wander to the trees along the roadways, the shrubs bracketing the monuments, and the lawns that connected the elements of a section.

Many Midwestern cemetery designers and civic leaders adopted this approach after seeing how Adolph Strauch restructured Howard Daniels's design for Spring Grove Cemetery in Cincinnati. He instituted firm rules that enhanced the coherence and unified the beauty of the burial sections by emphasizing family monuments. In 1871, city officials in Ironton, Ohio, a small booming river town on the border with Kentucky, decided they needed to follow the lead of cities like Cincinnati in establishing a modern cemetery—one that imitated Spring Grove.

Today, visitors enter Woodland through a lovely, arched 1912 gateway, pass by the superintendent's house, and travel up a long road surrounded by woods before reaching a bridge that rises over a ravine holding a state highway before entering the burial grounds. Woodland exemplifies early twentieth-century cemetery consultant Howard Evarts Weed's assertion that "the first impression of a cemetery should be so pleasing that visitors will wish to be buried therein."[19] The trip in this space between city and cemetery gives visitors a momentary pause between the routine activities of their lives and the contemplation of their mortality and remembrances. Similarly, in Spring Grove Cemetery, visitors meander through a series of ponds before they reach the burial sections.

My Irish American great-great-grandfather, Ambrose H. Collier, began working at Woodland as sexton in 1876. My forefathers managed the cemetery for the next thirty-eight years. Ambrose's son-in-law, Nathan Sloan, became sexton on Ambrose's retirement in 1886, helped by his two sons, Edward and my grandfather Frederick, and for a while by a brother, Perle. Nathan supervised the cemetery until his death from tuberculosis in 1892. Edward was promoted, staying there until he moved in 1907 to the cemetery in Marion, Ohio. Grandfather Fred took over; when he left for Youngstown in 1914, the family's reign ended.

I don't know much about Ambrose. My dad thought Nathan

was the first in the family to be a cemetery sexton—he was the first
Sloane—taking up the profession when he returned injured from the
Civil War. As with many family stories, this one is partly true. Nathan
was a war veteran, but he does not seem to have been injured in the
war. And he only got the job because Ambrose had it, two decades
after the war ended. Still, in 1925, a decade after the last Sloane superintendent had left, the local newspaper wrote glowingly about the
state of the cemetery, stating that much "of this credit is due to the
Sloane family," since they had maintained the cemetery for so long.[20]

Landscape to Lawnscape

Woodland and its generations of lawn and garden cemeteries represent a transitional period in the evolution of the cemetery's relationship to nature. These cemeteries compromised the design values of
the early rural cemeteries while presaging the further taming of the
natural landscape in the twentieth-century memorial parks. On one
hand, their plantings seemed more artificial and overwrought to critics. In 1893, Bellett Lawson, superintendent of Chicago's Oakwoods
Cemetery, deplored the planting of richly colored flower beds, arguing that they were "extremely out of harmony with the surroundings." On the other hand, the complementary balance of culture and
nature, so integral to the rural cemetery model, skewed increasingly
toward culture as larger and more monuments spread throughout
the sections. Giant family obelisks, massive rocks, soaring angels on
high pedestals, and, most dramatically, larger and larger mausoleums
overwhelmed the natural setting in many places.

As a response, Lawson advocated for "beautifully kept lawns, or
open spaces surrounded by, or dotted with trees and shrubs bear-
ing foliage of different hues, and shades of green," where the "very
somberness of the surroundings indicates repose."[21] Lawson's wish
came true, not just in the cemetery but throughout the urban landscape. In his beautiful, complex history of landscape and memory,
Simon Schama briefly outlines the change from the jumbled wildness of the mid-nineteenth century to the smoothness and predict-

ability of the lawn. "Turf, acre after acre after acre of it, became the landscape of settled civility," whether in the "bowling greens of urban parks," the "heavily rolled cricket pitches of the British Empire," or the "suburban yard."[22] And the victory in the suburbs was especially cruel since, while the "grass occupied an unbroken space in front of the house," the culture required that the family not use it, not "disport itself in public view," leaving the lawn "a dead space, an empty green stretched before the dwelling."[23]

Forest Lawn Memorial Park in Glendale, California, pioneered the suburbanesque memorial park concept. The rolling lawns of the memorial parks were restricted spaces, the use of which was heavily regulated and the visual interruption of which was rarely allowed. More and more bushes and shrubs were sacrificed to unclutter spaces so visitors could see the monuments and feel more comfortable in these spaces, which resembled their yards and parks. Eventually, lawns were filled with almost invisible flush-to-the-ground individual memorials and large, carefully selected institutional memorials. They left little room for trees and shrubs. The landscape was designed to ease maintenance, feel egalitarian, and simplify the setting. Instead of a lawn integrated with diverse flora and fauna, a lawnscape emulated the endlessly repeated front lawns of the suburbs.

Even today, Forest Lawn is a remarkable space, filled with intriguing and kitschy memorials surrounded by acres of lawns dotted with large, lovely trees. Its design spread rapidly throughout the country, with virtually every cemetery opening since the 1920s imitating most aspects of its appearance. Its suburban location was also a critical feature of its success. Even as spreading cities engulfed Oakwood, Woodlawn in the Bronx, and other reform cemeteries, memorial parks were sited in a new ring of suburbs sprouting up on the fringes of the city. Indeed, the neighborhoods around the older cemeteries were becoming less desirable in this era of suburban flight, creating new financial pressures for management.

The memorial parks that followed Forest Lawn often were founded without the financial resources of the original, and soon faced similar difficulties as the older urban cemeteries. In 1976, Oakwood absorbed

White Chapel Memory Gardens, in the Syracuse suburb of DeWitt. The decision was purely economic. By its 125th anniversary in 1984, Oakwood was adjacent to urban neighborhoods reeling socially and economically. White Chapel was on the verge of receivership due to mismanagement. My two older brothers helped my father as he tried to invigorate public interest in Oakwood as a historic monument. At the same time, they viewed suburban White Chapel as a possible financial lifeline that with careful use of economies of scale could support the larger, and much more costly to maintain, original site.

White Chapel had been itself an undercapitalized, speculative venture, one franchise in an aborted attempt to establish the first national chain of memorial parks. A poorly designed imitation of Forest Lawn, it sat in a wide-open space easily accessible from a major road in a quickly expanding suburb. The owners, like others across the nation, hoped to draw in the first generation of suburban residents while also attracting urban residents fearful of growing social turmoil.

The first time I visited in the 1970s, I was surprised by the sparseness of the grounds. Although the memorial park was over twenty-five years old, the sections had little tree canopy, virtually no differentiation in the landscape, and no specialness. Each section had a central theme, represented by a single institutional monument. The grave markers were set flush in the grass. Almost no bushes broke the lawns, allowing large riding mowers to move quickly over them. The terrain was slightly but uniformly sloping, giving the site an especially monotonous feel. When I visited again in 2010, a few flowers poked up out of the bronze plaques, and, as I was there near Christmas, some wreaths were on graves. Standing at the top of the slope, looking out over the very prominent adjacent shopping mall, I saw none of the sensitivity and imagination of earlier cemetery designs, just a utilitarian space with almost no diversity in its plantings.

Nature had been tamed, even stunted. In some sense, we had come full circle. Just as the eighteenth-century urban graveyards had utilitarian designs, the memorial parks generally used a narrow natural palette that provided little more than a monotonous terrain for the deposit of the dead. At Forest Lawn, one can still enjoy a lovely canopy of mature trees, but too many other memorial parks are just unattractive lawns with few trees and bushes placed near street intersections. Ensuring sight lines for visitors seems much more important than engaging them with nature.

Indeed, in conjunction with Oakwood's centennial in 1959, my father opened new burial sections high upon a hill that were easily accessible from Colvin Street, planting younger, more evenly spaced trees and shrubs among the lawns. I wondered why he had not opened sections closer to the office at the bottom of the hill, near the gate, amid the older sections with their mature landscapes. He responded that new lot holders only wanted easier access and more openness. They wanted to be able to drive to their lots without passing through as much of the cemetery and being surrounded by death. They did not want to be enveloped by nature, as had older generations. Entering and enjoying a place of death and memory now held less attraction in a society bent on avoiding death.

Instead, they wanted green grasses, trees, and shrubs. So, within the new lawnscapes, pressures to ensure that lot holders saw only manicured green grounds with no weeds pushed superintendents to use any available weapon to help preserve the illusion of an ordered landscape. As a result, a new weapons race propelled the introduction of a multitude of herbicides and other chemicals. In the early twentieth century, *The Cemetery Handbook*, a compilation of useful information for superintendents, included a curious array of "weed exterminators" that look like medieval torture items. While one was for "injecting poisons into the roots of weeds," the others were manual devices for "cutting lawn weeds."[24] When labor was relatively cheap, and chemicals were still mostly experimental (especially on large spaces like those in cemeteries), most cemeteries relied on the workers to extract weeds.

By 1962, maintaining those lawns depended on a massive array of support systems, including "lawn mowers, rubber hoses, municipal water systems, chemical fertilizers, herbicides, and pesticides."[25] In a brief "agenda" for maintaining the cemetery landscape, G. J. Klupar, executive director of the Chicago Catholic Cemeteries, called for spraying and fertilizing in the spring and fall, and for "weed control" starting "in the spring and [continuing] through the summer." Later, he is more explicit, calling "weed eradication" "essential in a well-kept cemetery."[26] One achieves such a state by saturating a "reel-type mower" with weed killer or rolling a "chemically impregnated roller" behind a mower, or attaching a spreader to a "power mower," although one might adapt a "gang mower" to hold "five or seven reels" "designed to accommodate a 100-gallon tank" of weed killer. The modern cemetery was becoming a sophisticated, industrialized landscape.

Visitors could see the green aboveground, but an equally insidious invasion was happening under the ground. Starting with the need to get bodies home to their loved ones during the Civil War, embalming spread.[27] When Americans began rapidly urbanizing after the war, the older traditions of holding the wake in the home became more difficult as houses shrank and families spread out. Embalming was adopted by many Americans. As Jessica Mitford has graphically described, embalming requires the insertion of about "three to six gallons of a dyed and perfumed solution of formaldehyde, glycerin, borax, phenol, alcohol, and water" into the body to disinfect and preserve it.[28] Unlike the undertakers they replaced, the new funeral directors sold services as much as they did products, like the casket, which was now available in a wide variety of wood and metallic options. By the middle of the twentieth century, funeral directors were embalming more and more bodies and laying them out in hardwood caskets, which cemetery crews lowered into steel or concrete vaults placed inside graves.

Advocating for Nature

Throughout this evolution from a landscape tainted by few environmental hazards to one increasingly dependent upon them, a small number of voices in the industry argued for a return to a gentler nature. In 1894, superintendent Thomas Meehan reminded his peers that Cincinnati's Nicholas Longworth, who he asserted was the "father of modern strawberry culture," was not buried in an elaborate mausoleum or beneath an ostentatious sculpted monument, but instead "sleeps beneath the spreading branches of a noble elm tree."[29] Meehan used this example in a speech to the national superintendents' conference, where he argued for reasserting natural elements instead of the Victorian-styled, vine-draped, complex, and complicated monuments of the last generation.

John Plumb, superintendent of New York City's Woodlawn Cemetery, took the argument even further at the same conference a generation later in 1932: "The memorial of most enduring life is a tree. Tombs and temples of ancient kings have crumbled and passed away, yet we have living trees which were old when they were erected."[30] While Plumb was no environmental advocate from the early twenty-first century, his vision of a place where trees served as memorials reminds us that one of the key challenges to the modern cemetery, the natural woodlands burial ground, is both a rejection of one generation's practices and a continuation of another's.

2

ECOLOGICAL SIMPLICITY

Roughly a half century after Plumb suggested a tree was the perfect cemetery memorial, English activists began arguing that the entire conventional cemetery was an environmental mistake, explicitly rejecting the devastation they associate with contemporary burial techniques, and the other modern policies and practices that it symbolized. They promoted natural death and burial as an alternative. A death should conclude with interment in the "woodlands" or a "natural" burial ground, an idea that some advocates term a "green" cemetery. They focused on reconnecting humans with nature, in both the process of the interment and the design of the burial ground. Although constructed by humans, the grounds represent a rejection of human cultural artifacts. Indeed, advocates have striven to create burial places nothing like the conventional memorial park lawnscapes with their bronze markers and white marble monuments.

The American pioneer of the woodlands concept, South Carolinian Billy Campbell, has asserted that he and his fellow conservation cemetery managers are "reclaiming the memorial park movement and moving it into the 21st century."[1] They are hoping for more than just an adaptation of existing conventions. They aim to develop burial grounds that merge with nature, leaving behind no visible cultural traces save perhaps deteriorating wooden or native stone memorials. While these burial grounds so far have attracted only a small number of followers, they represent a growing trend toward simplicity in today's death rituals, which, as we will see in the next chapter, has already begun to elicit a quick response from conventional cemetery managers. They symbolize the demand for choices defined by the user, not the institution, and for representing people's principles rather than a shallow civil culture.

Currently, the green cemetery movement is a pretty big umbrella, promoted in the United States by the Green Burial Council, which Juliette and Joe Sehee established in 2005.[2] Members range from Campbell's Ramsey Creek Preserve, with its aspiration to create a permanent woodlands conservation area, to single sections within existing cemeteries that meet the Council's minimum definition of green burial. As I shall try to chronicle, the current state of the movement raises two questions: First, how can or will societies remember their dead in a natural cemetery without memorials that seamlessly morphs into a conserved wild space? Second, can the movement actually achieve its goal of diminishing the modern cemetery's environmental impact within an existing institution that includes natural burial as just another consumer option? I believe natural burial is more likely to follow the path of cremation: gradual social acceptance, with a corresponding diminution of its radical challenge to conventional burial.

Bringing Woodlands Conservation to America

As with the earliest crematories, the first US natural burial grounds embodied ecological principles. Billy Campbell says that the idea for Ramsey Creek Preserve came out of an epiphany he had in 1988 after reading about the Fore people in New Guinea. He "suddenly realized that burying people in a simple way in the wilderness—America's sacred groves—would be a means of preserving open space and to give families a stake in the land."[3] As a result, he formed Memorial Ecosystems, which purchased a thirty-three-acre parcel outside his hometown of Westminster, South Carolina. Opening in 1996, his new burial place required families to agree to the following principles: a simple shroud rather than an elaborate casket, no embalming, no concrete vaults or metal caskets, and any memorialization limited to

FIGURE 2.1. Crenshaw memorial alongside Ramsey Creek, Ramsey Creek Preserve, Westminster, SC, 2017.

local native stones. In return, Memorial Ecosystems promised to use its profits to create a conservation area set aside permanently (once the burials were completed) as a woodlands grove. Of course, the timing of such a conversion depends on how fast the gravesites are filled, and that would probably be decades from now, at least.

Although Campbell cited a premodern culture as his inspiration, Ramsey Creek exemplifies the contemporary ecological sensibility of Aldo Leopold and Rachel Carson, English environmentalists Marion Shoard and Paul Kingsnorth, and other critics of industrial society's impact on the earth. Indeed, in his first newsletter discussing the endeavor, Campbell referred to Leopold's role in developing the concept of "restoration ecology."[4] The Preserve's principles produce a powerful new paradigm by combining lessons from the nineteenth-century reform and rural cemeteries, the English natural burial movement, and several environmental successes—including, importantly, the creation of the national parks and forests systems. The Preserve combines an ecological sensibility with a nostalgic, Romantic view of nature.

While contemporaries thought of the reform cemeteries as environmentally advanced, the new conservation cemeteries or natural burial grounds challenge virtually every element of the conventional cemetery. Nature moves from a backdrop to the central motif of the grounds. At the Preserve, instead of an elaborate gate, a simple gravel road, bracketed by large boulders, frames the entrance from Cobb Bridge Road, leading visitors to a parking area next to a visitors' center. Once parked, visitors move through the grounds along a set of winding paths. No cars are allowed inside, just small electric golf carts. A series of small pavilions are planned to ring the middle of the property for the use of visitors, but no massive mausoleums, grandiose chapels, or ostentatious monuments.

Near the upper edge of the property, the bed of the eponymous Ramsey Creek flows through the grounds, adding the noise of nature. The site is designed, but in ways that remind me of New York's Adirondack Park, where my brother and I hiked when I was in my teens. That beautiful area is noted for its winding paths and simple framed buildings. Ramsey Creek uses similar building types and pathways to provide just enough infrastructure to allow access even as it maintains the natural condition of the grounds.

The allusion to state and national parks is not surprising, given conservation cemeteries' aspiration to use burials to ensure the preservation of this woodland grove. For the past two generations, environmentalists have railed against the wasteful sprawl of suburban development, leapfrogging across the countryside destroying habitats and plowing up farmlands.[5] In evoking the concept of the conservation area, they are drawing upon a widespread interest to secure land from development. Yet many groups hoping to preserve land do not have the funds to purchase the acreage as encroaching suburbs increase land values. By combining the principles of the natural burial movement with those of the conservation movement, social entrepreneurs can achieve what in other circumstances is almost impossible. They can use burial fees as continuous operational funding as they develop a permanent fund to support the preservation of the conservation area.

However, to be a successful conservation area, the cemetery must not leave many cultural traces that would "ruin" the landscape. That is why the simplified principles of the natural burial movement are such a critical ingredient in the concept. Such concerns had precedent in some reactions to the successes of the reform and rural cemeteries. Pioneering landscape architect and park designer Frederick Law Olmsted raised the specter that the rural cemetery had become a place "of the grossest ostentation of the living."[6] Just as he worried that large family monuments disrupted the simple natural environment, English reformers initiated the natural burial movement and the woodland cemetery to reaffirm humans' place as a part of nature, in life and death.

The Natural Burial Movement

With the initiation of the British Natural Death Centre in 1991, English social activist and inventor Nicholas Albery and his psychotherapist wife Josefine Speyer hoped to promote a natural approach to death that would mirror the natural childbirth movement of the 1960s.[7] While their initial focus emerged from their efforts to humanize the way people died, especially by promoting hospice care as an alternative to technologically driven hospital care, the movement quickly broadened to include funeral rituals, and finally to gravesites. After 1993, when Ken West opened the first natural burial ground in the city of Carlisle (in northwestern England), the movement quickly spread.[8] Enough people ascribed to the cemetery reform movement by 1994 that the Centre created the Association of Natural Burial Grounds (ANBG) to oversee and regulate the establishment of new natural burial grounds by writing and enforcing a code of conduct. By 2015, ANBG listed over 250 "woodlands burial grounds" in Great Britain.[9]

But what exactly is a natural burial? Definitions and interpretations vary. The ANBG code of conduct begins with an admonishment to conserve "local wildlife and archaeological sites," ensure the permanency of the site, and use only "environmentally acceptable" burial containers such as a shroud or wooden coffin.[10] They encourage

TABLE 2.1 Guiding Principles American Green Burial Cemeteries, Green Burial Council, 2014

1. A rejection of embalming and other parts of the preparation of the body perceived as unnatural

2. A rejection of cement vaults and steel caskets as both unnatural and unnecessarily wasteful of the earth's resources

3. A rejection of hardwood caskets perceived as a waste of a precious natural resource

4. Embracing the conservation ethic by which the return of the body to the earth feeds the woodlands without imposing human artifice and artifacts, such as ostentatious memorials and monuments

5. Accepting nature as the site of the burial through the family's acceptance of a simple yet dignified burial process with a shroud or a softwood casket, a tree, shrub or local stone as the memorial

6. Encouraging limited visitation accessibility to preserve and protect the woodlands

simple ground burial over cremation. They aspire to the environmental conservation of resources and land while creating a sacred space.

As clear as these general principles seem, the definition of a woodlands cemetery remains elusive. As Andrew Clayton and Katie Dixon have reported, "[n]o single model governs their ownership, location, design, or management, and therefore the experience which users have may vary considerably."[11] Many components of practice are still debated, especially as the model has been transplanted outside Great Britain. In Britain, most of the natural burial sites are quite small (under five acres) and have had limited influence on dominant cultural practices. Still, the movement has gotten widespread press, has spread across the globe, and has provided a growing number of people with a new burial option.[12]

The successful launch of Ramsey Creek led to an increase in woodlands burial grounds and sections around the United States. The Green Burial Council, the US organization that certifies green cemeteries, has established three types of sites that adhere to its principles—conservation cemeteries, such as Ramsey Creek; natural burial grounds, a slightly less rigorous category; and hybrid cemeteries, where conventional and reform ideas merge. (See chapter 3.)[13]

As of 2016, five conservation burial grounds had been certified since Ramsey Creek—two in Ohio, and one each in Georgia, Florida, and Washington—while twenty-three natural burial grounds have been designated. These grounds are significantly more likely to be owned by a non-cemetery institution and to represent the establishment of new grounds, compared to the hybrid cemeteries that are typically an addition to an existing cemetery. The natural and conservation/woodlands burial grounds inter a tiny fraction of Americans who die each year, yet their influence comes from the rejection of standard practices: a rejection arising from environmental concerns.

The natural burial movement merges two powerful streams of cultural reform that I highlighted in the introduction: the critique of the cemetery as an element of the modern way of death, and the environmental destruction of the traditional countryside through unfettered urbanization. The two strands combine concerns about authenticity, community, and environment to create a coherent critique of current practices in the death industries, including the now pervasively accepted practice of cremation.

Environmentally Unfriendly Modern Way of Death

The first stream of the critique has extended Jessica Mitford's explosive 1963 attack on the death industries.[14] Mitford argued for a simplified funeral that included transparent pricing, no embalming or the other inauthentic rituals, and inexpensive cremations. In essence, she objected to the mechanics of the death rituals, but more importantly detested that the family had lost control of the process to largely unemotional professionals. The result was that the cost of death was obscene, and the experience felt inauthentic even as the body was made to look as lifelike as possible. Mitford famously rejected her publisher's request not to describe an embalming; rather, she used the ingredients list to remind readers of its outrageous chemicals.[15]

The battle against contemporary practices, and especially the use of chemicals throughout the industry, continues. Environmental activists have increasingly argued that the conventional burial process is both dangerous and wasteful. In the nineteenth century, arsenic was used in embalming, leaving a harsh legacy. Later, formaldehyde and other chemicals remained environmentally unfriendly. Some estimate that annually US cemeteries consume 30 million board feet of hardwood, over 100,000 tons of steel, approximately 1.6 million tons of concrete, and over 800,000 gallons of embalming fluid, including significant quantities of formaldehyde.[16]

Cemeteries are not alone in their embrace of chemicals, of course. Most large recreational sites, such as golf courses and parks, use daunting amounts of chemicals on their lawns, flowers, and other plants. As Rachel Carson sadly asserted in 1962: "Gardening is now firmly linked with the super poisons."[17] By 1984, Americans were applying "more synthetic chemical fertilizer to lawns than India applied on all its food crops."[18] Indeed, by 2015, the United States had an estimated 40 million acres of bio-homogeneous lawns, making lawn grass by far the nation's largest crop (more than three times as much as corn or hay).[19]

My father used a variety of targeted pesticides in Oakwood to attack fungus or other growths that threatened the beauty of the grass, trees, shrubs, or other plants. He was not alone. By the 1960s, cemetery magazines were filled with advertisements for various pesticides, herbicides, and other chemicals that could eliminate weeds, control animal pests, and keep grounds sparkling. In Rachel Carson's words, such chemicals "give a giddy sense of power over nature to those who wield them."[20]

Confirming the environmental impacts, however, is difficult. When the World Health Organization conducted "an introductory briefing" in 1998 on the environmental and public health impacts of cemeteries, they did not find substantial evidence of specific environmental dangers from burial practices—though they didn't consider lawn care. Yet they did caution, among other things, that given the chemicals used in embalming and possible mercury or other hazards in the teeth and other spots in the body, human bodies should not be buried within 250 meters of a spring or well.[21] Other studies have found that the use of such resources clearly has an impact, though it is hard to connect that impact to specific health outcomes.

Even if scientists cannot find a direct correlation between burial and pollution, natural burial ground managers demand that people bury their dead in a place without a lawn. Reformers fret about the cemetery as part of the broader lawn culture that is dependent on pesticides and other chemicals that are harmful to the birds and other fauna and that diminish eco-diversity. English nature writer Richard Mabey, in his lovely book on weeds, writes that even these most inventive and persistent of plants cannot withstand the repeated destruction brought about by the modern mower, especially combined with chemicals.[22]

While no one has developed a formal measure of how well a cemetery supports ecological diversity, my experience suggests that the older, more topographically and plant diverse rural cemeteries are better homes for birds and other wildlife than the more bio-homogeneous memorial parks, and both would fall short of the bio-diversity in any green cemetery.[23] Woodland burial grounds would sit at one end of the continuum, the least biodiverse memorial parks at the other, with significant variation in between. The more lawn, the less diversity in plantings, and the more the landscape seems constructed and inauthentic.

Reconsidering Cremation as an Environmental Good

While cremation has been promoted as a solution to the waste and cost of burial and entombment, natural burial advocates view it as part of the problem. Their critique is quite a reversal from Mitford, who argued that the practice combined "economy and simplicity," putting the process back in the hands of the family. She even encouraged people to consider the supposedly inexpensive cremations of private agencies as an alternative to traditional burial, although she later retracted this endorsement when confronted with some agencies' unsavory economic practices.[24] Perhaps she was only a decade too early to believe that a more radical solution was possible.

The contemporary reformers' concerns about cremation partly reflect cremation's success in replacing burial throughout the world. As noted, the process has gone mainstream. In 2011, for the first time, over one million deceased Americans (42 percent) were cremated, and by 2015 the number of cremations had surpassed the number of burials for the first time.[25]

The numbers are startling. When Mitford was writing in the early 1960s, roughly 60,000 Americans were cremated—just 3.6 percent of all deaths. The 2015 national rate of 48.6 percent of all deaths (roughly 1.1 million) actually obscures quite dramatic regional differences, with some states having much higher rates. While in Mississippi fewer than 20 percent of 2014 deaths were cremated (which is still over five times the national average in 1960), in Nevada, 75.9 percent were cremated.[26] Cremation has become an integral part of American interment practices. We might even say that cremation has become standard practice.

While they oppose the practice itself, natural burial advocates might view cremation as a model for finding public acceptance. When indoor crematories were introduced in the United States in 1876, many advocates viewed cremation as a more rational, healthful process than ground burial. Ironically, they even argued that ground burial was dangerous—not only to groundwater supplies, but also as repositories of disease. Science soon proved the worries about contagion wrong, but cremation retained the image as not only less expensive, but also more environmentally friendly than ground burial.[27]

Today's critics firmly reject its friendliness. They dismiss the practice as part of the broader unsustainable modern way of death. Ken West summarized the objections to cremation in his 2010 guide to natural burial:

> In truth, cremation is wrong in many ways, not least because it reinforces our reliance on fossil fuels to the very end; it wastes the benign biodegradable components of our body and the coffin and turns them into harmful emissions; it wastes technology to manufacture the cremators and abatement equipment. It also removes us from that important state, that of being natural.[28]

Ecologists identify two specific hazards: 1) environmental pollutants, especially "cremercury," a term for the mercury in teeth from dental amalgams; and 2) the "wasted" fuel and other energy used to complete a cremation. Scientists Montse Marti and José Domingo conducted a review of all the studies of cremation emissions.[29] They found quite varying results, but they concluded that "if mercury emissions from crematoria are not properly controlled, these facilities could [be] a relatively important source of atmospheric pollution." A 2013 UN study found that worldwide cremation accounted for less than 1 percent of mercury emissions—though that still amounts to 3.6 tons of mercury.[30]

Second, while the Mitfordian critique focused on the modern way of death's expense, wastefulness, and inauthenticity, environmentalists worry about adverse impacts like the amount of carbon dioxide released by cremation. One estimate holds that a single cremation, which lasts between two and three hours and during which the crematory is heated to 1,600 degrees, releases roughly 540 pounds of carbon dioxide into the atmosphere. With over 1.1 million Americans cremated annually, the amount of CO^2 released is startling: roughly 594 million pounds (269,434 tons), or the equivalent of 287.5 million pounds of coal. These numbers depend on the type of fuel used, and reformers are trying to leave less of an impact by using alkaline hydrolysis or liquid nitrogen. Still, even if they succeed, we are left with Ken West's worry that cremation "removes us from . . . being natural."

"A Vast, Featureless Expanse of Prairie"

If the first stream critiques the cemetery and cremation as elements in the modern way of death, in the second stream, critics fear the cemetery's symbolic role as part of an attack on the broader natural environment. In the 1980s, English writers Marion Shoard, Richard Mabey, and others critiqued the effects of the industrialization of English rural agriculture on the traditional countryside. They applied the powerful arguments of early environmentalists such as Rachel Carson, rejecting the use of chemicals and pesticides on lawns and in trees. Shoard protested the failure of law to protect the hedgerows, streams, meadows, and, yes, woodlands, resulting in the countryside being turned into "a vast, featureless expanse of prairie." Thanks to a lack of regulation, a remarkable amount of English land has given way to a "grass monoculture" that, as with the lawnscape of the memorial parks, "cannot sustain our traditional wild flowers, birds and animals": an argument reminiscent of Carson's attack on DDT.[31] Paul Kingsworth, like Shoard, refused to blame just big business for this travesty; the British government played a crucial role in the destruction, with government policy abetting corporate greed. Each writer argued for reclaiming ancient woodlands or fringe spaces left after development, and conserving them, perhaps by using them as burial grounds.

At almost the same time, an urban planning and design movement with similar concerns was emerging in the United States. New Urbanism has been defined by its attack on unfettered growth that gobbles up farmland and open space for disconnected, sprawling subdivisions. Advocates argue that urban planners, real estate developers, and suburban homeowners jointly have been erasing the nation's natural heritage, placing a wide range of wildlife habitat at risk. Their early efforts drew upon the ideas of ecologist Aldo Leopold, especially his "land ethic," which provided a principled argument against the indiscriminate loss of land to development. Eventually New Urbanism would focus more on regulating development itself, but the underlying desire to sustain nature in the face of seemingly inexorable human expansion continues to play a key role in their thinking—as it does in the broader environmental movement, including the emerging green burial movement.

In 2005 former Jesuit minister and current cemetery consultant Joe Sehee, with his wife Juliette, founded the Green Burial Council as an American version of the British Association of Natural Burial Grounds (ANBG), with the mission to certify natural burial places. His GBC adapted the British code of conduct to create the certification criteria for green cemeteries and provide a source for promotional information about the movement. The GBC distinguishes between "conservation" and "natural" burial grounds, with the former being more restrictive. Even so, conservation burial grounds are remarkably individualistic, varying in size, organization, and some of their practices. Organizationally, for instance, Foxfield Preserve in Wilmot, Ohio, the first conservation burial place in that state, is also the first in the nation established by a conservation agency. Located roughly forty miles south of Akron, the cemetery is set on forty-three acres of former farmland owned by the Wilderness Center, an educational conservation organization. By repurposing the farmland into woodland burials, Foxfield echoed English conversation efforts. By its fifth anniversary in 2013, the Center reportedly had sold 200 plots and held fifty burials, all supporting land conservation. Conversely, Honey Creek Woodlands, twenty-five miles southeast of Atlanta in Conyers, Georgia, is set amid 8,000 acres owned by the Monastery of the Holy Spirit, a Benedictine order. The order has designated the whole acreage as a conservation area, splitting a small section out for the burials. Here, all visitors save the survivors are forbidden from entering the burial ground, to protect the lands.

Conservation burial grounds are the most radical green alternative to the conventional cemetery. They reject the aesthetic and rituals of the modern way of death, replacing them with older, simpler, more natural, environmentally sensitive practices that are largely devoid of (but not hostile to) religion and culture. The strictest of the burial grounds reject monuments, benches, and other hard cultural artifacts. This decision places them in opposition to the cemetery, where the connection between art and death has been close for centuries. Other conservation burial grounds construct simple chapels and allow families to erect memorials of local native stones, but strictly limit their interventions in the landscape. Even though some American conservation burial grounds are less strict than the purest British ones, most still largely rely solely on nature as the mediator of death and memory.

The second category, the natural burial grounds, are generally a bit more willing to compromise about conventional burial rituals, but remain committed to core values such as the conservation of the land and the return of the body to nature. For instance, Penn Forest Natural Burial Ground, located outside Pittsburgh on thirty-two acres, is conserving part of its land while using the rest for burials. It allows nontoxic embalming and a variety of memorial stones (of wood and

FIGURE 2.2. Pathway through the woods, Ramsey Creek Preserve, Westminster, SC, 2017.

local stone, set level to the ground—perhaps the only thing such a burial ground has in common with a conventional memorial park). It emphasizes that the burial ground looks, feels, and is completely unlike a conventional American cemetery. Perhaps for this reason, this category is the fastest-growing one, having increased in new cemeteries by over 30 percent since 2014.

The site hosts a mixture of young and older trees set in open woodlands. The managers aim to maintain and sustain the landscape "to look like typical Pennsylvania forest and meadow lands" in perpetuity. Such language echoes across the websites and promotional materials of many such grounds; most of it is copied or adapted from the Green Burial Council or pioneers such as Ramsey Creek. Managers slightly alter components to fit their site and values. Penn Forest, for instance, offers to sell "memorial boulders, benches and other hardscape items" to lot holders. And although they point out the environmental dangers of cremation, they allow cremation burial and scattering.

While Penn Forest literally hopes to restore the forest, Duck Run

Natural Burial Cemetery aims to create a "natural park." Located on 113 acres in the Shenandoah Valley, roughly fifty miles northwest of Charlottesville, Virginia, the land does not have the natural texture of Penn Forest. The pastureland that had served as a dairy farm is still open, only dotted with trees. In reclaiming a space previously used for industrial food production, Duck Run emulates many of the English burial grounds. As Ken West details in his guide, the natural burial movement is a fluid creation in which the type of appropriate land-scape is still evolving. One reason the movement shifted from "wood-lands" to "natural" is that many places around England no longer have woodlands, and are simply trying to preserve the pasturelands or other natural spaces.

The green burial movement retains many conventional American cemetery practices. The burial grounds bury bodies, though not in en-vironmentally unsustainable containers. They create memorial sites, though they abhor ostentation. They promise to keep careful records of burials, so each grave is sacrosanct. They create pathways so that families can visit their loved ones. As they age, most of the conser-vation burial grounds plan to have a chapel like the one at Ramsey Creek. They plan to build shelters that perhaps remind us of the Adi-rondacks or other state and national parks. They state that they will develop rituals that draw on the religious and cultural heritages that have shaped conventional cemeteries.

They remain burial grounds, with critical differences. Looking back to premodern practices, they largely reject bodily preservation, artistic ostentation, and anything else that smacks of conventional so-ciety's focus on consumption. They do not want tall spires competing with the trees, massive mausoleums overshadowing the shrubbery, and people's names drawing attention away from the blueberries or the hawks.

Debating Nature versus Culture in a Sacred Space

Walking through Oakwood or another of the great nineteenth-century cemeteries, I think there is joy in coming upon a lovely statue or intricately designed panel. Natural burial ground advocates don't agree. In their strictest definition, the only acceptable memorial is a living part of nature, such as a native tree. Yet right from the start, this interpretation has been debated, with types of memorialization serving to define different styles of natural burial.

Such a debate strikes at the heart of the modern cemetery, which has from its beginning served as a gardenesque space as well as a community and individual repository of memories. Burial grounds have combined nature and culture for millennia, providing some of the most stunning architectural and artistic achievements, from the tomb of Mausolus to a variety of beautiful sculptures and memorials I will discuss later.

The natural burial movement's rejection of memorials seems tied to the broader desire to create a burial site not associated with consumption culture. In this decision, the originators of the movement drew upon concerns of environmentalists worldwide that consumption creates waste, degrades environments, and destroys natural habitats. Yet how does one balance the environmental good with the cultural heritage of a society?

In 2010, Billy Campbell challenged the ANGB on this topic.[32] English correspondents asked Campbell to defend the practice of allowing local native stone memorials in his American woodlands landscape. They reminded him that most English burial places do not allow them. They use only trees as markers of the grave, since they are biodegradable and are part of the original landscape. They believe memorial stones intrude, introducing artifice into nature.

Campbell argued for the desirability of "artistic stone memorials." The Preserve allows only memorials "made of stone from the same geological strata as [the Preserve]." The restriction ensures that the stones, which can only be carved with minimal information, will not violate the conservation ethic and will meld into the environment. Campbell's reasoning is that "returning stones to the forest floor is a good thing ecologically." The area's forest, unlike in England, has not been logged out. It is dense and provides a full canopy; therefore, saplings have little chance of surviving. The stones also play a crucial role as homes for "ant colonies, snake eggs and various small mammal and invertebrate(s)."

Campbell also admitted that the memorials were necessary in America, as they would "improve the comfort level of those potential clients that might not consider a grave marked only by a tree or by wildflowers, and who were fearful of not being able to find the grave of a loved one." Given a "cultural context where ostentatious funerals are the rule (the average funeral and burial in South Carolina is approaching $8,000), and where traditions (if only a few generations old) die hard, we found that we risked losing a large number of potential clients without at least the option of some minimal type of stone marker." The Preserve is an experiment, and only slowly attracting customers, partially because of worries that it would not include the traditional components of the cemetery.

Finally, Campbell asked his English counterparts, "But what about the role of art [in the burial place]?" Campbell reminded them of the petroglyphs of the American Southwest and the ancient Dreamtime art of Australia, then inquired why environmentalists celebrated these sites. He wondered if art was acceptable only "in a lonely landscape dominated by non-human nature," not in a "world totally reworked by humans," where the "need to 're-wild'" the environment made environmentalists averse to any human intrusion. He assured them that the Preserve would not include "carved angels" or "sheep dotting the landscape," while arguing for stones of "indigenous materials" that "heighten the sense of sacred space."

The ANGB rejected his position. Even though Campbell had called upon ecological principles, the Natural Death Centre writer noted that "You cannot fill the countryside with memorial stones for the indefinite future—but reforestation can continue for the longest term." The rejection of human intrusion was, in the writer's words, the "essence" of the woodlands concept, and was "not to be lightly surrendered." The principle of returning to a natural state allows no exception, given the deeply constructed nature of contemporary burial practice. In this view, the balance between art and nature was simple; art has no place in a natural setting.

I am surprised by this rigidity. I live in Los Angeles, where reforestation requires far more resources than the addition of a stone to the desert or the shrubland. The Centre's argument seemed not only

to valorize the constructed nature of the vast majority of their woodland sites (which are recovered farms and other spaces already altered
by humans), but also conceived of the woodlands cemetery in very
specific English terms, not applicable to much of the rest of the natural world. If the movement is to have the impact that it wishes, recognizing the human desire to be remembered and the wide variety of
natural environments seems crucial.

Further, the rigidity exposes a very narrow view of culture. The
English woodlands landscape is a cultural landscape as much as the
streets of London are. This is especially true in a woodlands landscape
that has been recreated for the purpose of burial, and embodies the
memories of those surviving. A finding in a 2007 study on the decisions people made about those memorial trees highlights the difficulty
of defining an authentic "natural" environment. Some lot holders are
filling natural burial grounds with a mixture of "native" and "exotic"
tree types, ranging from the sturdy oak to flowering and fruit trees
like the magnolia and pear. In this case, the natural burial ground,
like the traditional cemetery it rejects, becomes a place where family
members express their cultural preferences, hoping their choices will
ensure that their loved one's grave has "presence" as the distinctive
tree matures, even at the expense of altering a native, natural landscape.

The study found that such "presence" was important to many. For
example, one person chose a tree with red leaves, so that it would
"stand out." Other choices reflected the family garden or the season when the person died. One respondent reported that the chosen
tree "flowers in the spring when he was conceived," and "has ber-
ries around the time of his birthday." Even though the families were
choosing to bury their loved one in a space where no names are in-
scribed, no dates of birth and death etched into stone, they were still
hoping their gravesite would be memorable, and personal. The collective framework of the woodlands conflicted with their hope for some
individual symbolism. The need for some individual trace suggests
the hybrid cultural meaning of these sites—both rejections of traditions, and continued embraces of elements of those traditions.

When the pioneering woodlands burial ground manager Ken West wrote his guide to natural burial, he recognized that memorialization was not an easy topic. While he argued for a prohibition on all memorials save trees, he proposed three levels of memorialization in natural burial grounds: natural memorials such as trees; communal memorials, ideally on the edges of the site; and individual memorials, from which the "habitat must suffer."[33] West argued for prohibiting individual memorials, or at least putting time limits on them, in part because "after 30 years very few [mourners] will renew the right." West is less aggravated by communal memorials, which can even serve a positive purpose in sites that "cannot allow access to grave for operational reasons." Clearly, though, culture had to be subordinated to nature.

The debate over erasing culture from the burial ground, and replacing it with an "authentic" nature, suggests the strength of the principled stand the AGNB has taken. It mirrors their belief that humans should be simply part of nature. Yet they also contradict the thousands of years of commemoration prior to the development of embalming and the other characteristics the reformers detest—suggesting the power of the environmental sensibility. Campbell, for instance, allowed local stone memorials at the Preserve.

Internationalizing Natural Burial

The effort to define a new style of burial is not exclusively Anglo-American. For example, "tree-burial" started in Japan in 1999.[34] While Americans have some concerns about the amount of future burial space,[35] the Japanese are severely short on it, and it is very, very expensive. A family plot might cost roughly 3–4 million yen, or between $28,000 and $29,000 in 2016 US dollars. And that does not include the very high cost of a funeral. Almost all Japanese are cremated, and most are placed in the rear of their family monument in densely crowded cemeteries managed by Buddhist temples. The family name and the Japanese character for the household are engraved on the front of the stone. The names of those interred there are placed on the sides.[36]

"Tree-burial" essentially mimics English natural burial grounds, where a person's ashes are interred with a tree as their primary grave-stone, although small wooden markers are also used. At the pioneering site in the city of Ichinoseki, in northeastern Japan, a Buddhist priest, Chisaka Genpo, developed a 20,000-acre forest burial ground populated with large native trees, such as cedar, beech, birch, and maple.[37] Over its first fifteen years of service, over 1,500 Japanese elected for tree-burial.

However, the original tree-burial ground is truer to the principles expressed by the English than those that have followed. There are fifty other tree-burial places, but they often are not systematic in their policies about grave marking, with some very intensely used spaces planting one tree for multiple burials. They were also not "actively involved in environmental restoration and conservation."[38] They were not restoring a forest, just offering another service.

Similarly, the intense competition for burial space in Taiwan has led to woodland and parkland burials. Over 90 percent of Taiwanese in Taipei are cremated, but even so, the columbaria have filled up or are filling rapidly. Taipei authorities have sanctioned the burial of ashes in biodegradable urns around an existing tree or a newly planted one. The first woodland burial ground opened in 2003, with others soon following. Seven to ten months after the original burial, the sites are reused, and no permanent memorialization is allowed. As a result, authorities estimate that such burials take up only 10 percent of the space of a traditional grave.[39]

Such natural burials produced similar concerns in Taiwan as in the United States and Great Britain. While authorities argued that such burials reunited the remains with nature, provided places for recreation, sustained religious practices and family traditions, and were being accepted by growing numbers of people, reluctant critics worried that their ancestors were being caught in the tree's roots, placed mementoes near the graves that were often not cared for, and demanded identifying stones on new graves. One parent placed multicolored windmills around a grave so she could keep "my baby entertained"; other families filled the space with Buddhist figurines, crucifixes, toy cars, and toy houses during the Chinese remembrance celebration of Qingming.[40] The result is that while the woodland burials mirror those in Great Britain, they depart from the movement's original principles.

In the Netherlands, new green cemeteries also vary in their adherence to the movement's principles. The Bergerbos cemetery was apparently the first to attempt to follow many of the English ideas. The Kluijtmans family opened the privately owned burial ground on roughly sixteen acres of pine forest in 2003, in Sint Odiliënberg, in the southern portion of the country near Belgium and Germany.[41] By 2009, the burial ground had interred over 500 individuals, some cremated. An estimated 90 percent of those were buried using natural methods—not unusual in the Netherlands, where embalming is largely unknown, having been outlawed until 2010. In many ways the burial ground mirrors the English ones, with no true gates or fences, a focus on welcoming facilities, and the freedom to plan your own funeral. When a nudist asked about being buried naked, the owners checked the legality, and allowed it.

Bergerbos both differs dramatically from the traditional cemetery and emulates its practices. On the one hand, the grounds are intentionally disorganized, compared to the carefully designed rows and sections of the traditional cemetery. The only exception is a section set aside for babies and children (something many traditional cemeteries also do). Intriguingly, the Dutch do not allow "traditional headstones," but "it is possible to mark the grave." Researchers who have studied Bergerbos note that, much as in South Carolina, tensions have developed when some lot holders have pushed the boundaries of what is acceptable, with others complaining about the result.

Since Bergerbos is a mature forest, trees are impractical as markers (they would die under the canopy), so lot holders have fashioned a number of alternatives: They place "nesting boxes in the nearest tree," "material objects" on the gravesite, and the name of the person and a candle (some in elaborate holders) in a constructed space near the entrance. The "material objects" are the most-debated items, with a white eagle sculpture drawing negative comments, while a "boulder and plants" are viewed as more appropriate.[42] As these examples suggest, the natural burial movement is still in flux worldwide, with each society adapting the movement's principles to its culture. Still, the examples as a whole demonstrate the wide reach of the movement, and its growing intensity.

Reinventing Disposition with Technology

While the international natural burial movement has turned away from technology in a return to premodern and personalized natural rituals, others are exploring new technologies that diminish the environmental impact of disposition. The two most advanced efforts are resomation and promession, but the one that combines nature and technology most controversially is human composting. Each picks up the ecological ethic espoused by the natural burial movement, moving a step away from traditional practice. Each also raises the "yuck factor," since they use processes that many people feel might violate religious or cultural values.[43]

Proponents liken the process of "resomation," "aquamation," or "bio-cremation" to cremation, but argue that it demands dramatically less energy.[44] As with proponents of electric cars, these reformers are offering consumers a similar outcome for much less impact on the environment. Instead of burning, this process employs "Alkaline Hydrolysis," a "water-based chemical process using alkali in water at temperatures of up to 180C (350F) under high pressure only to safely and rapidly yet sympathetically reduce the body to ash." After two to three hours (similar to the length of a conventional cremation), the body is reduced to the bones. The bones "are dried and processed to a powdery substance," packaged, and returned to the survivors. The rest of the body simply disappears into the sterile fluid, which is safely disposed of into the sewer system. Proponents argue that the process uses eight times less energy than a conventional cremation, and has dramatically fewer adverse emissions as well.

The process was perfected in the 1990s for the disposal of animal carcasses. Only recently have funeral directors argued for its use with humans. The Mayo Clinic began using it a few years ago for cadavers, and the UCLA medical school has recently adopted the practice as well. In 2008, the UK Cremation Society approved its use among its members. The US National Funeral Directors Association has at least tacitly supported its use. By 2016, Colorado, Connecticut, Florida, Georgia, Illinois, Kansas, Maine, Maryland, Minnesota, Oregon, and Wyoming had legalized the process, with nineteen other states considering legalization.[45]

However, in 2011 the Ohio Department of Health effectively stopped an operator from using the process by refusing his request for burial permits, arguing that the process was not legal in the state, and was still not in 2016.[46] Religious spokespeople have been more direct in their opposition, on the grounds that allowing human remains to "go down the drain" is against church doctrine. "We don't call for the separation of a person's remains," Tom Berg, Jr., of the Columbus Roman Catholic Diocese stated. Instead, the church requires "that they should be kept together and buried together."[47] These concerns mirrored similar objections voiced 150 years ago about cremation.

Other opponents are equally emotional in voicing worries about the lack of dignity in the process. In 2013, a New Hampshire lawmaker disapproved of a motion that would make the process legal (again), stating emphatically that this process was a "vulgar, heinous, barbaric act of disposing of a dear loved one."[48] Lawmakers voted to move the legislation forward, since no one was being forced to use the process.

The second new technique is a variant of cremation as well. In "promession," a term coined by Swedish researcher Susanne Wiigh-Masak, a body is freeze-dried by bathing it in liquid nitrogen and then vacuum-drying it. The result for an adult is roughly 40–60 pounds of "fine, hygienic, odorless powder which serves as compost."[49] My description is a condensed version of the process's five stages, which should end with the powder having been transformed into high-nutrient soil. One key stage is the removal of any metals from the powder to ensure that nothing hazardous is returned to nature. Wiigh-Masak has created a firm that has affiliates in Sweden, the United Kingdom, and Korea, although she has not yet received legal permission to use the process in North America.

While resomation and promession advocates depend on technology to reach an environmental solution, other reformers want to use nature as the medium for returning the human body to the earth. Katrina Spade has pioneered a disposal method that would merge premodern and modern practices into what she calls human composting. Spade is the founder of the Urban Death Project, which has received a considerable amount of press, partly because of composting's connotations. Spade herself was quoted in the *New York Times* as remarking that the term "makes people think of banana peels and coffee grounds." She retorts that humans are "nutrients" that "could grow new life after we've died."[50] The Project seems to extend the woodlands burial ground concept toward a fully environmental solution, creating a process that mimics the natural disposal of the body.

In essence, a body would be placed in an environment of "woodchips and sawdust," which would speed decomposition. Over about a month, the body would turn "into a nutrient-rich compost." This process would occur in a three-story glass building, the core of which would be a cylinder for the bodies. A stylish revolving walkway would allow mourners to carry a body to the top of the facility for placement in the core. Presumably, the bodies would descend through the core, with a portion of the final compost available for the family to take home.[51] Spade hopes such facilities could eventually be built in communities, "like libraries."[52]

Moving from idea to production means the Project has "to navigate an array of obstacles."[53] These barriers include legal issues, including state regulations that limit human disposition to burial, entombment, cremation, and in a few states, resomation. But perhaps even more difficult will be overcoming cultural and religious objections, summarized nicely by one comment on the Project's website: "A pile of bodies is usually called a 'mass grave.' Please stop what you're doing." All three methods raise significant concerns on religious grounds, but even more broadly, worries about the treatment of human remains. Advocating for the remains to go down the drain and to be spread on the fields seems to evoke dystopian novels as much as it channels environmental principles.

Yet Spade is working with ecologists at Western Carolina University, and using her architectural background to design a handsome facility. Perhaps surprisingly, the process has not raised objections from the National Funeral Directors Association. Indeed, James Olson, the chair of the group's green burial work group, has called the concept "wonderful," and reminds us that not long ago most Americans reacted to cremation in the same way.[54]

Designers Jae Rhimm Lee and Mike Ma have taken a similar approach, and have received a sometimes visceral response. In a TED talk that has been watched over 1.3 million times, they propose an "infinity burial suit."[55] The suit is infused with mushroom spores that clean the toxins from the body after burial, reducing the environmental impact of burial. The concept came to market in 2016 through a new company, Coeio, which sells the suit for $1,500. Their first adopter was Dennis White, a Massachusetts man suffering from a terminal illness. As with each of these approaches, the human body is treated less as a sacred object of veneration than as another element of the biosphere that needs to be reintegrated into nature.

The conventional cemetery, then, faces a powerful critique from multiple sources, all connected by a common environmental concern about the modern way of death. Promoters of green burial grounds, resomation, promession, and human composting ask, are the cemetery's practices environmentally responsible? Their answer is an emphatic no. They hope to replace the conventional practices with more sustainable, natural, and sensitive ones. A growing number of cemetery managers have responded by co-opting environmental concerns into their practices.

3

CO-OPTING NATURE

In 1876, Pennsylvania physician F. Julius LeMoyne built and operated the first American crematory. His success followed similar experiments by Europeans, and opened a new age in the disposition of the dead—though at the beginning cremation was viewed as a radical reform. Indeed, the Catholic Church outlawed the practice in 1886, and the *New York Times* editorialized against the adoption of cremation several times in the decade after LeMoyne's success. Those early efforts to dissuade people from accepting and adopting the new disposition method echo the controversies surrounding current attempts to develop natural burial grounds, resomation, promession, and human composting (under another name, perhaps!). Each of these innovations offer radical alternatives to burial, entombment, and cremation, much as the cremation movement did when it was the upstart.

The history of cremation, though, is also helpful in providing insights on how cemeteries, at first generally opponents of the practice, came to view it as another consumer option, one they could monetize by providing crematories, burial lots, cremation urns, niches, and other associated services. Even though cremation began as a rationalist social reform movement built on a severe critique of the conventional cemetery, it was integrated into the modern death system. While the first five US crematories were all built by local reform societies, by 1939, "roughly 60 percent of the crematories in North America were run by cemeteries."[1] Similarly, while pre-existing burial grounds have been important to the British natural burial movement from the outset, with the pioneer Ken West managing one such cemetery, many US cemeteries are adopting the minimal requirements to be "green" service providers. Indeed, two bedrock principles of the movement, only natural memorialization and no cremation, are both being jettisoned in the move to the cemetery. The cemeteries offer natural burial "lite" as another service option, much as funeral directors and cemetery managers folded cremation into their existing services and stripped the practice of much of its revolutionary symbolism.

In adjusting to the concept of natural burial, cemetery managers have once again demonstrated their ability to evolve even as they sustain their deeply conservative institution. Cemeteries, like universities and other *longue durée* institutions, are long-term cultural spaces and slow to change.[2] For instance, in the early twentieth century, cemetery managers rejected modern art even though their figurative statues soon seemed outmoded, and "cemetery art" was prohibited from most art exhibitions. They did not feel the new abstract aesthetic reflected their institutions' values, or what their lot holders wanted cemeteries to embody. Eventually they did integrate abstraction in places, but they never allowed it to become a dominant aesthetic.

In our contemporary period of uncertainty, cemetery managers, however, have quickly recognized that natural death and burial offers them an opportunity to diversify their offerings, and further, to reach a segment of the market that might otherwise turn away from cemeteries. A growing number of them have integrated elements of the natural death philosophy into existing properties practicing traditional rituals. They are constructing natural burial sections adjacent to conventional ones. As table 3.1 shows, 80 percent of the Green Burial Council's certified cemeteries are not new burial grounds but located in existing ones. A similar percentage is operated by existing cemeteries, not reform organizations. In other words, on one side of the road, a family could be conducting a traditional funeral with an embalmed body, metal casket, concrete vault, and waiting sod, while on the other side a family is carrying the un-embalmed body in a bamboo casket to a grave that will have only limited memorialization

TABLE 3.1 Green Burial Council (GBC)
members by categorwy, 2016

GBC categories	Conservation	6	11%
	Natural	23	40%
	Hybrid	28	49%
Cemetery owned?	Yes	46	81%
	No	11	19%
New cemetery?	No	45	79%
	Yes	12	21%
Total		57	100%

and intentionally will disappear into a landscape where the grass is only rarely mowed and is not tended with pesticides. Indeed, at Prairie Rest, a natural burial section under construction in Greenwood Cemetery in Milwaukce, the potentially lovely spot is a few steps away from a conventional burial section with family monuments and presumably traditional burials. The section is located on the cdge of the cemetery, and is largely separated from the other sections, but it is merely an extension of the grounds.

Leaders of the green burial movement have not cxpressed serious concern about this development. The Green Burial Council certifies them. Pioneering leaders like Ken West, as well as many others within the movement, view incremental steps like these as not only acceptable but praiseworthy. West, for instance, eloquently argues against memorialization in his guide, but he also provides other categories of memorialization.[3]

If cemetery managers can co-opt the concept of natural burial by adhering only to those principles that fit thcir consumer orientation, then the movement will become quite different than what the original reformers had imagined. Just as early cremation advocates called for the end of the cemetery as a place harboring contagion and disease, natural burial purists condemn the cemetery as a reservoir of toxic chemicals and wasted natural resources. If cemetery managers can blunt these criticisms by incorporating natural burial as they did cremation, the cemetery can continue to provide both old and new practices without debate. These new practices may eventually complement cremation and traditional burial, but their impact on any environmental degradation associated with burial will be diminished.

Natural Burial in Cemeteries

Burial grounds within existing cemetery landscapes are quite varied in their locations and in the principles behind them. They differ in size, although most of them are quite small. They are very recent, with most having opened in the past five years or still being under construction. Some are quite lovely, while others show their youth, with landscapes that are still immature (or in the planning phase). Almost all of them are described in terms that are environmentally sensitive, such as White Haven (NY) Memorial Park's pioneering designation as a certified member of the Audubon Cooperative Sanctuary Program, and emotionally touching, such as Pine Forest (NC) Memorial Park's decision to inaugurate a green burial section in response to a local man's plea as he struggled with terminal cancer.

The Green Burial Council's "hybrid burial grounds" are required to make a very limited commitment to the original natural burial principles. They have to be in a conventional cemetery and offer the "option" of burial without the use of a vault or outer burial container and allowing shrouds. I suspect that many conventional cemeteries could meet these minimum requirements. A family came to my father decades ago and said that they wanted to bury a relative according to Muslim requirements, which meant they could not use any container. Jack made sure New York State did not prohibit such burials, and the funeral went ahead. So, did Oakwood offer the "option of burial without a vault or outer burial container," and thus was a green cemetery in the 1970s?

I do not mean to underestimate the sincerity and the commitment of these cemetery operators. Yet how do we measure environmental and social change? What demands do we make of the people and institutions proclaiming they are pioneering such changes? Three similar goals that extend across the cemetery natural burial sections are summed up in the Glen Forest, Ohio, rules: They should offer an "eco-

TABLE 3.2 Comparing rules in green sections and entire institution of sampled hybrid cemeteries, 2016

	Green section			Whole burial ground		
	Yes	No	Unclear	Yes	No	Unclear
Nontoxic embalming allowed	1	3	2	0	6	0
No embalming encouraged	6	0	0	0	6	0
No metal/hardwood caskets	4	1	1	0	6	0
No non-biodegradable vaults	6	0	0	0	6	0
Cremation interments	2	1	3	0	6	0
Cremation scattering area	0	4	2	1	3	3
Only local stone memorials	5	0	1	0	6	0
Only natural memorials	0	6	0	0	6	0
Hardscape (benches, etc.)	2	4	0	0	6	0
No non-native plants	3	2	1	0	6	0
No non-native flowers	3	2	1	0	6	0
No pesticides/herbicides	3	0	3	0	6	0
Family-assisted burials	2	1	2	0	6	0
Visitors welcome	6	0	0	6	0	0

nomical alternative to modern burial"; encourage "tasteful, hands-on involvement of family and friends" in the funeral; and make "burial more eco-friendly."[4] To judge from a sample of twelve hybrid cemetery websites, the last goal is uniformly successful, while the other two are unevenly achieved. In one case, the managers point out that even though the green grave is more expensive, the family should save money on other elements of the funeral (no vault, etc.). And the rules at another cemetery seemingly invite family and friends to be involved, but limit that involvement to lowering the casket into the grave. Further, several burial grounds prohibit the use of any stones save those available from the management—something that would make Hubert Eaton of Forest Lawn smile, since that was one way he controlled the landscape of his pioneering memorial park, and added a revenue stream. (See table 3.2.)

All of the sampled hybrid cemeteries' websites indicate that they adhere to the basic requirements of a green burial ground within a designated section or sections. They also prohibited all but biodegrad-

FIGURE 3.1. Prairie Green, Greenwood Cemetery, Milwaukee, WI, 2015.

able vaults and did not use pesticides and herbicides within the green sections. Two-thirds prohibited hardwood and metal caskets and dictated that lot holders use only local stone for their memorials in the green sections. Half of the websites clearly stated that they prohibited pesticides and herbicides and planted only native plants and flowers. Although several websites criticized cremation, few prohibited cremation interments. None of the green sections allowed the scattering of ashes, although a few did in other parts of the burial ground, and no green section prohibited all memorialization.

The green sections are completely different than the cemeteries and memorial parks they sit in. None of those burial grounds discourage embalming or prohibit metal/hardwood caskets or conventional vaults. All of them rely on non-native plants and flowers. They all embrace cremation by providing spots for interment, offering niches in mausoleums, and many selling expensive "artistic" urns. Only one clearly states that it has a scattering area—which surprised me since many conventional cemeteries are now setting aside such spaces.

I cannot get the image out of my head of one family entering a mausoleum while another walks calmly down a tree-shaded path. While I applaud Pine Forest's half-acre Garden of Renewal with its Path of Clark's Reflection, I also note that its price list includes "cremation rocks" and "Trigard markers which capture color photos of your loved one right in the bronze."[5] And White Haven, a pioneering memorial park in New York State, has developed not only a meadow for green burials as well as a Nature Trail with places for cremation burial and memorialization (and "pet friendly hiking trails" as well), but also has multiple mausoleums and traditional burial sections.[6]

The green options seem just another product line the cemetery is using to hedge its bets in this environmentally aware age, co-opting a radical concept into a consumer choice that allows them to pick and choose which features match their market. Cemetery websites don't tout green burial over conventional burial; they simply offer choices. Not one of the green section websites I surveyed offered a green option that cost less than their standard grave. One cost the same, and another was less than a grave only because the monument was included in the regular lot price. One green lot cost almost four times their most inexpensive traditional grave. The DIY features so prominently discussed in the natural burial movement—for instance, the family digging the grave—are almost entirely absent from these websites. The only explicit discussion of family assistance was related to planting appropriate native trees and plants, but even that did not happen with the burial service.

Will these green burial sections—created by well-meaning, thoughtful, innovative cemetery managers—undercut the larger message of the natural burial reformers? Or should we applaud them since they could reflect a fundamental and unexpected change reshaping the cemetery?

Hybrid Cemeteries at Either End of LA

For a more granular look, let's explore two Southern California hybrid cemeteries: Hillside Memorial Park and Joshua Tree Memorial Park. Hillside is a seventy-year-old Jewish cemetery with an array of "distinguished residents," including such notable Hollywood people as Jack Benny, Milton Berle, Nell Carter, and Cyd Charisse.[7] Located on the Westside of Los Angeles and snuggled up next to the San Diego

FIGURE 3.2. Gan Eden, Hillside Memorial Park, Culver City, CA, 2016.

Freeway, the memorial park is surrounded by suburbs and high-rise commercial buildings on one side and residential areas on the other. The park is dominated by famed African American architect Paul Williams's 1951 memorial for early twentieth-century crooner and film actor Al Jolson, who was reinterred here from a Hollywood cemetery. Classical columns surrounding Jolson's tomb sit at the top of a long cascading waterfall dancing down the hillside that gives the memorial park its name.

In November 2015, Hillside opened a green section, Gan Eden (Hebrew for the Garden of Eden). Hillside's promotional material states that adapting Jewish funeral practices to green principles is relatively simple, since the dead are buried very quickly and in contact with the earth.[8] The new section perfectly exemplifies the contradiction inherent in a green burial section in a pre-existing memorial park. It is tucked into a small space in the southeastern edge of the grounds, and bracketed on both sides by large traditional burial sections and garden mausoleums. The "Valley of the Prophets" mausoleum has a large circular central building with two garden crypt arms jutting out from it. What looks to be a new cremation niche columbarium stands at the end of the green burial section, with a wooden pergola seemingly intended for non-native grapevines or a similar planting overshadowing the columbarium.

One enters the green burial section by passing through an opening in a stone wall engraved with the name of the section in English and Hebrew. The wall is interrupted halfway across to reveal natural grasses growing among the graves. The section itself is quite narrow compared to the wide expanse of green lawn dotted with small dips where bronze markers are carefully set in rows going up the hillside. Instead, here the memorial park offers small rocks as tombstones. The one stone that has been engraved has Hebrew at the top and bottom, the decedent's name in bold letters (but still very tastefully presented), and a seven-line statement of her qualities that ends with the statement "deeply loved, deeply missed."

Tall grasses are planted between each of the burial rows, creating a strong, natural look and boundary from row to row. On each side of the section, the park has planted bushes that are still very small, presumably with the intention of further separating the section from the surroundings and making the experience unique for lot holders. Unfortunately, inside the boundaries, the natural grasses compete with small lawns that cover the grave areas. Instead of the messiness of a meadow, we get a carefully culturally constructed lawnscape interrupted by native grasses and the rocks. The rocks themselves mimic the bronze markers in being set in straight rows within the lawns. In Southern California, which was just ending six years of drought in late 2016, the very green lawn, the very green trees, and the very healthy and high native grasses all are evidence of the imposition of a European-style lawn landscape into our semiarid chaparral ecosystem. The section seems truly a hybrid, with an appearance that fits with the conventional cemetery's image, and procedures that simplify modern funeral practices in an effort to make them appear environmentally sound.

Joshua Tree Memorial Park is just about as far away from Hillside as one can get in Southern California, over 140 miles east. And rather than being beside one of the world's busiest freeways with hundreds of thousands of cars passing daily, it is just a few miles from the entrance to one of the region's most breathtaking landscapes, the eponymous national park. On Google Maps, the memorial park is a dot of green in a sea of brown desert and shrublands. Water is everything in Southern California. The green lawns of the memorial park—exactly what drove people like Billy Campbell to create a new paradigm— stand out like a natural disturbance in the surrounding landscape.

The materials that Joshua Tree presents regarding green burial do not discuss adapting a green burial to an arid climate, but instead use the boilerplate provided by the Green Burial Council to discuss the dangers of traditional practices and the wonders of the alternatives.[9] Nor does it discuss any possible conflict of interest between promoting the park's garden mausoleum while advocating for a simplified process. Instead, green burial comes across as another product on their seventeen-page price list, including a $12,000 bronze vault and a $3,000 oak veneer cremation casket. The price list, however, does not include any specific terms for green burial and memorialization, nor does their pamphlet mention differences in price or availability.

These two California hybrid sites are very different, but they are generally typical of the green sections across the country. These sections are qualitatively less green than the other two categories. They tend to mirror conventional cemetery landscapes much more closely than the other categories, while they adhere to the essential funeral practices that define them as "green." Strikingly, their literature is much less likely to discuss the controversies around cremation than virtually all of the conservation and natural burial ground websites. Perhaps they don't mention it because cremation has become such an important part of most cemeteries' business, especially in states such as California, where over half of all deaths are cremated.

Cremation Gardens

Although at first most cemeteries discouraged or prohibited cremation interments and every one prohibited the scattering of ashes, a
few broke against the tide and opened crematories, developed special
sections on their grounds, and built niches into their mausoleums for
cremation remains. Time passed; the process became more widely
accepted; and cremation services became commonplace. Still, the
Catholic Church did not approve cremation as a burial process until
the 1960s, which was the same decade my dad installed a small cremation garden in Oakwood. Located at the end of the valley, deep in the
newer sections, the garden consisted of a granite birdbath surrounded
by rose flower beds. It was an accessible but not overly ostentatious
location that a casual visitor would not notice—I think on purpose.

In the decades since, cremation has become both a terrible worry
and a new source of innovation in the cemetery industry. The old
cremation gardens were mostly standard burial section designs with
lawns, flower beds, and, as at Oakwood, a small monument or feature.
The newest cremation sections tend to be more natural, or at least appear more natural. One lovely example is in Forest Home Cemetery,

FIGURE 3.3. Cremation Garden, Forest Home Cemetery, Milwaukee, WI, 2015.

in Milwaukee, which had a "master gardener" design a "Victorian Garden for cremation." Small columbaria are separately located in a circle around the garden. A path leads the visitor around the fountain to a short allée of trees that ends in a pergola. The plantings are less ornamental and bio-homogeneous than in the rest of the cemetery. Longer grasses and the vines creeping up the pergola suggest a very different aesthetic. The setting is contemplative, fitting well with the rest of a cemetery filled with beautiful deciduous trees in glowing colors the day I visited.

The cremation garden at Forest Lawn Memorial Park at Hollywood Hills (CA) is an excellent example of how cemeteries have integrated cremation into their traditional business model. This attractive garden, called Woodlands, was designed as a rock garden for strolling. A short "meandering" path is surrounded by native plants set in decomposed granite.[10] The designer, J. Stuart Todd, Inc., kept as many of the existing trees as possible to give the garden a mature look. The combination of a thirty- to forty-foot tree canopy and the native brush plants creates a tranquil space that backs up against the Sennett Creek Canyon, a preservation easement.

However, Forest Lawn placed artificial rocks designed to hold up to four cremation urns throughout the garden. The manufactured rocks work surprisingly well in relationship to the real ones. Of course, the artificial rocks allow Forest Lawn to monetize the space. The 526 rocks, plus the 212 spaces in the two columbaria, create a total capacity of 3,000 interment spaces, which in 2014 sold for up to $4,500 a rock, and the niches $3,600. If that was not sufficient, the garden setting also is interrupted by a small two- and three-story gray granite columbarium curving through the middle. The columbarium breaks the flow of the pathways through the space, and it emphasizes the artificiality of the "garden." If the columbarium had been constructed as the fence along the back edge of the garden, the site would have felt much more unified and aesthetically different than the lawn sections that surround it.

The decision to place the columbaria at the center of the garden suggests the trouble memorial parks and cemeteries are having balancing nature and art in the landscape. An article describing the new garden suggested that it would be a "place for permanent memorialization designed to appeal to those who might otherwise scatter a loved one's cremated remains to the winds somewhere in the great outdoors, only to regret later having done so." The language — "scatter . . . to the winds," compared to "permanent memorialization" — suggests the tension. Old justifications for designs that create high-capacity interment spaces are competing with aspirations for more natural landscapes that embody a stronger environmental sensibility.

After decades of cemeteries dismissing scattering as no better than a pagan ritual, cemeteries are now opening scattering gardens. Although another attempt to recapture revenues lost to the family's control of the cremated remains, these new scattering grounds also fit with the natural burial sections and other activities to both be more environmentally sensitive and attract people who have felt alienated from the cemetery. Given that many older cemeteries were designed on topographically uneven terrains, they often have areas that are not easily turned into traditional burial sections, such as the "woods" at Oakwood. These "waste" spaces suddenly can have a new purpose, and become revenue centers, as scattering gardens. Although not yet in Oakwood.

At Cave Hill Cemetery in Louisville, Kentucky, management utilized an underused space near the cemetery's primary landscape feature, the falls between their "Twin Lakes," as a place for a scattering garden.[11] A tall black granite, domed, upright monument is sandblasted with the words "Twin Lakes \ Scattering Garden." Small bronze plaques are attached that commemorate those memorialized there. Since the garden sits in a part of the cemetery founded in 1846, the landscape is fully matured, with large trees and ample brush set against the lakes and falls.

The lovely Forest Lawn Cemetery in Buffalo has committed to fully integrating cremation into its business model and landscape plan.[12] It offers multiple options to families, including a "private scattering stone garden," the option of purchasing a lot for the express purpose of scattering, a "community scattering space," and more traditional alternatives such as mausoleum niches, including in the unique open-air Frank Lloyd Wright–designed Blue Sky Mausoleum. The scattering gardens purposefully are not overbuilt, in keeping with the idea that the cemetery is a natural oasis within the city. Indeed, the cemetery has six and a half acres near its center set aside as a contemplative space for lot holders and visitors to re-engage with nature.

The reluctance to authorize scattering is evident in the opposition to it by all of the cemeteries where Sloanes have superintended. Although three of them have crematories, and all of them offer both in-ground and niche burial for ashes, only Woodlawn (Bronx) has a recently established scattering repository. David Ison, Woodlawn's director of sales and marketing, articulated the general position of cemetery managers regarding scattering: "Scattering of cremated remains is really romanced in movies," he said, but "if you want to come visit your dad or your mom, if you pour them into the ocean, you don't have a place to visit."[13] Like the new hybrid green sections, this language reminds us how central institutional control of the remains is to the continuation of the cemetery.

So far, environmentalists are less concerned with the space the cremated remains take up in the cemetery than the process by which the body is cremated. Some crematoria (including Oakwood) have installed scrubbers to limit mercury emissions. Crematory companies are trying to build more efficient, less polluting machines, but the turnover in machines will take a generation or more, and even then they will continue to use energy. (One intriguing example of innovative thinking is the Redditch Borough Council in Worcestershire, England, which has proposed using excess heat from crematoria to warm an adjacent leisure center, with pools and other activities for the community.)[14] Environmental claims have had no discernible impact on the rising rates of cremations around the world, but then few people have seriously considered the environmental costs of a cremation.

We have too few evaluations of the impacts of ground burial, entombment, cremation, and the alternatives to know whether the significant negative impacts that critics claim of traditional burial are true, or conversely, if the proposed savings suggested by the advocates for the alternatives will occur. But the prevalence of the debate suggests the power of the environmental sensibility in shifting cultural discussions.

Future of Culture in the Cemetery

Much as cremation offered a trenchant critique of burial and entombment in the late nineteenth century, the natural burial movement is today's most radical alternative. From the perspective of the conventional cemetery manager, natural burial, if fully implemented, returns us to a natural landscape with few cultural mementoes. It scuttles most of the culturally constructed elements of the cemetery, including the large and elaborate individual, family, and institutional memorials as well as the ornate chapels that have served families for centuries. Even more radically, the cemetery becomes a way station rather than a permanent feature. Burials are not intended to leave a record of the community, but instead serve as the material for the creation of natural spaces where signs of individuals are erased.

In their efforts to adapt to green burials, cemetery managers have veered sharply in different directions. Some managers clearly view green burial as another consumer option they need to provide but that does not alter their basic business model. They adopt selected principles of the natural burial movement, rejecting those that threaten their underlying principles and perhaps revenue streams. Other managers are testing whether there is a market for a fully developed alternative to conventional burial, with the promise of new revenues but also a new template for the cemetery.

The biggest threat looming for virtually every cemetery is the loss of income as cremation rates grow and fewer people inter even those remains in the cemetery. The promise of the natural burial movement is that it strips away the environmental hazards now associated with the conventional cemetery and offers a return to simplicity. This revolutionary change, though, fundamentally rejects the cemetery as a repository of memories, characterizing it as a nature preserve. The cemetery might remain a place of consolation and contemplation—but after a few decades, will it still? If the natural burial movement succeeds, what happens to the idea that the cemetery is for mourning and memorials as much as it is for preserving nature?

That tension is, for me, the most important discussion we should have about natural burial. But there is a second tension: When is a natural burial simply another cemetery service rather than a challenge to the culture of the modern cemetery? Those cemeteries that are creating a cultural adjacency between conventional and natural do not find a conflict in placing these graves just yards apart. Instead, they reassert the cemetery's control of the body and the memories within their institutional framework. These hybrid green cemeteries retain the role of the cemetery as a mourning and memorial space, but at what cost to the original movement and its principles?

PART 2

———

MOURNING

FIGURE P2.1A–C. Evolution of mourning spaces. Images are of Oakland Cemetery, Atlanta (GA); Riverside Drive, Los Angeles (CA); and Green-Wood Cemetery, Brooklyn (NY).

Mourning helped define nineteenth-century society. The ways people dressed, socialized, even decorated their homes were affected by the deaths of family members and national leaders. Today, mourning affects us less in the way we dress or decorate our homes than in how we use social media, interact with the public, and where and when we perform the rituals of death and commemoration. In between these two periods was a time when society tried to limit ostentatious mourning, isolate the dead in the cemetery, and privatize memories.

In the nineteenth century, visiting the cemetery was a weekly routine for many families. Yet by the end of the century, fewer people were visiting, and those that did visited less often. A few decades later, many people viewed the cemetery as a nuisance or burden, perhaps useful only as a park or bird sanctuary.

Current society is torn. Many people, especially older generations, still embrace traditional rituals. Other people, especially younger ones, focus their mourning at the public everyday memorials and on social media. Members of either group create memorial sites at an Internet cemetery, watch a video professionally produced by the funeral home, and attend a memorial service where mourners create collages of photographs, slideshows, and other personalized ways of remembering.

How does the cemetery fit in this world? Not as easily or seamlessly as in the past, so cemetery managers have tried to develop ways to attract people and to sustain their attraction. Some managers have built up popular events such as the Day of the Dead, while others employ historical tours and recreations. A growing number of cemeteries are using digital platforms to provide ways to reattach themselves to fragmented communities. But do any of these activities provide enough income for the cemeteries to survive as the number of people being conventionally buried declines?

4

CONSOLATION

On some Friday mornings, my fifth-grade teacher, Miss Thraves, would tell me to clean the classroom's erasers. The job was messy, but only respected students were asked, so I was honored. I would go to a small table in the hallway. In the center of the table was a vacuum that sucked the dust out of each eraser as you swept it across the vacuum's opening. I was standing there on November 22, 1963, when the principal came by and told me to go immediately into my classroom. Soon after, Miss Thraves announced to the class that President Kennedy had been shot, and school was closing for the day.

All my Danforth Elementary classmates and I walked to school in 1963. I don't remember how I got home to the cemetery that day. I just know I ran to my mom. We turned on the black-and-white television in the living room. A short time later, Walter Cronkite was telling the world that the president was dead. Over the next three days I barely left that room except to eat and sleep. I watched as America mourned one man and Jack Ruby killed another.

As with millions of older Americans, two particular moments are frozen in my memory: the moment when I heard about the shooting, and the sight of the president's three-year-old son, known as John John, saluting his father's coffin as it rolled by on its horse-led caisson. I was awed by his poise on his third birthday, by his mother's veiled grace, and by the family's composed public grief. I felt it was exactly how Americans had been taught to meet a death—with a balance of emotion and modesty, showing an appropriately well-mannered *public* face that hid *private* sadness.

The president's funeral and gravesite provide a way to think about the dual meanings of the cemetery as a mourning site. Kennedy's funeral could not have been more public and communal, with an estimated 300,000 people in attendance and another 175 million watching on television. People still pause near the grassy knoll in Dallas and consider the events of that day. Hundreds of thousands of visitors go to the president's library in Boston. Yet the most visited shrine to Kennedy's memory is the gravesite in Arlington National Cemetery. Millions have visited over the years. Most act just as the Kennedy family did in 1963, with somber respect. The gravesite is a communal public space serving as a contemporary tourist site for selfies and group photos, not unlike those at the White House, Capitol Hill, and other tourist sites around the National Mall.

The gravesite, however, is also a personal place of mourning for members of the Kennedy family. Because of its public role in our nation's memory, we forget that the gravesite is a family lot holding the bodies of three fathers, a mother, and two deceased children. These two functions came into conflict when the eternal flame and the surrounding landscape had to be reconstructed to make visitors' circulation more efficient. For that work, the bodies needed to be disinterred. After the work was done, the Kennedy family came secretly to witness the reburials, without crowds, television, or other media coverage. Doubtless a Kennedy grandson or granddaughter, a great-nephew or -niece has recently stood over the graves of John, Bobby, Edward, Jackie, and the children. The visit did not make the news or get noted on Twitter. Instead, it was one of millions of visits mourners make to cemeteries to seek solace and to remember.

The modern cemetery is created for a family member mourning a loved one as well as for a visitor admiring its artistic monuments or a bird-watcher eagerly searching for a new species or a group seeking connection to their community's past. Distinguishing these two realms—public and private, personal and touristic—is almost impossible, and the cemetery has served both from its earliest days. Green-

Wood Cemetery in Brooklyn was a tourist stop in the 1840s, just as it is a mourning space today. Young people have journeyed to Jim Morrison's grave in Père Lachaise for decades, as Parisians grumble at the graffiti and intruders as they walk to their family's chapel or gravesite. The cemetery offers an amenity to both mourners and visitors. The grounds are a place of great sorrow and consolation, while also a record of a community's history and a natural and sculptural garden. These public and private purposes are not separate, but complementary sides of the same cultural institution.

Today, these roles seem, at least to many critics, to have become even more blurred together than ever. The purposes seem be more likely to conflict and collide, say when a scantily dressed jogger passes a funeral in progress. However, even if our secularized society seems to acknowledge the sacred less and less, the modern cemetery remains a public institution intended to serve as a place of private grief, as well as a typically private institution that encourages the public to visit. The two sides make up "the secret cemetery," a place where people learn to mourn, socialize, contemplate, and confront their own mortality.[1]

Mourning from Black Corsages to Memorial Services

Even by age ten, when Kennedy died, I understood that death was a private sorrow and a public event. I had seen many funerals pass by our house on their way into the cemetery with a grieving widow crying as they passed, and had watched on the streets of Syracuse as a funeral procession motored by. My parents had made it very clear that when a funeral passes, you stop what you are doing, doff your cap if you are wearing one, and stand respectfully until it proceeds. You do not need to know the person, and the funeral doesn't need to be going to Oakwood, you just show your respect. In the Syracuse of my youth, I watched as families stopped, men removed their fedoras, and women quieted their children. This simple act was an accepted part of town and city life, since all deaths are a public sorrow even as their effects are mostly private.

FIGURE 4.1. Mourner, Montparnasse Cemetery, Paris, 2016.

Standing by the side of the road, I was learning to mourn. Later, I watched as my father cried after the death of his best friend, Grant Lewis. I admired him as he struggled to keep his professional composure throughout the funeral and afterward. Cemeteries are educational places because death forces us to experience sorrow and grief. How we manage or perform mourning is a result of a socially constructed, dynamic process that creates a "paradox of mourning." We want to "sustain relationships with the (beloved) dead." We wish to keep them close, talk with them one last time, hold their hands, and kiss their faces. Simultaneously and "paradoxically, [we want] to collaborate in bringing these relationships to an end." The pain of the loss combined with the need to survive presses us forward.[2]

Indeed, the tragedy almost demands that we "function in some way redefined by the absent one(s)" even as we remember them.[3] For most of us, learning to mourn starts at home. In a past time of high death rates, especially of infants and children, death was a dreaded yet accepted presence. Families kept the memory of the dead nearby as they hung postmortem photographs in their living room and visited their loved one's grave to share news about the living world. Many families erected small shrines to the deceased in their living rooms, such as the shadow box memorial for Clara E. Reid.[4] Clara had lived four months before succumbing to death on January 23, 1908. Her family constructed a small, framed box with a postmortem photograph in the center, a casket plate centered below it, ringed with dried lilies of the valley, small roses, and other flowers. The gold-painted frame sharply contrasted with the whites of the flowers and the baby's clothing.

The public relationship to mourning changed during the twentieth century. While millions watched JFK's funeral on television, and for a long time people continued to stop in the street as funeral corteges passed, the public's connection to private grief was formalized and depersonalized. Instead of entering a home to find postmortem photographs and casket plates hanging from the wall, these vestiges of a passing era were disappearing even when Clara Reid's shadow box was photographed. Postmortem photographs were soon replaced with ones of the baby while alive, and then — save for in African American, ethnic (especially immigrant ethnic), and rural communities — the shadow box and other such memorials were no longer made, or were placed only in private spaces within the home.

Mourning still began at home, but more often it stayed there, rather than becoming public as it had in the nineteenth century. Some mourners still construct variations of a home altar around a special image or item. Some people draw upon their faith and make a kind of altar on their mantelpiece or place an offering near a photograph of the deceased. In my case, I created two collages: my favorite photographs of Beverlie, which I placed on the door of my bedroom, and a selection of Beverlie's photographs of flowers that I put in the living room. Even in the middle of my grief, my modernist constraints were obvious — I kept the personal (photos of her) private, and the public (photos by her) on display.

White middle-class families like mine have been more restrained in this way than other communities, although their degree of demonstrativeness has ebbed and flowed. They joined the larger society in being more open about grief before the 1890s, and became less so between the 1920s and the 1970s or 1980s. As late as the earliest decades of the twentieth century, they were likely to hang a memory box, but soon the small salute of John John and the careful composure of Jacqueline Kennedy would be considered a much more appropriate portrait of public mourning.

This type of public grief was once common. Widows wore black not as a stigma, but as a sign to all that they were in a period of sorrow. The clothes made death public. A few years ago, though, I realized that a colleague had recently had a death in their family. Yet he was not wearing anything that signified his loss. Just as signs of class have blurred over the past century, grief has become harder to discern. Society encourages us to act normally in public, and to act so we don't embarrass those around us. We are encouraged to hide our grief, and to "move on."

The "denial of death" proclaimed from the 1950s on was a comment about public mourning, not private. By 1952, famed etiquette writer Amy Vanderbilt could advise families that after a death, they should discuss "practical issues like wills, bank accounts, and any medical formalities," rather than more emotionally charged ones. As she cautioned, "funerals and mourning should be kept short," and the "emotional mood after a death should be as light as possible."[5] So, we should not be surprised that the Kennedys went ahead with John John's birthday party after the president's funeral. Indeed, in many families today, children no longer attend funerals or visit the cemetery, in order to limit their experience of death and loss.

Historian Peter Stearns believes this shift accompanied a dramatic change in the living's relationship to death and the dead. Between 1900 and 1960, the American death rate declined almost by half (from 17.9 per 1,000 to 9.5).[6] People lived longer, were healthier, and more rarely experienced the death of a close relative, friend, or colleague. We can see the change in cemeteries like Montreal's Mount Royal. In 1859, 33 percent of all burials there were children under two, and 22 percent were of people over forty. By 1924, the baby burials had declined to 22 percent while the over-forty burials had soared to about

50 percent.[7] Stearns argues that in the face of these changes, Americans could not possibly "maintain customary attitudes and rituals when the incidence of death was shrinking so massively."[8] Not surprisingly, two surveys of college students in the late 1980s found that though most of them had gone to a cemetery for a funeral, fewer had gone to visit a grave.[9] Death, the longtime scourge of the young, became increasingly a part of aging, and so less a part of life.

Visiting the Grave

Still, the cemetery remains a place apart, the last stop of grief for millions of people. I don't get to Cambridge often, but I never go without spending some time with Beverlie. I am like the millions of others who remember and mourn over the graves of a wife or husband, son, friend, parent, uncle or aunt, or someone else special to them. When we go to the cemetery, we carry with us the social traditions in which we were raised. We sit or stand and talk to the person about our lives and our memories. We tend the grave, replace the old flowers, and dust the top of the monument. We might leave a small memento — a photograph, stone, figurine, or stuffed animal. Most cemeteries discard such items after a week, but people continue to bring them to personalize the grave. In the Jewish tradition, people put stones atop the monument; management leaves those alone.

Why do we act as we do at a cemetery? A study of grieving visitors in English cemeteries found that "memorial behaviour [*sic*] seems to be culturally learned" through visits to the cemetery.[10] For many visitors, the grounds are "special sacred spaces of personal, emotional and spiritual reclamation where the shattered self can be 'put back in place.'"[11] Mourners can recreate a "home" for the deceased; cultivate a "garden" for them; and erect a memorial, which often is the symbolic representation we speak to when we visit. Visitors thus hope to use the gravesite as a way to "'control' death" and keep the memory of the "departed 'present' and 'alive.'"[12]

The cemetery thus can be a place that "facilitates some degree of control over loss, allowing some escape from the anguish of separation," especially in the early period after the death.[13] The visit to the cemetery thus plays a crucial role for society as well as a safe place to inter the dead: "Maintaining the dead as members of society maintains the continuing life of the living. Should the dead really die, in the belief of those who put them to rest, then they, too, must die." The cemetery plays a key role in keeping the dead alive in people's memories. "The cemetery is an enduring physical emblem, a substantial and visible symbol of this agreement among men that they will not let each other die."[14] All agree, then, that the cemetery has provided, and continues to provide, a highly valued service for a large number of people everywhere. However, today, fewer people seem to believe the society they live in depends on sanctifying the memory of those who have passed.

Ethnographer Carolyn Ellis's story illuminates how we learn to mourn.[15] In July 2001, as Ellis drives to the family graves, her ailing mother complains that the cemetery administration has refused her request to place a larger American flag on the grave of her husband, who had been a veteran. They also will not let her plant or place flowers on the actual gravesite, allowing them only on top of the monument—"They say they're too hard to mow around." Ellis feels emotionally distant from all these concerns, but still convinces her mother to visit a Wal-Mart and buy new plastic flowers. Carolyn arranges the flowers in the small regulation urns on the family lots, and she weeds the graves while her mother watches from the car.

During subsequent trips, she learns why the graves are so integral to her mother's life. In tending them while her mother watches, she feels "more fully connected to my deceased relatives, the pain of loss, and my memories." She recognizes that "this is what my mother feels here." When her mother passes away a year later, the family gathers together and "[cheers] her on her journey." Preparing for the funeral, she heads with her sister and sister-in-law back to Wal-Mart to get new flowers.

The significance of a cemetery visit comes through at that moment: "It feels good to be working together on Mom's behalf, knowing how important tending the graves was to her. It feels good to be with women who loved her as I loved her. Tending graves seems to be women's work. Odd, how good it feels to be at the cemetery this time." Ellis ends with a promise to make a future trip just to see and tend the family graves with her siblings and their spouses.

Each step—buying the flowers, driving to the cemetery, walking to the grave, arranging the flowers, speaking to her dead brother, father, and aunt, walking back to the car, and discussing the flower arrangements with her mother—is carefully orchestrated to fit convention and to address Ellis's emotional needs. Such a visit could have occurred at any time, among just about any ethnic or religious group. The visitation is a learning, grieving performance, and the process is part of virtually every human society.

Ellis's initial resistance to the cemetery visit is emblematic of the growing number of middle-class white Americans who shun the cemetery. The rise of cremation combined with this new avoidance of death meant that fewer mourners drove or walked through the cemetery gates. Even as early as 1935, Charles Benisch, superintendent of Maimonides Cemetery (NYC), noted that fewer people were coming to cemeteries to visit graves, leave flowers, and see the "smiling faces" of their loved ones.

Benisch came to his conclusion after driving through Brooklyn's Green-Wood Cemetery on "a beautiful afternoon early in October, with the foliage and shrubs and trees aglow in yellow and gold." Even though he had driven "through the grounds from north to south and from east to west," he had not met "a single man, woman or child other than cemetery employees." Green-Wood's superintendent lamented in response that he recalled when the cemetery "was one of the points of interest for foreigners and people from other states visiting New York. In those days a number of carriages were stationed at the entrance to the cemetery for the convenience of those visitors." And on Decoration Day (Memorial Day), "police reserves were required to keep the crowds from over-running the lots and graves." Benisch worried that "we have gotten out of touch with our patrons," and with the growing distance between public life and grief, cemeteries have lost some of their value for society.[16]

Sustaining Older Traditions

Such a distancing of the private from the public has not been universally true. Ethnic immigrant communities and African Americans have continuously made grief public and expressive. These largely working-class communities often have retained their more emotional relationship to death as part of everyday life. Among mid-twentieth-century Italian American families, for instance, "[w]eekends at the family plot in the cemetery were anticipated eagerly by all of the family, and on Sundays a favorite pastime was to stroll among the stones and comment upon those deceased and the families' displays for them."[17]

Similarly, many African Americans still embrace the wake and after-funeral reception, as well as the elaborate church and cemetery services. Their abiding Christian faith shapes their grief and their relationship to the cemetery. Many African Americans visit the cemetery at least on Father's or Mother's Day, Memorial Day, and the day the person they are mourning died. They often tend the gravesite just like Carolyn Ellis's family does, especially where segregated African American cemeteries do not receive the same treatment as the white ones. People have been known to bring new relatives to the cemetery to introduce them to a deceased family member.[18]

The differences between many white and black funerals were obvious at Oakwood, which had a large African American clientele as well as a long-standing white one. Over the years, I watched a number of funerals from my truck, waiting for the services to end. The African American funerals were often emotional scenes with distraught parents and publicly grieving families and friends. Perhaps because too many had died too young, the funerals seemed sadder. One time, a mother suddenly broke away from her family as the body of her son was being lowered into the earth. She threw herself into the grave, demanding to go with him. We watched as family members gently but forcibly got her out of the grave and into a waiting car. Some families didn't want to leave, staying even as we filled the grave. We would

FIGURE 4.2. Day of the Dead altar, for Zachery Nathan Champommier, Hollywood Forever, Los Angeles, CA, 2014. (For more information, see JusticeforZac.blogspot.com.)

start by shoveling dirt carefully around the casket, trying to offer the deceased as much dignity as possible.

I knew at the time that sometimes black families stayed because they didn't trust the cemetery management. I didn't blame them for their skepticism, since the African American, Asian, and Latino relationships to the white cemetery have been marked by endemic and systematic institutional racism. Racial restrictions started early. In 1690, New York City's Trinity Churchyard proclaimed that "No Negro shall be buried" in its churchyard.[19] Over two and a half centuries later, in 1952, a funeral home in Texas refused to hold a wake for a local Latino soldier whose body had been repatriated from the Philippines in 1949.[20] Freshman senator Lyndon Baines Johnson interceded, and Felix Longoria was buried at Arlington National Cemetery. Even the first African American Oscar winner, Hattie McDaniel, was refused a grave at Hollywood Memorial Park when she died in 1952.

The American tradition of afterlife segregation of African Americans continued even after such discrimination was outlawed in the

1968 US Supreme Court decision *Jones v. Mayer*.[21] In 1970, the *New York Times* published an editorial chastising Hillcrest Gardens in Fort Pierce, Florida, for advertising free plots for servicemen but refusing to bury black veterans. Federal District Judge William O. Mehrtens of Miami mandated that Hillcrest bury Pondexteur Eugene Williams as a result.[22] And even so, in 2016, a cemetery in Texas initially refused burial to a Latino, although it, like the Florida memorial park, reversed its decision when faced with public scorn and possible legal action.

Of course the irony of this discrimination is that these racial and ethnic communities have been more loyal to the tradition of burial than other ethnic and religious groups. Indeed, Forest Lawn Memorial Park in Glendale, long a bastion of Caucasian-only burial, now has a large Asian and Latino clientele. As the nation becomes more demographically diverse, cemeteries have had or will have to engage these communities as clients.

Such groups remain loyal because the ritual of the grave corresponds with their imagery of death and afterlife. Especially among African Americans, Latinos, and evangelical Christians, burial is a passage to a separate realm, a "homegoing" that signals not only the end of life, but also a new beginning. This powerful belief in the passage "home" means these groups are more likely to bury or entomb their dead in the cemetery. They fear if they cremate they will have no passage.

An especially vivid example of the continuing importance of the passage as a part of ritual occurs in New Orleans. The seemingly touristy "jazz funerals" are simulacra of a long-standing tradition of "second line" funeral processions. Second lines are held to show respect for those community members who had "successfully negotiated lives of integrity in a highly inequitable society" and "those who had died too young."[23] They have been occurring for generations, and have adapted to changing conditions. Organized by a neighborhood social club and joined by any number of neighborhood residents and others, the second line is public by definition, since its participants parade along the streets, visiting the deceased's home and other key places. The funeral is participatory, incorporating bystanders, thus breaking any barrier between audience and performer. Using music, dancing, poetry, and even memory T-shirts (see chapter 8), the participants ensure that these folks will not be forgotten even as they are missed.

A Diversity of Celebration and Consolation

This passionate ritual of passage partially explains why these same communities have retained their connection to the cemetery, and why these cultures embed a reverence for the grave into their public festivals. These ethnic religious festivals range from holy days when European neighborhoods stopped what they were doing to honor a saint, to Qingming, the festival in which Chinese families reconnect the living and the dead by honoring their ancestors. The cemetery plays a vital role in these celebrations, whether as the last stop on the parade through a town in Italy or as the central feature of the day for the dead in Mexico. By going to the cemetery as a community, people remind themselves that the dead are with them, even as they plan for the future.

For thousands of years, cultures have been setting aside a day or a few days to reflect upon family, their ancestors, and mortality. The ceremonies cluster around either the fall harvest period or the opening of spring. Roman Catholics celebrate All Hallows' Eve (Halloween), All Saints' Day, and All Souls' Day, starting October 31, while Qingming is held in the fourth lunar month of the year. But even as they share many underlying qualities, these ceremonies are hardly static. The Chinese, for instance, added flying kites to their millennia-old Qingming ceremonies between 770 and 476 BCE. As another example, Day of the Dead ceremonies started as a mash-up of indigenous and Roman Catholic practices in Southern Mexico and elsewhere when Europeans colonized the New World in the sixteenth century.[24]

In each case, and similarly with the Japanese Bon and Korean Chuseok Festivals, the central activities entail ensuring that families' graves are maintained and communing with ancestors at their graves. Each festivity focuses on the gravesite as a repository of family and community memories, with the dead metaphorically welcomed back, and offered gifts in hopes of their safety and the family's good fortune. The Chinese began celebrating Qingming, literally "pure and brightness," in Honolulu, Hawaii, when they started immigrating there in the late eighteenth century. The tradition requires that a family fulfill its obligations to its ancestors by completing a three-step grave-sweeping process: First, family members must clean the grave, including "weeding, cleaning, and painting the gravestone"; second, they must make offerings of meats and fruits "to the earth gods and the ancestors"; third, they should burn "incense, joss sticks, and paper money."[25] They fly the kites apparently to mark the lifting of the dead, although the origins of the practice are lost to history.

The most popular such festival today in the United States is the Day of the Dead, a combination of All Saints' Day and All Souls' Day. In premodern Europe, communities viewed death not as "the end of life, but rather the continuum of life, necessary for regeneration and rebirth." So, while All Saints' Day was associated with the remembrance of children (evolving into Halloween, with its combination of candy and ghouls), All Souls' Day was for courtship and marriage.[26] In these ways, the festivities revolved around the dead, but were also important markers for building and sustaining families, and thus the whole community.

However, the spiritual foundation increasingly is competing with secular celebrations. Halloween has almost entirely lost its relationship to the cemetery and its concern for dead children. Jack was always nervous on Halloween, less because mourners wanted to commune with their deceased family members than because adolescents would come to do crazy things and vandalize monuments. The worst Halloween of my youth was when a local radio deejay announced he would be at the gates of Oakwood at midnight. Baron Daemon did not show, but several hundred, mostly older, adolescents did. It was a long night at the Sloane house, which sat directly in front of that crowd. In general, though, Halloween was just a day for candy, not ghosts.

Day of the Dead, for centuries a ceremony deeply ingrained in the cultures of Catholic communities around the world, has also been transformed. The change of All Saints' Day and All Souls' Day into the Day of the Dead primarily occurred in the Spanish colonies, but Dia de los Muertos ceremonies are now deeply ingrained in many communities throughout the Americas, Europe, and elsewhere. Initially, Dia de los Muertos became a vehicle of Chicano pride in the border towns and cities where Latinos were discriminated against and treated as intruders in American society. Activists claimed the ceremony as a means to "generate cultural awareness, ethnic pride, and collective self-fulfillment" for their communities.[27] The result was that Catholic elements have been downplayed, while those connected to indigenous cultures have been emphasized.

This secular celebration of Chicano pride has become popular in the United States in recent decades, and is broadly celebrated. It has become a civic celebration endorsed by a diverse set of institutions, including the church, nondenominational cemeteries, and local community groups. For instance, in Los Angeles and San Francisco starting in the 1970s, the day is organized not by the church but by two Chicano artist groups, Self-Help Graphics and La Galeria de la Raza.

Cemeteries were central to such festivities in Mexico, but they were largely ignored as the ceremonies became more secular (St. Mary's Cemetery in Sacramento was an exception). Beginning in the early twenty-first century, cemeteries began to once again hold Day of the Dead celebrations.[28] Even though successful, the festivities reflect the complicated cultural role of the cemetery in contemporary society. Some cemeteries holding celebrations have large Latino clienteles and intend their festivities for them. Others, such as Hollywood Forever in Los Angeles, view the celebrations as part of a larger engagement with a diverse audience dominated by young Anglo and Latino adults.

In either case, though, these ceremonies are often not even on All Souls' Day. In 2016, for example, Calvary Cemetery, a large institution in the heavily Latino eastern portion of Los Angeles, held its Day of the Dead celebration four days prior to All Souls' Day. The celebration was intended for family and especially children, and included homemade altars, a procession and, at noon, dancers and music. The cemeteries know they need to compete with alternative ceremonies and other entertainments, so they shift the festivities to a weekend day to make them more convenient for participants.

The shift from small community cemeteries to large suburban sites may have also affected the relationship of these festivals and the cemetery. When many of these festivals were initiated, burials occurred around the block or at another site nearby. As new burial grounds were banned in some places, such as Manhattan and San Francisco, and others moved into more spacious grounds in the suburbs, the link between mourner and cemetery shifted, affecting not just the individual visit but also the community celebration.

Memorial Day: A Secular Ceremony

In a nondenominational, mostly Protestant cemetery, All Souls' Day was not very important. For my dad, the most active religious holiday was Easter, although in Syracuse, if it came early, the grounds were still covered with snow. Many families would still come out to stand by the grave, bring lilies to lay on the gravestone, and dust off the snow. Christmas was mostly about making sure that the wreaths had been placed on perpetual and annual care lots. The cemetery was again often snow covered, with most trees leafless, so the red ribbons and green fir of the wreaths were a vibrant, if lonely, sight.

The most important holiday by far was a secular one—Memorial Day. This day was the one day families were sure to visit, the one day, in the words of sociologist W. Lloyd Warner, that "the cemeteries were a place for all the living and the dead." Said Warner, "the bright-colored flowers and gaudy flags gave [the cemeteries] an almost gay appearance," letting Death take "a holiday, not for itself but for the living, when together they could experience it and momentarily challenge its ultimate power."[29] Just like the celebrants eating and talking over the graves of their ancestors in Mexico on All Souls' Day, many families gathered on Memorial Day to remember even those who had no connection to military service.

Though few Americans recognize it, African Americans initiated

FIGURE 4.3. Memorial Day, Tod-Homestead Cemetery, Youngstown, OH, circa 1950.

Memorial Day in Charleston (SC) in 1865.[30] They held what would become a standard remembrance that included a parade, speeches, prayers, and picnics. Confederate and Union survivors, family members, and the public embraced the concept very quickly. When General John A. Logan proclaimed that the Grand Army of the Republic (the Union soldiers' organization) would celebrate "decoration day" on May 30, 1868, the ceremony reached the national stage. That year, thousands of Americans left flowers and flags on the graves of soldiers from both sides of the Civil War. As early as 1888, "the day's pace had been clearly established: solemn memorial services and grave decorating followed by peppy parades" and other events.[31] I can still remember the day in the late 1950s when my mom took me aside and pointed to a frail old man, telling me he had served as a drummer boy in the Civil War. By 1971, when Congress made it a national holiday on the last Monday of May (convenience victorious once again), the day had long been institutionalized throughout the North and South, and encompassed veterans' deaths from all American wars.

Private cemeteries celebrate Memorial Day even though we have a national veterans cemetery system. I have never been in a large modern cemetery that did not have a veterans' section. Only with the American Civil War and the Franco-Prussian War were soldiers interred in "proper cemeteries for all ranks." After the terrible toll of the two world wars, "each death had to be commemorated," so veterans' cemeteries joined battlefield cemeteries as memorials to the soldiers' sacrifice.[32] Still, long before the veterans cemetery system expanded in the twentieth century, Memorial Day celebrations "consisted of thousands of people walking through streets carrying flowers to [private] cemeteries."[33]

As a boy, my dad worked even longer hours than usual in the weeks before the holiday. Resurrecting the cemetery's grounds from the damage caused by the snowplows and the freezing and unfreezing of soil in graves was aggravated by the sudden lush growth of grass that sprouted in the relative warmth and plentiful rain of the spring. Just before the day arrived, we all helped with putting out the flags on each veteran's grave, weeding the flower beds, emptying the trash bins, and mowing the last bit of grass (often by twilight).

I don't even notice Memorial Day these days. I do take time when realization dawns to remember my dad, think about my brother who served in Vietnam, and consider the remarkable sacrifice of the nation's veterans, but I don't go to parades or visit the cemetery—and I am not alone. The cemetery gate at Oakwood through which the parade used to enter now faces an interstate highway, its lovely iron gates gone and squirrels its only visitors. The veterans' section remains, with its cannons symbolically protecting the graves of the long-lost sons, brothers, and fathers who gave their lives to retain the Union. Families still inter their loved ones in Oakwood's, Woodland's, and the other Sloane cemeteries' veterans' sections—for there is seemingly always another war, with ever more casualties.

5

MOURNING IN PUBLIC

By the beginning of the twentieth century, the cemetery was no longer the attraction it had been, as the cultural scene was crowded with new museums, parks, and other amusements where people didn't have to contend with the presence of death. Imaginative cemetery managers had to adapt, and the person who changed most adroitly and controversially was Hubert Eaton of Forest Lawn Memorial Park. He created a new synthetic model of cemetery operation, combining an aggressive sales program to a very specific targeted audience (middle-class white Christians), a commitment to traditional artistic memorials and a mostly egalitarian style of memorialization, a suburban aesthetic, and more than a bit of showmanship. He believed the cemetery or, as he renamed it, "memorial park," should be a popular place, a place of celebration, even happiness.

Recognizing that American attitudes toward death had shifted (or had begun shifting), and that death was receding from the culture as we developed a death taboo, Eaton summarily banned death from his burial place.[1] Drawing upon those who felt that Memorial Day "should no longer be a day of mourning and sorrow but a day of celebration," he merged these values into an attractive site that combined popular amusement, cultural education, and a profitable cemetery operation. He rejected the images of the somber Christ and the falling leaves from a weeping willow, and the mementoes of a lock of hair hung in the parlor. Instead, he brought 40,000 people together to celebrate an Easter sunrise service (already in 1926 being broadcast by radio to the "farthest points of the Southwest"), and made Forest Lawn the region's second-largest tourist attraction even after Disneyland opened.[2]

When Hubert Eaton dictated that death be banned at Forest Lawn Memorial Park, he smartly and innovatively grasped a significant change in early twentieth-century American cultural attitudes. With the institutionalization of dying and with death rituals, the dead had been isolated and mourning privatized. Death had become a taboo. His memorial park concept embodied that shift. However, as Eaton's successors were putting the finishing touches on his Glendale site after his death in 1966 and expanding to five more locations, the contradiction of a cemetery serving as a tourist destination by rejecting traditional emblems of death had adverse consequences. First, Forest Lawn remains a popular destination, but competing with more sophisticated cultural and entertainment approaches that superseded its mid-twentieth-century amusements was difficult. While Disneyland could reinvent itself, one cannot rip out statues, take down mausoleums, and reconceive the notion of the cemetery. Forest Lawn's unveiling of the large painting of the Crucifixion and Resurrection or its collection of original replicas of Michelangelo's statues seem better fit for the 1950s than today.

Second, the cemetery is a place of death transformed into memory. By joining society in trying to suppress the place of death in life, and even banning it, Eaton came perilously close to bifurcating the memorial park into the two components embodied in its very name. On the one hand, the memorial park remained a place of memories; even as on the other hand, it became an amusement park. If people found they didn't like the attractions in the park, would they stay for the memories, especially if they found an alternative outside the gates?

For many people, the answer has been no. They have found an alternative space where death can be "revived" and mourning embraced as part of a natural death.[3] These people started bringing mourning back into public through physical (real world) and digital (virtual) everyday memorials. For them, lives needed to be publicly honored and death part of everyday life. And they wanted to do it themselves, not rely on the Hubert Eatons to tell them how or where to do it.

Three key characteristics of these memorials are that they are public, they appear every day, and they are participatory. They can be sited in any place and occur at any time, which is why I term them *everyday memorials*—sometimes called spontaneous shrines, makeshift memorials, or grassroots memorials. They are not seen just on ceremonial days in a sacred space created and supervised by professionals. They are the opposite of cemetery memorials, which today are typically located in private, monitored spaces that allow the public to visit but have a long list of rules constraining their behavior. At an everyday memorial, an adolescent friend of a drunk driver who died in a crash can leave a beer to honor his or her memory—an act that would be viewed as inappropriate at the cemetery. Similarly, posts on a memorial Facebook page may hold emotions and stories that would be very difficult to "leave" at the cemetery.

Without belaboring the meaning of "public," when I say everyday memorials are in the physical and digital worlds, I am equating the virtual world of the Internet to a real public place like a library or train station.[4] Viewing the Internet as simply a media platform, like radio and television, narrows our understanding of how people use it. There are consequences to this narrowing. A *digital public space* such as Facebook or a chat room, just like a *physical public space* such as the street, needs a "set of civic rules, intuitive or formal, governing its wide-ranging, information-based activities." These "civic rules" become sensitive and place-specific when negotiating the delicate issue of sorrow. People do constrain their expressions of grief in some circumstances, but in general free expression is encouraged—the antithesis of prohibitory cemetery regulations.

Even given informal agreements over civic rules, the return of public mourning is a contested shift from the modern way of death. The vast majority of us pass away in a hospital at an old age after physicians make a heroic effort to sustain life. Millions of survivors will continue to use traditional rituals, following the well-worn path from hospital to funeral home to cemetery. Many people are wary of everyday memorials, due to the perceived intrusion into the routines of ordinary life. Yet these intrusions are exactly why everyday memorials have become so much more prevalent in this moment of cultural hybridity where traditions and innovations coexist. While we wish dying and death were controlled experiences, death is traumatic, especially among the very young and the middle aged.

Because our death rate declined dramatically over the past 150 years, and we made remarkable progress in limiting the old killers like epidemics and infant mortality, the traumatic death of people under the age of seventy or eighty is now surprising, even devastating. Yet such deaths—defined as suicide, murders, sexual violence, and unintentional injuries (including motor vehicle crashes)—take the lives of a frightening number of people, especially those younger than fifty: Roughly 190,000 people die from traumatic deaths each year in the United States alone, with just under 60 percent of them under the age of fifty-five. That number cannot compare to the full annual death toll of 2.2 million, but these deaths are not occurring in a hospital room or a hospice; they are often occurring in public and leave their family grasping for meaning.

Two of the prime culprits are no surprise. They are motor vehicles and guns. Gun-related deaths have continued to soar, with 36,252 Americans in 2015 either the victim of a homicide or suicide, which makes up roughly two-thirds of gun-related deaths.[5] To put that figure in perspective, throughout my lifetime I have been reminded repeatedly by advertisements, billboards, and other media that too many people die in car crashes. Yet roughly the same number of people, 38,022, were killed in motor vehicle crashes as by guns. Very recently, a shocking third culprit has emerged. Drug overdoses have gone from half the number of people killed by either guns or motor vehicles in 1999 to over 50,000 deaths in 2015. Stunningly, in that same year these three traumatic causes of deaths claimed over 126,000 deaths.[6]

Numbers are insufficient to explain why we are so devastated. While children were once measured by their economic value, over the twentieth century, as child labor vanished from America, they became socially "priceless."[7] In the old days of sky-high infant mortality and epidemic disease, a child's death was awful but a normal part of life. Not anymore. Indeed, as a society, we no longer understand why anyone save the elderly needs to die. The death of a younger person is so unexpected, seemingly so unnecessary, that the people around him or her are dazed, angry, and traumatized. Given those numbers and this cultural perception, the occurrence of everyday memorials on our streets and online platforms seems logical.

The resulting trauma has compelled many people to commemorate death outside the cemetery gates. Everyday memorials merge ancient practices like a shrine with new technologies like social networking sites. Whether crying in front of a computer or lying forlornly next to a ghost bike (a nonfunctioning bike painted white and placed at the site of the death of a cyclist), mourners, especially young ones, are unwilling to wait for an institutionalized response—they act immediately, in their own way, to engage other people in their sorrow.

This chapter (together with chapter 8) argues that wars, killings, overdoses, and crashes propel the acceptance of physical and digital everyday memorials. While the two types are quite different, there are surprising similarities in the ways people use them to mourn friends, family, and celebrities. Indeed, since both styles of everyday memorials became commonplace for traumatic deaths, they have been adapted for a wide range of demographics and causes of death. However, sudden, catastrophic deaths beg for an immediate, public response, such as a social media post, a roadside shrine, and an R.I.P. mural can provide. Everyday memorials are mechanisms for solace and support, especially when the deceased is a young person.

In this chapter, I explore the *activity* of public mourning in contemporary society by examining the emergence of everyday memorials as spaces of public mourning. I will follow the adaptation of ancient forms to contemporary society in shrines, murals, and tattoos, and consider how mourning becomes a part of digital media. In chapter 8, I will re-examine everyday memorials by looking at the design of memorial vinyl decals, ghost bikes, Internet cemeteries, and other everyday memorials as *objects* of mourning. Both types reflect our culture's demand for immediate reactions, a growing unwillingness to bow to institutions, the emergence of the DIY culture, and the reality that for many of these mourners the death they are mourning is the first of their lives.

Two cautionary notes: First, expressing public grief is not new. Not only have mourners given deeply felt eulogies for millennia, but we need only look at books by C. S. Lewis, Joan Didion, Thomas Lynch, Elizabeth Alexander, and others to remind us of the rich efforts to describe and discuss grief over the years. Or, we could look at the anguished grief expressed in plays from *Antigone* to *Othello*. Or, we could remember the black mourning dresses and postmortem photographs of the nineteenth century. Many contemporary writers have suggested that ceremonial rituals related to death are declining, yet the growth of public and digital everyday memorial sites suggests that perhaps society is adapting rituals rather than abandoning them.[8]

Second, while everyday memorials represent a shift away from privatizing grief and a return to public mourning, they are not disconnected from traditions. Indeed, they incorporate many traditions, and often complement institutional mourning. The new reforms in grieving draw upon older models and continue older traditions by often using components of traditional rituals. Many families and friends will attend a funeral in the cemetery or memorial park as well as contribute to an everyday memorial on a roadway or online.[9] While for some people, everyday memorials may replace traditional mourning spaces, for most they complement them because they serve different purposes. Unlike the conventional ritual associated with church, funeral home, and cemetery, they are more responsive and reflective of our consumerist, interactive, individualistic society.

Emergence of Everyday Memorials in Contemporary Society

This combination of personal, public, and political was evident in the response to the death of Princess Diana in a 1997 car crash in Paris. Appalled by the death of this lively woman, angered by both the paparazzi's relentless pursuit of her and the royal family's apparent disregard for her, Britons poured out their hearts in the messages, flowers, and mementoes they left in front of Kensington Palace. Eventually, over ten tons of material was left outside the palace, and Queen Elizabeth was compelled to appear and publicly mourn Diana. While Britons had previously laid flowers and other items at the site of collective deaths, such as the unfortunate deaths of ninety-six fans in Hillsborough in 1989, the extent of the informal memorial for a single individual was unprecedented.[10]

The events outside Kensington signaled a shift that was reinforced when John F. Kennedy, Jr., and his wife perished in a plane crash two years later, and then further by many other celebrity deaths. They all popularized and publicized the use of a roadside shrine as a means of public mourning. Shrines appeared for Ronald Reagan, Michael Jackson, Joan Rivers, Robin Williams, Amy Winehouse, Prince, and a host of other celebrities who have perished since. Indeed, everyday memorials have become a standard media illustration for a tragedy in the news and popular media. Romantic, sentimental shots of a single rose or an assemblage of candles, flowers, and a teddy bear have graced newspaper and digital media front pages as a signal of public sorrow.[11]

While roadside shrines are the most prevalent of the everyday memorials, they are only one type of them. Some of the others, such as memorial tattoos, are also derived from ancient practices, while others, such as ghost bikes and memorial vinyl decals, are responses to or the incorporation of modern technologies. Table 5.1 describes the various types, listing them by how they differ on a scale of private to public, individual to collective—though many types blur boundaries. Pavement memorials, for instance, can be plaques honoring the deaths of individuals in the Holocaust and the "disappearances" in Argentina, but they also can be more abstract shapes used to warn drivers that a pedestrian was killed in this crosswalk. Still, a memorial tattoo on the torso remains more private than a ghost bike. And memorial vinyl decals (small memorial stickers placed on motor vehicle back windows with simple commemorative motifs including the person's birth and death dates), although quite visible, often have just enough information for those who knew the person being memorial-

TABLE 5.1 Types and characteristics of digital memorial sites, categorized by personal to public

Type	Platforms	Description	Audience	Focus	Origins
More personal					
Home archives	Websites, photographs, videos	Online sites where families can store images, videos, material related to deceased	All demographics	Personal, Families	Twenty-first century
Support sites	Websites	Streaming services offering consolation types of support, often volunteer supported	All demographics	Personal	Mid-1990s
Social media	Facebook, MySpace	Memorialized pre-existing sites of newly deceased users	All demographics, skews younger	Personal, Celebrity	Early 2000s
Memorial videos	Funeral homes, cemeteries, families	Initially amateur, now amateur and professional video life narratives	All demographics	Personal, Political	1990s
Memory projects	Websites	Art and other websites/web connections that memorialize lives	All demographics, skews younger	Personal	1990s
Memorial blogs	Websites	Individual or group sites where people write about health, dying, death, mourning	All demographics	Personal, Political	1990s
Internet cemeteries	Websites	Free and paid sites where individuals construct a memorial for a loved one	All demographics, skews older	Personal	1995
Online memorials	Websites	Typically paid sites where individuals/ families construct a memorial for loved one	All demographics, skews older	Personal, Celebrity	Circa 2010
Dark tourism	Websites, photographs, videos	Physical tourist sites around death transformed into digital memory sites	All demographics, skews younger	Personal	1990s
More public					

FIGURE 5.1. Memorial vinyl decal, Los Angeles, CA, 2008.

ized to recognize them, while a Facebook memorial page potentially draws a much wider audience.

One reason that everyday memorials became so prevalent is certainly the media's focus on them around the death of highly visible celebrities.[12] Even so, they have been adopted widely within the culture, and have appeared in response to ordinary people's deaths from a broadening range of causes. I argue that the media's attention would not be sufficient to explain the widespread adoption, although the "highly visible" celebrity deaths constantly reinforce their relevance.[13] People's use of everyday memorials signals a broader resurgence of public mourning that reflects other trends in our postmodern era.

The media's fascination with the metastasized celebrity culture leads them to understate the history and true extent of society's embrace of everyday memorials. Historically, mourners left flowers on the grassy knoll in Dallas in November 1963, bouquets outside the Dakota after John Lennon was shot in 1980, and teddy bears and flags near the rubble in Oklahoma City in 1995.[14] Further, while mourners left everyday memorials at the site of national tragedies, such as at Columbine High School in 1999, they also placed them at other, less widely publicized tragedies, such as outside a supermarket where a shooting occurred, near a home where a family mourned their murdered child, and in the aftermath of a fatal nightclub fire.[15]

R.I.P. murals for the ordinary and locally famous who had died from gunshots and AIDS were being sprayed or painted in the 1980s in New York City. Memorial tattoos derive from old traditions of mourning or celebration ("MOM") that go back at least centuries. Even online memorials, such as virtual cemeteries, originated two years before Princess Diana's death, and they were the successors to e-mail exchanges and grief bulletins that went back at least another decade.

Indeed, contemporary everyday memorials are successors of a millennia-old tradition of religious shrines, and have adopted specific items connected to traditional mourning, such as candles and flowers.[16] The acceptance of mourning at such memorials in the broader mainstream American culture reflects a borrowing from primarily Catholic countries, such as Greece, Ireland, and Argentina. Shrines to saints have been incorporated into many churches and churchyards in Catholic North America, particularly in Quebec and Mexico. Offerings are made to the shrine by passersby, who leave items much as contemporary mourners do at a roadside memorial, ghost bike, or Internet cemetery.

The jump to a more secular, regulated use took many decades and varied across cultures. By the eighteenth century, Mexicans had transformed saints' shrines into "descansos," shrines to ordinary people that focused on their lives, not a saint's.[17] Those shrines began as places for pallbearers to rest as they trudged to the graveyard carrying the body. When Texas and the other territories of the American Southwest were taken into the United States, the ritual came with them. Later, the concept was adapted to leaving a cross where an auto crash had occurred. States eventually codified the practice in the 1940s. Legendary photographer Robert Frank published a photograph of a roadside cross in his classic 1958 exploration of the byways and towns of the nation.[18]

In 1953, the American Legion in Montana institutionalized the informal practice of placing white crosses along the road after six people were killed in a 1952 Labor Day weekend car crash. Historian Kenneth Foote remarks that some "particularly dangerous stretches in Montana came to resemble small cemeteries, with rows of crosses marking dozens of fatalities."[19] The practice declined (or was prohibited) with the spread of the interstate highway system in the 1960s, probably because the shrines were thought to be distractions for motorists traveling at higher speeds. Today, conflicts are almost constantly occurring between municipalities, which believe the shrines are violations of the engineering dogma that distractions cause crashes, and families and friends, who are often just as adamant about sustaining the memory of the deceased.[20]

Even as everyday memorials have a long history and tradition, they have become a much more common part of our national culture recently. As early as 1998, roadside shrines had begun "showing up more" frequently in Illinois and around the country. As the sister of one auto accident victim recounted, "It's no different than Princess Diana, the Oklahoma bombing, the Capitol shootings. *Everyone needs to be remembered.*"[21] Mourners have raised them for innumerable people, especially children and teens. And, while we associate them primarily with traumatic deaths on the roadway or by a gun, mourners are using them for any number of causes of death. They represent the pure emotion of the moment, the unwillingness to hold one's reserve or to wait for institutionalized rituals. They suggest a deep need to perform a public act of mourning that transcends the private nature of the modern rituals of mourning and burial.

Just after Beverlie and I moved into a condominium on the Westside of Los Angeles, I came across a very simple shrine for Michael Nemis, who lived from 1985 to 2001. His family and friends had appropriated an electrical pole on a side street. Near Christmas, they decorated it with red ribbon, wrapped it in Christmas paper, and wrote notes of love and remembrance up and down the pole. Periodically, they came and replaced the materials, updating them for the season. Clearly, the electric company didn't approve, since the materials were torn down regularly, and the company finally replaced the pole with a new one. The family was persistent, wrapping material around the new pole for nearly the entire six years we lived there. The site became the object of pilgrimages for family and friends. I cannot find any information about the life and death of this young man, but he still "lived" through this memorial.

Keeping the deceased's memory alive is a paramount objective of everyday memorials. The mourners celebrate the lives of those who died both by leaving material objects (teddy bears, angels, flowers, beer bottles, etc.) and by talking about them, even talking with them. A parent said when her child's friends are "feeling down or they've got a problem or whatever, they'll go up there and sit at the cross."[22] One Philadelphia mother noted that she stops by her son's R.I.P. mural regularly, since she can "speak to him. Face to face. You know? I can come here and speak to him in person."[23] Such consolation at a public everyday memorial is indicative of how everyday memorials complement, yet also replace, the gravesite for people who are perhaps alienated or too distant from the cemetery.

The alienation usually stems from a combination of the gravesite's inconvenient location and the cemetery's restraints on individual expression, in contrast to the positives of the alternative public memorial. A group of African American mothers, interviewed in Philadelphia about their children's R.I.P. memorials, have largely stayed loyal to the cemetery as a place of burial and commemoration, and yet are active participants in everyday memorials. One mother simply states that she "doesn't like to go" to the cemetery, preferring the R.I.P. mural near her house. Another mother reports that she goes out "at least two or three times a year, on his birthday, the anniversary of his death, you know, like the holidays." But she passes his portrait on the mural every day on the way to and from work. The reintegration of death into the neighborhood makes the memories more accessible.

Some people especially prefer the mural over the cemetery, since they can bring whatever they want to the wall. Their "Halloween and other grave decorations challenge cemetery rules" that are intended to "dictate how lively the world of the dead is permitted to be," but they can leave anything at the R.I.P. mural.[24] Also, when they are there they are part of the life of the neighborhood. They "often speak of

FIGURE 5.2. Roadside shrine, Culver City, 2006.

the 'liveliness' of the block [where the mural is located] — mentioning those who pass on their way to the bus stop 'hang out' on the street corner or slow down in their cars."[25] Authorities placed a bench in front of the mural, which reinforced the interactive nature of the experience: One mother talked about sitting on the bench to "talk to your loved one," while people go by; she was amazed that "so many people know my son. People I didn't know." Such interactions would rarely happen at a gravesite, since most mourners go there alone or in pairs and are unlikely to run into passersby along the relatively lonely streets of most cemeteries. Murals and other everyday memorials are not destinations; they are part of the lived space of a community.

Remembering through Social Media

Complementing the physical everyday memorials are the digital media sites where mourning and grieving are expressed in new modes. What some call "thanatechnology" (derived from "Thanatos," the Greek god of death) "has changed in ways that were once unimaginable" over the past two decades.[26] Support networks, e-mail, blogs, social networking services (SNS), and other digital platforms have all enabled the sharing of personal grief (see table 5.1). These sites have been an extraordinary help to some people, though this part of the online universe is not immune to its dangers.

Much of the focus of research and discussion of online mourning has been Facebook and the other social media or SNS, but those sites only built on earlier experimentations with physical, postal, and e-mail groups and sites.[27] One example, GriefNet, a nearly all-volunteer "support community," started in 1985 with a bimonthly bulletin on grief resources. It went digital in 1994 and grew to encompass multiple services, including fifty "e-mail support groups" by 2011. The original community splintered into groups focusing on specific types of losses, such as parents who had lost children or the recently widowed. This organization embodies the entrepreneurial spirit of many early efforts on the web, but it also demonstrates the clearly desperate desire of many people to find help in confronting grief.

The early digital support groups were complemented by the emergence of blogs that narrated dying, death, and grief—as in the case of Kirstin Paisley, a blogger and Facebook user who explained to her readers in 2008 that she had found "a strange thing on the back of her left ear." That was the start of her struggle with melanoma. She went from positive diagnosis to final illness over the next three years, and her evocative blogs over that period form a meditation on death in the digital age. Paisley, a seminary student, forthrightly and honestly described her deteriorating condition, the ups and downs of diagnosis and treatment. Elizabeth Drescher, a religion scholar who studied Paisley's writing, sees those posts as part of a broader discussion of life, death, and spirituality. For them, as for millions of others, the digital realm provides a practical advance and a complex social space for spiritual discussion.

These venues all thrived on the interaction between organizers and participants. DIY culture is often described in terms of arts and crafts, but GriefNet is DIY at its heart. The organizers allowed users to identify when they needed new groups, and how they wanted those groups organized. Long before Facebook, this site and others created spaces where people could "talk" in ways that helped them confront and better understand their sorrow. Similarly, later, Paisley was not simply writing into the ether, but responding to readers' comments and concerns.

Friends and followers of Paisley's blog and Facebook account attentively interacted with her, giving her sympathy from near and far. Yet in the end Paisley worried about the role of digital media: "Finally, as digital media become more and more defining in our lives, how will the spiritual practices and religious rituals long associated with healing, care of the dying, death, and bereavement be adapted to integrate the reality of digital participation at the end of life?" Her concerns resonate with me: Will we be more sympathetic because of the accessibility of digital media or less because of its abstraction? Would I have had as intense an experience gazing at my great-grandmother's grave in Santa Barbara on a website as I had standing in front of it?

Perhaps the most used and potentially emotionally unsettling embodiments of such concerns are the Web 2.0 SNS, especially Facebook, where people meet one another and develop elaborate networks of virtual "friends." In 2016, Facebook had over 1.7 billion active users, who had an average of 338 friends and were uploading over 350 million photos per day.[28] Even though younger users are now said to consider Facebook passé, the experience there is indicative of how digital companies and users cope with death.

In 2009, Facebook went through another of its seemingly never-ending platform updates. Quickly, some users heatedly complained that Facebook was automatically suggesting that people friend people who were dead. The company immediately responded by heavily publicizing the ability of a family to "memorialize" a page. Max Kelly, the company's security chief, noted that one reason that Facebook had allowed such memorialization from close to its beginnings was the sudden death of a colleague in a bicycle accident. Facebook, like many other SNS, had presumed its clientele would be young, healthy, and long-lived. Suddenly, this young company needed a plan. With memorialization, a person's site remains visible to their friends, and still available to them for comments, but it is not open in the usual sense of the word. All "sensitive information" is stripped out. Trolls cannot randomly intrude, nor can they pick up inappropriate information.[29]

By 2012, an estimated 30 million Facebook users had died.[30] Such memorialization reflects a broader engagement with dying and death on the Internet. Virtual cemeteries, digital videos, memorial websites, and other approaches have emerged to respond to users' needs and desires. In a time when many younger users feel alienated from conventional religious and cultural traditions, these outlets provide new avenues for mourning and memorializing.

Even though a majority of Facebook users today are women, a study of Facebook memorial pages found that a disproportionate number of them were for young white males who perished by sudden traumatic means (car crashes, murder, or suicide).[31] Visitors to the pages most often wrote a message in the second person ("you are with the angels"), a form of "direct communication from the mourner to the deceased."[32] This personal link is reminiscent of a person sitting or standing at a grave and talking to the deceased about how family members were missing them, giving them the news—so how is the interaction on Facebook anything new? What may be new is the way that, as with so much of life in the twenty-first century, death online seems at times like a spectator sport. While visitors are talking to the deceased, they are only rarely creating a collective mourning response when interacting with each other. Instead, each person values the site through his or her own experience on it. Further, some comments from visitors seem abstract, as if they were visiting multiple memorials, or they feel emotionally artificial, without a sense of authentic sentiment and originality. Yet within the spectacle is a deep sentiment that many people feel toward their family, friends, and even celebrities they know only through a virtual reality. At times, one's breath is taken away by a poem, reminiscence, or revelation.

The number of Facebook memorial pages is growing according to one estimate by as many as three million new pages a year.[33] Whether on Facebook or a variety of other digital media, SNS are a primary means for people to meet, introduce music to each other, and keep in touch with friends. The accumulation of photographs, responses to news feeds, and reactions to other people's posts create a diary of a person's life, including very emotionally revealing vulnerabilities, grief included.

Three broader social changes reinforce the use of SNS for expressions of grief. First, the rising rate of cremation means that fewer survivors will have graves to visit. One respondent noted of a friend who was cremated that "it's not like we can go to his grave or anything."[34] As people feel estranged from the traditional places of mourning, they search for new ways to share their grief. Second, the number of late adolescents attending college is also rising, so they are not necessarily at home when tragedy strikes. One friend reported being able to drive home from college to her friend's grave only on weekends, so she supplemented those with visits to his page on Facebook: "sometimes I feel it's really nice to have his Facebook still there." Third, talking about death or a dead loved one is still not that easy. Facebook allows one to keep a communication open. Said one interviewee: "It's like he's there. So you talk to him." Instead of being viewed as odd because you cry at night or talk to the deceased as you walk home (both of which I did after Beverlie died), you can join a group of friends on Facebook and hear their news even as they tell it to the person who has passed.

These sites are not just for a person's friends; they also serve family members, including parents, as they try to endure the pain of their loss. When a person dies, an entire circle of digital friends may be devastated, but parents may be especially hard hit: "The pages offer often wrenching views of young lives interrupted, and in the process have created a dilemma for bereaved parents, who find themselves torn between the comfort derived from having access to their children's private lives and staying in touch with their friends, and the unease of grieving in a public forum witnessed by anyone."[35] Some parents visit their children's memorial pages every day, finding that it makes their children come alive for them in a way that is impossible in virtually any other medium. The digital becomes an avenue for continuing relationships with the far-flung networks of a lost adolescent, as well as a comfortable place to simply remember their child's life from the privacy of home. As with the Philadelphia mother who preferred the bench in front of the R.I.P. mural to the long trek to the cemetery, the memorial page or other site can be accessed not just privately, but more easily.

Contested Social Territory

Everyday memorials are popular since they are flexible media for personal mourning and political advocacy. Friends can remind Facebook readers of a person's funny look in fifth grade, or they can rail at the failure of the state to protect bicyclists. Family members can post baby pictures even as others ask why a gang member, police officer, or anonymous driver killed their friend. Such spaces, though defined by ritual, can become politicized.[36] Everyday memorials are intended for those feeling the pain of the loss, and for the public, whom mourners feel should recognize the tragedy of their pain. Many such memorials focus on a deep sense of death and memory, yet hope to encourage policy changes, fix urban planning deficiencies, and raise public outrage. They respond to concerns about access to public space, safer public roads, crime and safety, inadequate building codes, and all-too-prevalent corruption. Some sites are political only by implication. They embody the change they seek, the failure the memorial represents, the dashed hopes of disappointed advocates.

FIGURE 5.3. Ghost bike, Houston, TX, 2014.

Anything having to do with death raises emotional responses. Through the centuries, Catholic cathedrals have clashed over where to bury a saint, cemetery managers and families have hidden the burial places of serial murderers (Jack did it only once, as far as I know), and developers have fought with communities about preserving cemeteries in the way of development, with mixed success. Contestation is simply part of the dialogue. Today, with so many changes testing traditions and conventions, these conflicts are as publicly evident as the new everyday memorials. That conflicts exist is not surprising; what is illuminating is how everyday memorials reveal elements of the tensions surrounding mourning and commemoration.

The outstanding characteristic of everyday memorials is that they occur in the public realm. Concerns about their very public nature are impossible to separate from broader worries about whether death belongs in the public sphere. R.I.P. murals can alienate people who believe mourning should be private, anger neighborhood residents who dislike the attention and crowds, and offend police officers. As one neighbor of the Philadelphia R.I.P. mural stated, "Why do I want to look at dead folks for? . . . In the church every day I look at dead people. Why I got to look at dead people out of my house?"[37] He was expressing a common question: Why is death present in my neighborhood and not confined to the cemetery?

The debate about the appropriateness of public expression flared in one Internet discussion when a participant wrote, "Actually, I feel like it's kind of disrespectful to go around advertising someone's death" by putting a memorial vinyl decal on the back of your car or truck. Another contributor argued that everyday memorials are "tasteless" and "tacky," going on to state that "Like the crosses that recently started appearing by roadsides on the site of where, presumably, someone died in a car crash. I really don't want to know. Leave the crosses and flowers in the cemeteries." These people worry that a long-standing barrier—between living and dead—is being breached, with possibly bad effects.

Not surprisingly, comments about the inappropriateness of memorial vinyl decals tumbled over to other ways people use their bumpers: "How are these different than all the 'My child is an honor student' except the child can't see how proud you are?"[38] Another angrily attacked "Baby on Board" stickers, questioning why anyone would "care that your own little piece of Big Carbon Footprint survive[d] to adulthood and take[s] natural resource[s] from my own Carbon Footprints!"[39] As these comments all suggest, roadside shrines, ghost bikes, and vinyl decals demand the public's attention. In our age of individualism, many of us simply do not want to be reminded of the deaths of others and our potential complicity in them.

The public nature of everyday memorial, of course, is the very reason why mourners embrace them. These people believe the critics have either missed the point or are selfishly trying to constrain them. A man whose son was shot and killed wrote on an Internet discussion board, "My greatest fear as a Dad is that the memory of him will fade and be forgotten." Similarly, a woman who had just lost a toddler lashed out at the person who posted that he did not believe in memorial vinyl decals by replying that perhaps "you do not want to face your own grief, and that is why you are having such a reaction to these stickers." Being in public allowed mourners to draw in diverse and disparate members of the community that more formal rituals might not attract. Further, they can express themselves in ways they cannot in other venues.

For their proponents, everyday memorials serve multiple functions, but most importantly, they allow public discussion of their grief, including their feelings that their loved one did not need to die. Walking through the Lower East Side in New York City, I passed a fence that had been transformed into a half-block-long roadside shrine to those killed in a gas explosion. Between the messages of grief was a poster accusing the owner of the building of arson and murder. The anger of the survivors' loss was mixed with their outrage. The memorials embody the emotions they experienced, and the dashed hopes of survivors.

The debates about R.I.P. murals, roadside shrines, and ghost bikes exemplify continuing social tension over who is worth remembering. Since so many everyday memorials are associated with traumatic deaths, and we are reluctant to acknowledge the cost of our traumatic society, the sorting out of worthy and unworthy dead is neither surprising nor new. Nineteenth-century city officials created separate cemeteries for those who died of epidemic and contagious diseases, as a way to protect society from them. In their day, their understanding of contagion may have made this segregation sensible, but these unworthy bodies were often quickly and callously buried without memorialization. Similarly, Catholic cemeteries have long prohibited the burial of suicides in consecrated ground. Whites have banned African Americans, Latinos, Chinese, and others from their cemeteries. The return of public mourning makes those often hidden acts of discrimination and abuse more visible, more part of the public record of the city. No wonder some people feel compelled to cart off a ghost bike or whitewash a mural.

The contested issue of who is worthy of remembering is most tragically visible in the cases of black men killed by the police. The Black Lives Matter movement has demonstrated that mourning can be a powerful political tool to reveal issues unaddressed by society, and can be a unifying message capable of propelling efforts to change systems. "Black Lives Matter aligns with the dead, continues the mourning and refuses the forgetting in front of all of us."[40] Although such deaths make up a small fraction of those who die from gun violence each year, they are politically charged. Roadside shrines, R.I.P. murals, memorial tattoos, Facebook pages, and other online memorial pages are all used to remember the lives lost and to publicize the concerns raised by the deaths. Perhaps the R.I.P. murals, painted usually by street artists right after the death in highly visible areas near where the deceased lived or died, are most effective in their use of portraits of victims such as Eric Garner or Freddie Gray to provide a setting for rallies, memorials, and other activities.

Many online comments on news stories about the R.I.P. murals express objections to them because they believe the people killed by the police are not worthy of public memorialization. Since the murals portray a difficult social issue and make a statement on a societal division, we should not be surprised that when the New York Times posted a photograph of a Freddie Gray mural, at the Gilmour Homes in Baltimore, Twitter trolls used the opportunity to demean Gray and his neighborhood. One woman, "Alison Wonderland," wrote, "Thank God Freddie can no longer supply crack to his mother, shoot up heroin & deal poison to our children." Another, perplexingly borrowing the name of accused rapist "Roscoe Arbuckle," spouted, "Gee, Mom. When I grow up, I wanna be just like Freddie."[41] Generally, such reactions highlight how grassroots memorials can quickly become controversial depending on the individual or group memorialized.

Conversely, police funerals are highly formal affairs with often hundreds, even thousands, of fellow officers participating from adjacent and far-flung departments. These victims, as a rule, are deemed very worthy. These militaristic funerals are powerful acts of mourning and politics, demonstrating the unity of the police officers and the value of any officer. Here, as with the R.I.P. murals, prior to the formal funeral, supporters, families, friends, public officials, and fellow officers often remember a fallen officer at a roadside shrine near where they died. These everyday memorials can be substantial as mourners add flowers, notes, and other materials to them. When a gunman shot five Dallas police officers in 2016, a police car was positioned to serve as the center of the everyday memorial, which drew hundreds of bouquets, wreaths, balloons, and mementoes. The shrine became one visual reminder used by the media to suggest the tragedy of the deaths and, once again, the special value of a police officer's life and sacrifice.

Whether a police funeral with hundreds of saluting officers, a silent ride in support of a deceased cyclist, or a loud protest rally held in front of an R.I.P. mural, everyday memorials serve the dual purpose of mourning and advocacy because they are public performative actions. While luminous ghost bikes are a less explicit advocacy statement than an R.I.P. mural, they have always had a powerful political meaning regarding a deeply contested issue. The first ghost bike was placed by a bicycle shop owner in St. Louis, who was outraged by a fatal crash near his store and sought to make motorists slow down and take care. The brilliant white of the newly painted bicycle festooned with flowers, mementoes, and notes is at first blush just a specific type of mourning space. Yet the siting of most ghost bikes is done ceremonially, with an accompanying ritual protest ride, with dozens, sometimes hundreds of cyclists—such as that after the intentional car crash in Kalamazoo, Michigan, that took the lives of five bicyclists.[42] In a way, ghost bikes are emblems of the urban planning reform movements, such as New Urbanism and Smart Growth, which call for cities to be friendlier to cyclists and pedestrians. The ghost bikes, then, represent a force for change as urban designers, planners, and policymakers try to shift policies around our motorways, influenced often by the resolute passion of community advocates.

As with other mourning sites that incorporate political gestures, ghost bikes are contested spaces symbolically representing a broader policy and planning debate. Just as the cyclists demand safer ways through the city, by advocating for bike paths, protected bike lanes, and other improvements, motorists have begun pushing back because they are worried this new infrastructure will slow their commutes and threaten their parking spaces. The ghost bike becomes a

FIGURE 5.4. Pavement memorial, Buenos Aires, Argentina, 2016. A pavement memorial or memory tile is place where an individual was "disappeared" during the military dictatorship in Argentina between 1976 and 1983. (Courtesy of Jacqueline Illum.)

symbol of their concern that a valued way of life, with single-family homes, ample street parking, and limited public amenities, will be transformed by a relatively small number of cyclists and their allies, who use the ghost bikes as an advocacy tool. As a result, ghost bikes are regularly vandalized or disappear.

Given the long period in which public mourning, as represented by everyday memorials, was viewed as inappropriate, state, county, and city agencies used to quickly remove roadside shrines, R.I.P. murals, and ghost bikes. Many municipal and state legislatures regulate aspects of everyday memorials, while others have prohibited them outright out of concerns over separation of religion and state, as well as traffic safety.[43] The primary justification for such regulation or prohibition is that private individuals are illegally appropriating public space, though concerns about distracting drivers, as well as visual blight when memorials deteriorate, are also considerations.[44] Some states, such as Maryland and Virginia, outlaw shrines but don't necessarily disturb them. Thousand Oaks, California, allows them for thirty days, while Atlantic City gives them only ten.[45] The variation is symbolic of the unevenness with which we confront issues of commemoration. Yet they all signify the importance of the continuing debates over everyday memorials.

As does the success that ghost bike advocates have had in getting municipal authorities to treat these bikes differently than derelict bikes. In New York City, for instance, after a public debate about whether the sanitation department should treat ghost bikes differently, the department's website now states: "The City does not accept requests to remove 'ghost bikes' that have been placed on public property as roadside memorials to those who have died."[46] This position sanctifies the bikes, separates them as memorials, and accepts, even supports, public mourning as a legitimate function of public property.

The Limits of Public Mourning

While they are public activities, memorial pages raise the question of how they contribute to a stronger community, in the real world and online. As I noted, since most visitors speak directly to the deceased, they are not creating a "collective memory" space, but instead are performing mourning much like at a traditional shrine. This inability to establish "a consistent dialog among the living," which is what gives rise to a sense of community, suggests the limitations of the Facebook platform to move beyond the simple, emotional, personal relationship of mourner and mourned. Here, "if the dead are virtually memorialized, they never really die."[47] Their personality and individuality are recognized and memorialized as the goal of the mourning process — not creating interactions that would also support the survivors and their community.

At the same time, the presence of "trolls" defacing memorial sites does suggest that when attacked, a more collective response may emerge. One study has shown that website memorials are regularly "desecrated and disgraced." Even more intrusively, sites like mydeathspace.com "link the profiles of the deceased MySpace user to articles related to their often violent and heartrending deaths with a forum on which unknown and even anonymous people can discuss their deaths." The site, only nominally about memorials and mourning, is a "desecrated virtual graveyard serving the curiosity and voyeurism of [an] anonymous public."[48] The presence of advertising that links the notice of an accident victim to an advertisement for car insurance or a suicide notice immediately below a mattress ad seems particularly macabre. Sentiment and spectacle collide throughout our media, but this site, which glories in the pain of others, seems a more crass violation of our society's strictures regarding the respect for the dead.

More devastating to families, who can just ignore such sites, is the willingness of "internet trolls" to vandalize memorial pages on Facebook and other platforms.[49] Certainly, the vast majority of people visiting the page of a newly deceased teen write messages of grief and solidarity ("she seemed a sweet girl"), but some especially visible cases have brought out horrible comments, such as "thank goodness for dead sluts." An especially vicious example, written by "infamous RIP Troll" Sean Duffy, about a fourteen-year-old who apparently died of an epileptic seizure, was "Help me mummy, It's hot in Hell," which he left on her memorial page on Mother's Day in 2011. He was jailed, but many other trolls justify their outrageous acts by saying that people leaving sentimental messages on memorial pages are "tacky," since they do it out of "boredom and a pathological need for attention masquerading as grief." As one author retorted, "RIP trolls are sociopaths, not cultural critics," and I couldn't agree more.

Importantly, when trolls attacked another highly visible site for Chelsea King, family members and friends acted to protect the page. King was a seventeen-year-old in San Diego who was raped and murdered in 2010. While she was missing, tens of thousands of people wrote on sites asking for help finding her, and after she was found, more than 100,000 people joined her fan site. So did the trolls, who left nasty comments about her. In response, family and friends created a monitored site where they could screen submissions, and friends responded aggressively to nasty comments on other public sites.[50]

As these conflicts suggest, returning mourning to the public sphere means it is open to conflict and contestation. While some mourners want to remember in public, others just want to leave the dead in the cemetery: "Maybe I just don't want to be reminded. But I also don't think I should have reminders forced on me."[51] Many people still cling to that older style of private mourning where the rest of the public is able to ignore or, after briefly acknowledging the loss, simply move on. But as even the presence of the horrible trolls represents, mourning is once again part of the public realm.

6

REINTRODUCING
THE CEMETERY

The active, participatory, engaged activities around everyday memorials contrast sharply with those in the cemetery. While people constructed their own memorials and brought friends and family to that space to mourn with them, the cemetery has remained a largely passive place where survivors are encouraged to mourn by themselves or among family. The figure of the sole mourner bent over a grave has long been the image associated with cemetery mourning. Throughout most of the year, cemetery operators would simply open the gates early in the morning, open and fill graves, direct visitors, and then close the gates at sunset.

The cemetery was not desolate. At the height of the cemetery's popularity in the nineteenth century, the number of visitors led cemeteries to print photograph booklets and guidebooks highlighting the beauties of the grounds and memorials. Also, as discussed, cemeteries have long held special ceremonies at Memorial Day and on All Souls' Day. The atmosphere in the cemetery, though, is serene compared to the involved interactions occurring at everyday memorials.

In the face of the rise of everyday memorials as participatory mourning spaces, the increasing popularity of cremation as a disposition method that provides family control of the remains, and the ongoing secularization of society, cemeteries have needed to become more active institutions. Those cemeteries that have, have re-engaged traditional audiences and broadened their activities and services to attract new ones by embracing the cemetery's role as a public mu-

FIGURE 6.1. Cast members, Grove Street Cemetery, New Haven, CT, 2000.

seum, and by adapting to the digital present. Their responses might upset the image of the somber and serious cemetery landscape, but they have begun bringing back visitors to the cemetery. Instead of just opening the gates to mourners, cemetery operators encourage visits by providing events and activities and providing survivors with specific programming to make their mourning less burdensome.

You've Got to Have Friends

An event Beverlie and I attended at Grove Street Cemetery in New Haven in 2000 was representative of these efforts to engage visitors. I gave a speech about the history of the cemetery, but the highlight of the day was four student actors portraying different individuals buried there. They first gave speeches, then they stood by the individuals' graves and answered questions, all in character. Volunteers and cemetery managers had joined together to do more than simply accept visitors, actively offering them historical, cultural, and natural events and tours that illuminate not only the cemetery's history, but the community's as well.

This effort, of course, was not new. Hubert Eaton recognized faster than almost any other cemetery operator that visitations were slipping. He argued that the cemetery was increasingly viewed as a "stoneyard," and the attractions of the nineteenth century were of little interest in the twentieth. He developed aggressive efforts to publicize Forest Lawn Memorial Park as a result. However, Eaton was not followed by other large cemeteries, and certainly not by the majority of smaller cemeteries. He was viewed as an outlier, even an outsider, whose memorial park was a bastardization of the somber cemetery ideal of the past century. My father and his fellow New York cemeterians were jealous of Eaton's financial success, but dismissive of his Hollywood attractions. His themed burial sections, museum, and shows were critiqued as more appropriate to the movie screen than a solemn sacred space. So, most cemeteries continued to publish small booklets of photographs as subtle advertising, and to rely on word of mouth and generational commitments to attract clients.

Somewhere in the 1970s, this attitude began to change. Not surprisingly, the shift was not straight from booklet to starlet, but took several stages. The first stage occurred mostly through the outside encouragement of new cemetery friends' organizations. Volunteers began the first of these organizations in 1978, when a group of people concerned about the condition of a Philadelphia cemetery met to form the Friends of Laurel Hill.[1] Their action illustrated two contrary trends in society. First, cemeteries had become too often the site of vandalism and desecration, which few organizations had the resources to fix. Second, a renewed fascination with colonial gravestones and the Victorian Age made cemeteries relevant again to architectural and art fans. Many organizations were founded in response to both impulses: a fear for the loss of these great artifacts and a love for them.

Laurel Hill Cemetery is the second-oldest rural cemetery in the United States, founded in 1836. By the 1970s, like many other older reform cemeteries, it had fallen on hard times. The cemetery had little unused land left and was losing most potential customers to better-funded and -located competitors. As home to many extraordinary but fragile nineteenth-century monuments and mausoleums, it also had massive maintenance problems. Drayton and Jane Smith joined with John Francis Marion to organize the Friends of Laurel Hill as a way to "assist [the cemetery] in preserving and promoting [its] historical character."[2] The Friends hoped to raise funds to help maintain this Philadelphia icon, home to numerous significant historical figures.

Other cemeteries quickly realized the potential of friends' organizations. Once the groups flourished, they did more than fund maintenance. Some began offering historical tours to highlight the natural, cultural, architectural, and other resources of the cemetery. The evolution of the New Haven group is instructive. Begun at the time of Grove Street Cemetery's bicentennial (1996), the group offered lectures, symposia, and ceremonial events related to African Americans and notable people buried in its grounds. By 2004, it had organized officially as the Friends of Grove Street Cemetery and initiated its first newsletter. A decade later, the group provided welcoming docents, organized horticultural and historical tours, and held special events related to Independence Day and Memorial Day. It had worked with the city of New Haven and Yale University to begin improvements outside the gate, and raised funds to preserve stones within it. Throughout, it continued to offer lectures.[3]

The historical and natural tours fit nicely with the traditional atmosphere of the cemetery. Small groups of people march through the landscape, stopping periodically to hear stories of presidents, murderers, philanthropists, and ghosts. Even if the topics vary dramatically, the sense of the cemetery as a historical repository of community memories remains. When one adds in the lectures, pamphlets, and other materials the cemeteries produce to support this element of their mission, it is reminiscent of the approach the reform cemetery founders took many years ago.

While the early friends' organizations were particularly supportive of Victorian-era rural and lawn cemeteries, now they can be found for large and small, urban and rural cemeteries. Many members start out by being interested in individual monuments of famous or historically important people, then become involved in protecting the cemeteries from the ravages of time, lack of income, and, especially for many urban cemeteries, unkind visitors. Like at Grove Street, friends' organizations hold events, sponsor lectures, and print brochures about individuals buried there and the architecture of cemetery buildings and mausoleums.[4] In some large cemeteries, friends' groups have a year-round schedule of tours and talks, supplemented by audiotapes and brochures. In smaller cemeteries, they may just conduct preservation work on gravestones and monuments. The groups signify a deep concern for preserving the history and physical artifacts that the cemeteries manifest, and for recognition of the cemetery as a historically important cultural institution.

Some friends' organizations have extended activities beyond the traditional subjects to more contemporary art events and even overcame a long-standing reluctance to recognize that many people associate cemeteries with ghouls, ghosts, and the darker side of tourism. A very few cemeteries, exemplified by Hollywood Forever in Los Angeles, have been willing to start holding events that have little or nothing to do with the somber and solemn purpose of the cemetery, rather viewing the grounds as a public space for a wide range of musical and cinematic events. And finally, after starting to view themselves as actors, not receivers, some cemetery operators have adopted digital as well as physical platforms.

A few cemeteries have taken the concept of the friends' group to a new level by creating a fund-raising nonprofit that can complement the operation of the cemetery. For instance, my brother Steve's old employer, Woodlawn Cemetery in the Bronx, created the Woodlawn Conservancy as an umbrella of their friends' activities, which range from tours to direct fund-raising appeals to support preservation. The conservancy started as Friends of Woodlawn in 1999 but has morphed into a preservationist and education arm of the cemetery that tries, in the words of their promotional film, to show how the cemetery is tied to "history, nature, culture, and community," and is thus deserving of special recognition, support, and preservation. In a time when fewer people visit the grounds, purchase lots, and even recognize the cemetery's existence, such groups play an important role in raising the institution's visibility.

The individual friends' organizations are indicative of a broader national interest in preserving this rich cultural heritage, dating back in some cases over 300 years. Many stones are falling apart due to acid rain, vandalism, poor maintenance, and simple aging. Some states have passed legislation mandating that municipalities assume responsibility for the maintenance of old burial places, but that usually means no more than minimal care. Family graveyards today face an even more uncertain future. Some old farm cemeteries are on isolated knolls surrounded by suburban developments; others have been lost.

The precarious state of America's oldest grave markers and burial places led in 1977 to the formation of the Association for Gravestone Studies (AGS).[5] The AGS has worked with local governments, national cemetery associations, and preservationists to raise public awareness. It has held workshops for caretakers to train them to use best practices in conserving stones, and to engage community residents in the history, art, and meaning of the cemeteries. In addition to holding an annual conference on a wide range of topics related to gravestones and cemeteries, the group has published a series of informative pamphlets.

The saddest aspects of this issue are chronic theft and vandalism. Thieves and vandals play havoc with the nation's memorial heritage. The most egregious examples of theft have been the very public robberies of prized objects such as specific sculptures and the treasure trove of Tiffany and other period stained glass windows that adorn America's mausoleums. The 1999 arrest of a prominent New York stained glass expert for the theft of a nine-foot Tiffany window, valued at $220,000, from Salem Fields Cemetery in Brooklyn was highlighted in the *New York Times*.[6] Other artifacts disappear with less celebrity. Iron fences, angel statues, and colonial gravestones are all attractive to art collectors. Law enforcement has taken the thefts more seriously as advocacy groups such as AGS have informed them of the historical importance of the stolen objects.

Most vandalism is about destruction, not theft, as we have experienced in 2017 with the anti-Semitic vandalism of cemetery gravestones.[7] Unfortunately, the conscious, malicious destruction of gravestones is not a new event. At the start of the reform and rural cemeteries in the antebellum period, trustees promulgated rules of order to stop visitors from picking the flowers or disrupting the tranquility of the grounds. A century later, two years after Oakwood's Centennial Monument was raised in 1959, vandals chipped off large sections, apparently just for fun.[8] In another typical spree, two teenage boys vandalized the Williamsburg Township (Ohio) Cemetery in 2002.[9] In just ninety minutes, the thirteen- and fourteen-year-olds toppled 150 gravestones, damaging roughly thirty of them—apparently out of simple boredom, not malice.

The problem is national. Cemetery magazines used to reserve a page for lists of vandalism examples, perhaps to remind superintendents that their problem was the industry's as well. As Joey Lyons, executive director of the Oregon Historic Cemetery Association, asserted, "I volunteer with Columbian [a pioneer cemetery in Portland] and other cemeteries because cemeteries are a place of peace, respite and love for the living. When that is violated, we are all damaged, not just the tombstones and structures."[10]

My dad was often bedeviled by vandalism, especially in the older, less traveled sections of the cemetery. Older family monuments were often constructed with a central iron pin holding together the various layers of the pedestal. Over time, these pins age and can rust, and the layers become vulnerable to the point that a person could topple a relatively large monument. Further, many mausoleums and monuments had separate decorative elements, such as a pineapple sculpture or a small statue. These items have been thrown down, damaged, or stolen.

Cemetery managers have realized that the best response to vandalism is to make the cemetery a vital part of a community engaged with the grounds. Just as urbanist Jane Jacobs argued that "eyes on the street" make a neighborhood safer, visitors discourage vandalism by their mere presence.[11] As a result, the friends' organizations combined with cemetery programming are intended to draw more people into the grounds. And, managers are beginning to realize they don't have to stop at history. Places such as Oakland Cemetery in Atlanta combine traditional tours about prominent African Americans, "love stories," local history, and art and architecture with a few nontraditional events such as a 5K run and their "Malts and Vaults of Oakland: Where Beer Meets History," which includes a post-tour tasting. Clearly the combination is their effort to appeal to new populations, especially African Americans, for whom they also have a special MLK Day service in January.[12]

A Public Museum

In a fundamental sense, cemeteries are public museums.[13] People appreciate cemeteries' monuments, gardens, and grounds, but these artifacts have not been curated to the best advantage and promotion of the institution. Remember, in the nineteenth-century reform cemeteries, monuments were approved by the cemetery but initiated by the family with little regard to the overall beauty and cohesiveness of the grounds, something late nineteenth-century commentators critiqued. That led to memorial parks' attempt to curate the grounds by constraining families, institutionalizing most visible statuary, and creating a coherent philosophy and aesthetic that was rigorously followed. They activated the grounds as a space to visit, but they rarely held specialized events and prioritized lot holders' privacy. For example, Forest Lawn Memorial Park promoted such attractions as large-scale paintings, sculptures, and other artistic elements, not family gravesites, even Walt Disney's.

In many ways, friends' organizations flipped Hubert Eaton's focus by making the individual graves the stars. Just as the cemetery guidebooks of the nineteenth century, the new tours began to highlight large mausoleums and specific family monuments. Beyond the topical tours, such as the beer barons in Woodlawn and dead distillers in Green-Wood, Mount Auburn holds a tour that focuses on "celestial beings," the cherubs and angels "posing on pedestals or tucked into the decorations of many monuments."[14] Woodlawn Cemetery in the Bronx held a series of tours in mid-October 2015 that highlighted "design stories" and "unlocking mausoleum interiors," both of which focused on its amazing selection of family mausoleums.[15]

One very popular avenue for attracting people was to highlight the natural world of the cemetery. The passion for Victoriana combined with the new environmental sensibility has reinforced the long-standing interest in natural urban environments, especially gardens. Cemeteries' diverse tree stands, flowering beds, urban animals, and designed spaces allow them to offer multiple types of tours and events. Woodlawn Cemetery offers a tree tour with a local noted horticulturalist, while Mount Auburn holds an 8 a.m. winter birding walk. Jack allowed a number of birders to come through the gates prior to the cemetery's opening because he viewed them as a safe group. A number of cemeteries offer self-guided tours of the grounds that include natural highlights. While the deer I bumped into at Allegheny aren't on any tour, when I stopped by the cemetery office to ask for a map, I mentioned them, and the receptionist responded laconically that yes, they are residents.

Smaller, less prominent, and less well-funded cemeteries, of course, face barriers to developing anything like what a Mount Auburn or Woodlawn can conceive and fund. The first Sloane cemetery, Woodland in Ironton, offers a well-received "ghost walk," attended in 2015 by an estimated 2,000 people.[16] But rather than the cemetery or a friends' group, the walk is sponsored by the Lawrence County Historical Society. Similarly, the Oakwood Cemetery Historical Society produces the tours at Oakwood, not the cemetery itself. Partly, volunteers mount tours because of a lack of funding at less well-endowed cemeteries. However, relegating the events to outsiders may also suggest that the cemetery managers have an older vision of their responsibility. My dad never considered developing tours or other events that might support the preservation of the grounds. He believed his obligation was to his lot holders.

I initially was surprised to learn of Woodland's ghost walk, since when I was growing up in the cemetery my parents were careful to separate the reality of life and death from the vampires, zombies, ghosts, and ghouls of fiction. My dad's feeling was echoed by the sexton at Orlando's Greenwood Cemetery, Don Price. While Price often gives "moonlight" tours of the cemetery, he has not done it on Halloween since the time that someone came in a cape, which he found disrespectful. As he told a local reporter, "Halloween can bring out the worst in everybody."[17] Instead of welcoming people at Halloween, Price joins volunteers to "sit atop the hill overlooking the rolling grounds and watch for trespassers." Across the country, other superintendents, like my father, have done the same thing. Halloween, long an important day in Catholic countries as the day children can return from death to meet the living, has become too exuberant a holiday for cemetery managers.

Still, ghosts and ghouls, along with the zombies and vampires in the movies, are not as ignored as they used to be. A number of cemeteries have embraced the rising interest in the paranormal. Greenwood Cemetery in Orlando allows the private tour group American Ghost Adventures to provide tours twice a year. Similarly, in 2013, the Onondaga Historical Society offered an "Oakwood Visions Ghostwalk" (in June).

While such tours about ghosts sometimes are held at night, organizers are very clear that they are not in the horror movie business. The Woodland tour is "NOT a scary/haunted tour," nor is the "Grand Torch Light" tour at Mount Hope Cemetery, Rochester (NY).[18] The tours and other such cemetery activities are shaped by the balancing act between attracting the public, keeping the events family friendly, suiting the solemn setting of the sacred space, and not offending anyone. Reaching out to raise the visibility of their historical, natural, and cultural offerings, cemeteries hesitate to push too hard against traditional public expectations.

A New-Style Decoration Day

In the broadest sense, thriving cemeteries seem to be those that adapt by taking the interests and concerns of their publics into account. That can mean embracing a cultural interest in the ghoulish, but it can also mean taking new cultural traditions and priorities to heart—particularly in more diverse communities. In creating new events or loosening rules, they are responding to criticism that cemetery managers need to "become intimately familiar with, and truly understand, the personal needs" of lot holders.[19] Celebrations and ethnic holidays such as Qingming and the Day of the Dead are powerful ways to introduce or reintroduce the cemetery to families, to connect with ethnic communities that represent a significant potential clientele, and to acclimate older lot holders to a new and often exciting event. For example, in northern Virginia, where a significant Vietnamese population has developed, National Memorial Park has recently opened an Asian Cultural Cemetery section—with a pagoda at its entrance and graves sited according to the principles of feng shui—in between sections reserved for Jewish and Islamic burials. The memorial park has allowed each community to preserve its traditional practices while creating a common cemetery for them all.[20] The result here and elsewhere is a mosaic: a distinct and legible pattern of commonalities made up of hundreds of different individual tiles—a typical American story.

A diverse clientele can change the way mourners experience the cemetery. In Los Angeles, I have seen mementoes in cemeteries that would have been unimaginable in Syracuse in my youth (or even, in many other places, today). Decorating a grave at holidays is a long tradition, but it used to mean somber wreaths and red ribbons at Christmas and lilies at Easter. But as early as the late 1970s, even the rigidly controlled space of Forest Lawn Memorial Park saw Christmas decorations such as Santa Claus, candy canes, and snowmen appear ephemerally in the winter landscape.[21]

Today, Asians at Green-Wood in Brooklyn burn their offerings at the funeral, while Asian and Latino Catholics at Holy Cross Cemetery in Culver City transform the burial sections with Christmas decorations, filling it with tinsel, wrapping, Santa, and real trees. This shift from the somber to the celebratory opens the cemetery to longer and more frequent visitation. When I last visited Holy Cross, dozens of families were decorating the graves and the mausoleum crypts as their family members watched, ate, and welcomed others. Less formal than Day of the Dead events, these types of celebrations serve the same purpose of engaging the lot holders, beautifying the grounds,

FIGURE 6.2. Christmas decorations, Holy Cross Cemetery, Culver City, CA, 2003.

and allowing a public, community mourning, in contrast to the privatized way of death.

Christmas has turned out to be just the beginning, as purple balloons wave over graves on Easter, orange pumpkins appear before Thanksgiving, and red heart balloons flutter on Valentine's Day. Small mementoes, such as ceramic bunnies and turkeys, also appear, if more frequently on children's graves. Such decorations remind us that the cemetery is a live place, visited by people year-round but especially on days with strong memories for them. The periodic relaxation of the usually strict rules around what people can place on the graves suggests that cemetery managers have come to recognize that at some times of the year emotional needs supersede maintenance concerns.

From the Somber Atmosphere
to the Attractive Event

Not only the ceremonies and rules of the cemetery have changed. Cemeteries' role in the public sphere has begun to change as well, reshaped by events that are not traditional in form or content. In my earliest days at Oakwood, joggers were unwelcome while walkers were embraced. I think that was because running was an unusual activity, and didn't fit at all with the nineteenth-century values of the institution. Indeed, the sanction against such recreation reminds me of Frederick Law Olmsted, who famously disagreed with politicians who wanted to add baseball fields and other recreational activities into his precious parks.[22]

However, a century later, recreation was well integrated into urban parks, and as jogging grew more popular, Jack demurred and let them run, although he continued his opposition to bicycles, fearing the litigation associated with accidents in the hilly grounds. Other cemeteries have more recently embraced runners. "Run Like Hell 5K & Run Like Heck 1K" is a race held each fall inside Atlanta's historic Oakland Cemetery, with 1,600 participants running through the gravestones.[23] The run is likely the largest cemetery running race in the country, though other cemeteries also have 5K races, including Woodland, Dayton (OH); Metairie, New Orleans; Rosehill, Chicago; and Lake View, Cleveland.

Such events have to carefully balance attraction with respect. On Reddit in 2014, a person asked if others thought it was "inappropriate" to run through a cemetery.[24] This provoked a fascinating and illuminating discussion, with most people cautiously supportive. All the commenters were runners, so the varied responses were especially insightful. One person noted (the following quotes are verbatim) that there are "plenty of other places to run," and running in a cemetery seemed "selfish." Others were much more affirmative, with several noting that "they're all dead. I don't think they'll mind." After someone mentioned the Oakland race, another person noted that he wouldn't use the decision by one cemetery to offer a race as a general rule, adding, "I certainly wouldn't run in a narrow gravelpath inbetween closely packed gravesites, not because i'm religious, but i wouldn't want to offend anybody just because i felt like running there." The cemetery has to confront the same concern about balance, which is why many cemeteries, Arlington National Cemetery included, prohibit all running.

For me, the joggers and especially the races symbolize efforts by cemeteries to use their grounds more effectively to service the public, and through that service attract new lot holders and community support. Historical and nature tours reach a very specific audience, while a running race may have a much broader appeal. Further, cemeteries are looking for new audiences, while also trying to remind everyone of their meaning and purpose, their relevance to contemporary society. A race suggests that a space is open to you, and belongs to the community, and you should consider yourself part of that community. Will the runners buy lots? I don't know, and that may not be the primary goal of the race. Historic cemeteries with little burial space remaining, such as Oakland, may be trying to position themselves as a public amenity, much like the local art and natural history museum.

A diversion such as a run extends the cemetery's public profile to one audience, while celebrating the cemetery's own art by exhibiting contemporary art might reach another. For Forest Lawn Memorial Park, Glendale (CA), the introduction of art exhibits was a logical extension of their museum, established in 1957. For many years, the museum was a mishmash of coins and busts, stained glass windows, and other items that Hubert Eaton had treasured. In recent years, the museum has been redesigned to hold exhibits, mainly on popular topics such as the work of Disney animator Eyvind Earle and the "original art for album covers, posters, magazine illustration and other visual-arts ephemera tied to the music industry."[25]

A much more experimental approach was being tested by Green-Wood in Brooklyn in fall 2016. The cemetery invited artist Aaron Asis to create multiple site-specific installations, commencing with one called "unSeen Green." This installation consisted of fuchsia parachute cord strung through and within the cemetery's Warren & Wetmore Gothic chapel. A reporter noted that the installation had "a light touch, not overtaking the delicate stained glass of the chapel or distracting from [its] architectural highlights."[26] Instead, the cord illuminated these architectural elements. Then, periodically, a musical performance was presented to further enliven the space.

A generation of cemetery owners and managers, then, has been altering the norm for how a cemetery can be a community space. The most dramatic example started in 2002 at Hollywood Forever. The owners were approached by a young man, John Wyatt, about showing a movie on the back of their large community mausoleum, with viewers sitting on a lawn named for Douglas Fairbanks. They agreed. Now, each summer and early fall, Wyatt and his Cinespia staff of four show a series of films ranging from classic family favorites, such as *Wizard of Oz*, *Vertigo*, and *Fantasia*, to edgier, more recent films, such as *Rushmore*, *Rocky Horror Picture Show*, and *Blue Velvet*—not what one would find in the typical family summer film series. In the summer of 2015, the organization showed *Apocalypse Now*, apparently for the first time ever outside.[27]

This willingness to potentially offend is perhaps the most surprising aspect of Hollywood Forever's efforts to re-engage with the public. Whether having a deejay, photo booth, and other activities associated with Cinespia, or having a band play inside the mausoleum during their Day of the Dead celebration, the cemetery owners actively push the boundaries of cemetery tradition. They have converted a 1931 Masonic temple on the edge of the cemetery into a concert hall hosting touring bands and a comedy show ("Comedy Is Dead!"). While many cemetery management teams have been willing to incorporate historical actors, very few have opened their grounds to the movie *Gremlins* or the band Majical Cloudz.[28]

Filling in the Dash

In almost every long article about Hollywood Forever, at some point the owner, Tyler Cassity, or an employee states, "We're more interested in filling in the dash between the date of birth and the date of death."[29] With this phrase, Hollywood Forever shifts the focus back to the individual, away from the institution. In recent years, Hollywood Forever has done this by using video and the Internet to create personal memories that are available online. Hollywood Forever's "LifeStories" are roughly five-minute video biographies created from photographs and other materials supplied by the family. They are shown first as part of an individual's memorial or committal service.[30] After the service, the videos are uploaded to the Internet so that anyone can access them. Hollywood Forever also constructed kiosks throughout the grounds where one could access the video tributes. In this way, the cemetery embeds the abstracted life of the person—which otherwise is viewable only through the Internet—into the cemetery grounds. The tributes are a deliberate response to the perceived blandness of twentieth-century memorial park bronze plaques and traditional cemetery granite slabs.

The success of Hollywood Forever's service is emblematic of a broader effort to integrate digital products into funeral and memorial service lines. For instance, funeralOne, an Internet service company that started out by offering prepackaged tribute software to funeral homes, saw rapid success.[31] The company's owner, H. Joseph Joachim IV, told the *Chicago Tribune* that the company had grossed $2.8 million in 2007. "Basically, a funeral director uses the software to upload photos of a client, select their profession or hobby, add a few details, such as date of birth and death or the names of children." Afterward, the funeral director directs the software to produce "a memorial video shown at visitations. Animated birds peacefully fly by scenic landscapes. The musical scores are symphonic. Most important, the product feels deeply personal." The first version, "Easy Tribute," debuted in 2004, with a more sophisticated version, "Life Tributes," launched in 2008. That same year, funeralOne claimed it had contracts with 5,000 of the 21,000 funeral directors in the country.

Cemeteries are also using the Internet to reconnect with current and future lot holders, highlight their assets in short videos, and personalize memories, such as those we showed at Beverlie's memorial service. These decisions are obvious choices at one level, although given the conservatism of the field, a number of cemeteries have allowed funeral directors to provide most digital services. At another level, the digital services tie into efforts to rethink the cemetery as more than a physical place where people can choose to go. Still, the traditional passive approach is difficult to change.

As with other efforts by institutions to manage digital technologies, cemeteries are no longer in control of memorialization. Families themselves use the Internet to tell their life stories on such websites as Find a Grave and Legacy, which host short biographies and obituaries.[32] Families provide materials that are turned into photographic time lines of the family tree and the deceased's life, a series of videos about the deceased's life and family, and a set of montages about an individual's or couple's life. The photographs range from carefully posed stills to informal candid shots of birthday parties and Christmas celebrations, often set to sentimental popular music. The stories typically extend from the deceased to their parents, families, and friends. Although available online, the videos retain a sense of privacy since they are typically a series of illustrations with little or no text. If you don't know the person, their life story is hard to penetrate beyond the ordinary tropes of childhood, education, marriage, and other conventional societal landmarks.

When funeral directors and cemetery managers digitize biographies, they are trying to keep up with their customers. When we memorialized Beverlie in 2007 with the two slide shows of photographs and music, we were doing something that has become ubiquitous at homemade services, and is increasingly common in funeral homes and churches. The end result is that the more commercial versions, unfortunately, tend to be close to saccharine in their sentimentality. Unlike at Beverlie's service, where I curated the music based on her tastes, the music tends to the melodramatic while the soft animation gives us dreamy close-ups of key people and relationships. I have viewed a couple dozen of these videos, and even though they are seeking to personalize the deceased, often they seem to have too little information or too little willingness to step outside the commercial treatment to fully portray the unique characters of those chronicled.

Returning to Somber Services

The decision by cemeteries to embrace their status as public museums, and their opportunities to offer services such as digital and Internet biographies, raises the question of whether cemeteries could more fully engage with their most natural clientele, survivors. Cemeteries are by definition places of mourning, but few cemeteries offer grief counseling and other activities as components of their efforts to re-engage with the public in this age of more participatory mourning. Indeed, the modern cemetery has largely been a blank canvas upon which mourners are allowed to paint their own sorrow, rather than an institution actively attempting to alleviate grief. Back to the founding of Mount Auburn itself, cemetery operators have believed that the setting and the gravesite are what they need to provide; but if they more assertively offered mourning services, would people view the cemetery as a place they *need* to visit, not just one they can?

Many cemeteries do offer a range of services, including referrals to local counseling services. Faith-based cemeteries seem more likely to link cemetery services with grief services, since their associated institution may already offer help to survivors. Integrating the grounds and the services is less prevalent, however. Sophisticated memorial parks will offer help at the time of purchase, funeral, and interment, but I don't get a sense that such services continue after the initial visit—beyond the types of informal shoulders that sextons and superintendents have provided to mourners for centuries.

An exception is the range of services at the Catholic family of cemeteries associated with Mount Calvary in Cheektowaga (NY) near Buffalo, which tries to bridge the gap between funeral home and cemetery.[33] Their "funeral celebrant" will assure that the memorial service is personalized to "reflect the personality and life-style of the deceased." Their grief and social support groups—"Hope After Heartache" and "Bridging Out in New Directions"—provide immediate and longer-term spaces where survivors can talk through issues with experienced people. They also have a lecture series and a "Laugh for the Health of It" club. Finally, there is the use of their grounds as a grief support system by offering twice-weekly "Stepping Out" walking clubs that traverse the grounds with others "who have experienced a loss."

The paradox is that cemeteries are trying so hard to make themselves part of the public realm through the development of traditional (and innovative) tours and events. Could they use that same outreach to better serve their primary traditional audience, their lot holders, who are by definition survivors of a terrible event? The postmodern cemetery could be radically different than the modern cemetery by offering its landscape as a restorative space of contemplation. Yes, such an act would be a return to the nineteenth century. However, today's population is largely uneducated about the cemetery as a place of consolation, and will need help to learn how to grieve, share, and support. The cemetery, working with groups like GriefNet, could once again take its place as a critical social and cultural institution by returning to its original mission.

PART 3

———

MEMORIALS

FIGURE P3.1A–C. Evolving memorial concepts. "Willow and Urn," gravestone carving, Ironton, OH, 1855 (2007); roadside shrine, Syracuse, NY (2009); laser-etched monument, Tod Homestead Cemetery, Youngstown, OH (2007).

Where eighteenth- and nineteenth-century gravestones bore startling visuals and lyrical prose, twentieth-century memorials often carried only the most mundane information about the deceased (name and dates of birth and death). As the twentieth century approached, standardization led to rows of granite family monuments. And individual memorials were reduced even further, to flush-to-the-ground grave markers. In a kind of recompense, memorial park innovators then erected "features" that evoke common values of family, patriotism, and faith—but do nothing to honor any individual.

Over the past fifty years, people have rejected both the requirement that commemoration occur only in private or in the isolation of the cemetery, and the standardization that has led to rote images and little information about the deceased. Now, many people believe mourning should happen in the public realm. People are using a wide range of old and new images, styles, and modes to celebrate and mourn along roadways, in front of houses, even on their cars and their bodies—especially when the cause of death is a trauma such as homicide, suicide, or a car crash.

Cemetery managers have responded by allowing a renewed informality in grave decoration and monument memorial design. Families can often now decorate their graves more expressively, as new laser technologies have given them the freedom to express themselves in granite. My father cringed when a lot holder erected a stone carved with a scene of the deceased golfing—but he adapted, as cemetery managers have been doing for decades. He would have adapted to laser-etched scenes, too.

7

A MEMORY PALACE

We don't know if famed British prime minister William Gladstone actually said, "Show me the manner in which a nation cares for its dead and I will measure with mathematical exactness the tender mercies of its people, their respect for the laws of the land and their loyalty to high ideals." Yet the funeral and cemetery industries have long used this statement as a justification for the elaborate rituals that now cost Americans roughly $21 billion annually.[1] From their perspective, the quote inspires people to show their ideals, exhibit their mercies, and demonstrate their loyalty to loved ones. And, through the modern way of death, the death industry often successfully promotes these values to their emotional and bereft customers. It makes them a presumption for millions of people suddenly confronted by the sorrow of death—including me.

However, what if we were to reverse the interpretation, and consider whether by exploring the history of memorials, we can uncover what values and laws shaped our monuments, and why people's (dis)-loyalty to these older values might damage the cemetery's status in the contemporary world? If we did so, we would find that historically the social values embodied in the cemetery's memorial landscape do indeed mirror those in society. Those social values would represent a largely elite and middle-class white perspective where family, nation, and god are called out and praised, race and gender play largely missing roles, and death is an increasingly shadowy figure. The cemetery would come across as a place of traditions, where sentimentality reigned over equity and diversity, and consolation overwhelmed realism.

Thus, until recently, few people expressed their difference and their outsider status in these culturally constructed and constrained spaces. People who deviated from middle-class values due to their sexual orientation, racial heritage, or religious nonconformity were either forced into their own burial grounds or coerced into hiding their difference. The initial memorial parks emerged in the early twentieth century as the epitome of this striving for conformity. Cemetery managers took increasing control of the visible expressions of normative values in large family and institutional monuments.

This memorial landscape prevailed throughout the first two-thirds of the twentieth century. The cemetery and memorial park reigned supreme, embodying the inequities of American society as managers strove to sustain a socially and environmentally coherent landscape. Eventually two separate shifts would begin to shake the foundations of this widely accepted cultural institution: cremation and the everyday memorials as symbols of the family regaining control over mourning and commemoration.

The early signs of this eventuality came even as Eaton's Forest Lawn became the standard model for new sleek and simple cemetery lawnscapes with their flush markers and institutional features, and critics were calling for the secularization of memory and art. The victory over the "stoneyards" of the late nineteenth century, where rows of obelisks and machine-cut statuary competed to stand out in increasingly crowded burial sections, came even as critics increasingly found cemetery and memorial art wanting. One group thought the old-styled memorials of standing soldiers and cannons set aside a flagpole were outdated and outmoded. They wanted instead for communities to celebrate their war heroes with "living" memorials integrated into secular society: memorial auditoriums, highways, and other elements of "living" society. Many civic leaders championed designing plazas, designating buildings, and memorializing streets as places of memory. Between 1949 and 1951, for example, my hometown built the

Onondaga War Memorial, a sports facility that included a listing of all the county residents who had died in recent wars.

Art and architecture critics reinforced the suitability of the "living memorial" even as they disparaged the cemetery monument. They believed cemetery art was no longer current; instead, even in its modern forms it represented a sentimentality and ornamentation misaligned with modern precepts. Famed cultural critic Lewis Mumford went so far as to state sarcastically: "The notion of a modern monument is a contradiction in terms. If it is a monument, it is not modern, and if it is modern, it cannot be a monument."[2] Three generations later, historian James E. Young similarly concluded that instead "of searing memory into public consciousness, [artists and architects] fear [that] conventional memorials seal memory off from awareness altogether." Such critics argued the memorial was "an evasion" and "abuse."[3] After centuries serving as a prime location for artistic creations, the cemetery was increasingly viewed as a cultural backwater of no real merit. These attacks did not shake the cemetery's dominance within the new modern institutions of death, but they did marginalize the cemetery as a cultural institution and, eventually, provide one basis for a reappraisal of the cemetery as an institution.

Planting Memories in a New World

The modern criticism belies the long history during which the cemetery held a treasure trove of amazing carvings and sculptures, stained glass, and artfully designed buildings. From almost the initial colonization of America, colonial carvers had the skills and found the materials to produce riveting gravestones, followed over the next two centuries by pioneering sculptors, glass makers, and architects who often started successful careers by making cemetery memorials. While our focus is the nineteenth to the twenty-first centuries, the colonial memorials play a critical defining role in the evolution of the form. Until relatively recently, most Americans did not have permanent gravestones. They were too expensive. And of those that were erected, many have been lost over the centuries as the graveyard got in the way of progress or through the physical deterioration of memorials made of wood and fragile stones. Still, we have been left with a collection of fabulous gravestones from the seventeenth and eighteenth centuries that provide a foundation for understanding the evolution of the memorial within the cemetery, and eventually outside it as well. Few groups of artifacts are more beautiful and more illuminating about colonial society than gravestones.

For early gravestones, carvers chose from a selection of illustrative motifs, added in the basic information, and then often inserted a few lines of poetry, observations, or information. But the form was not static. Scholars and avid enthusiasts have carefully chronicled the changing styles of carving from "mortality images—skulls, crossbones, hourglasses, and other signs of life's brevity—to cherubs, and then on to monograms and urns and willows." While these dominant styles coexisted with a wide selection of alternatives, the normalization of memorial art also started long ago.[4] The shift to cherubs followed by waves of willow and urns reminds us that the standardization of gravestone motifs was not a modern consumer phenomenon but a reoccurring effect of cultural consensus.

Laura Baldwin's gravestone is a magnificent example of the willow and urn style, although it appeared in 1825 on a family lot in Oakwood. I discovered it when I started working in the 1960s. Baldwin was the daughter of James Geddes, who engineered the Erie Canal, and wife to Harvey Baldwin, Syracuse's first mayor. By the time I saw the large three-panel marker, it laid flat on the ground, its text barely visible from age, grime, and overgrown grass. The top panel holds a very popular motif of the period, three weeping willows and two symmetrically placed urns. The urns are set between the trees, drawing on the fascination with ancient Greek culture then in vogue. The central oval panel holds the name and information about the deceased within an elaborate abstract wheel with sheaves of wheat (representing the divine harvest) at the outside edges. The bottom panel is an eleven-line epitaph.

I was initially drawn to the stone because the carver had omitted the "than" in the first line of the main body of the epitaph, and had

FIGURE 7.1. Laura Baldwin gravestone, Oakwood Cemetery, Syracuse, NY, 2010.

"Oh, what a Gem lies buried here"
This is
the Grave
of LAURA
the wife of Harvey Baldwin
and daughter of
the Hon. James Geddes &
Lucy Geddes. She died
Dec. 18th 1825. age
21 years.

In less than one revolving year, She was a Maid a Bride A Corpse
Adorned with every grace, & pofsefsing every personal
Charm & mental excellence.

In her spring time She flew
To that land where the wings of the Soul are
Unfurled.
And now, like a Star, beyond evenings cold dew
Looks radiently down on the tears of this world.

FIGURE 7.2. Laura Baldwin's epitaph, Oakwood Cemetery, Syracuse, NY.

been forced to add it by inserting a caret (^). I had never seen a caret on a gravestone before. The carver must have realized the mistake too late, or the client had pointed it out (even worse) and they decided not to waste the stone. I wonder how these two powerful men felt about buying a gravestone with a corrected mistake, and I have often thought about how wealthy and powerful civic and business leaders would react today.

While the caret was the initial attraction, I have come back to the stone again and again because of the sentiment in the startling and sorrowful first line of the epitaph: "In less than one revolving year, She was a Maid, a Bride, a Corpse." The stone holds a sense of palpable loss for this "Gem" who was "Adorned with every grace," and possessed of "every personal Charm and mental excellence." We can only imagine the grief that consumed her husband and family. The cruel reality of a young girl, marrying and then quickly dying, touches me even now.

Baldwin's elaborate and sentimental stone marks it as a product of its time and the wealthy families from which she was descended and into which she married. At the same time, the stone evokes a broader era in which deaths were publicly celebrated, and cemetery memorials told the stories of people's lives. Eulogists 150 years ago might speak for an hour to remember the deceased, and those remarks might be printed and published, depending on the local notoriety of the individual. Today, we have returned to memorial services that tell stories through words, music, and images. Yet cemetery monuments have been less and less likely to hold poetry like that accorded Laura Baldwin.

Viewed another way, the stone helps us understand the social world in which Laura Baldwin lived and died. Even on her gravestone, this "Gem" is largely remembered as a daughter and wife, as if such attributes were the only way to memorialize this young woman. In the poetry that follows, in that line of joy and grief, she remains a daughter ("maid") and "bride," even as she dies. The stone is like many other stones that marked women's graves by stating "here lies the wife of," "daughter of," or some other descriptor that reinforced women's subordination in a patriarchal society. In surveying the gravestones from 1825 to 2001 in an upstate New York cemetery, researcher Ernest Abel discovered that 75 percent of females had their familial relationship recorded on their gravestone, while only 16 percent of the males did. Further, 60 percent of the females were described either as "his wife" or "wife of," while less than 1 percent of the males were "husband of."[5] Although Abel shows that the situation improved in the twentieth century, we still have a long way to go before women are worthy of notice simply on their own terms.

A Rose Is Not Just a Rose

After two centuries in which almost all gravestones were upright individual markers, the availability of relatively inexpensive marble combined with a rising urban population and community dislocation propelled a revolution in three dimensions. New "water-powered machinery" lessened the cost and increased the availability of marble, allowing artists who previously carved flat stones to imagine more elaborate three-dimensional monuments.[6] Wider, taller, and rising toward the sky, the new generation of gravestones changed our perception of the cemetery. The landscape moved from rows of upright memorials of a relatively consistent height to a diversity of shapes and sizes.

The memorials were not the only shift. Colonial graveyards were filled with individual markers. Now, the new cemeteries held a growing number of large family lots that each had a sizable central family monument surrounded by rows of graves, only sometimes aligned with the ones in the next lot. While earlier graveyards embodied community in their very consistently sized memorials, this landscape offered new opportunities for artists, but also reinforced differences between the wealthy, middle class, and poor. The burial sections were no longer about the collective; they were now about family, although the organizers viewed the whole cemetery as a communal memorial.

The new emphasis on the family was literally materialized in the landscape. Many antebellum family lots were surrounded and defined by a fence or coping. These iron or stone boundaries explicitly denoted the extent and size of the family. The smaller individual markers surrounding the family monument typically held minimally ornamented scrolls or panels with the names and basic information of each family member. A growing number of cemetery managers felt the individual markers clashed with the family monuments, cluttering the memorial landscape and making grounds maintenance much more difficult. As the century progressed, they successfully persuaded lot holders to shrink the upright nature and the size of individual markers, and eventually to abandon them in favor of flush-to-the-ground markers.

The family monument came to dominate the landscape. The monuments announced the patriarchal family names in large letters (LONGSTREET, LEAVENWORTH, and CROUSE), which ensured that the family father's presence was acknowledged and their lineage secured. Fathers bought lots of ten, twenty, even fifty graves, so that long after their own death, later family members would be buried under the gaze of their family monument. When one of the grand families of Oakwood was going to have a funeral, Jack was especially careful with the preparations, although many times the funeral itself was quite small, since most of the once-grand family and their social circle had gone ahead.

The obelisks, pedestal monuments, and columns literally towered over the landscape, competing with the immature trees for space and attention. They introduced a period of diverse styles. The pedestal monuments were constructed with multiple layers of stone piled on top of each other, with the top layer holding a statue or other feature. The pyramidal layers created maximum stability for the increasing height. The broad bottom layer was often rough granite, while the upper layers were polished granite or marble. The most elaborate examples had four-sided panels in the middle layer so that families could put more names on the monument itself.

The variation of memorials was astounding. Lewis Redfield was a printer and one of the original subscribers who established Oakwood. When he erected his standing memorial on the hill facing Dedication Valley, he memorialized himself with a simple stanza:

LEWIS H. REDFIELD,
PRINTER.
A worn and battered form,
Gone to be re-cast
More beautiful and perfect.

Then, above the text, the sculptor included a bas-relief medallion portrait of himself.

Such a combination of text, image, and decoration was not typical, since most sculptures were intended to speak for themselves, as with Ball Hughes's realistic bust of the scientist Nathaniel Bowditch (1847) at Mount Auburn or the Longstreet family's pyramid in Oakwood. The Brower family (circa 1869) had an obelisk topped by a covered urn that could have come from Laura Baldwin's earlier gravestone. In contrast, the Granger family raised a square Gothic open colonnade of granite, marble, and sandstone with a peaked slate roof topped by a cross (now lost). "Granger" was spelled in upraised letters on a marble panel affixed to the two sides of the monument. Inside, the Grangers were entombed in raised crypts with panels atop each one. When it was built just after the Civil War, the white, bright marble must have stood out dramatically from the pink and grays of the granites.

Unlike today, both colonial gravestones and especially family monuments used a wide palette of symbols. Some popular colonial symbols, such as a crossed bones or upraised hand with a finger pointing to heaven, continued into the nineteenth century. They joined a remarkable array of figurative and literal symbols that could be incorporated in the larger canvas of the family monument.

When Henry Denison passed away in 1882, his family raised a towering monument topped by a sculpture of a mother and her children. The pedestal proudly proclaimed the family name at the bottom. Each side of the Gothic-styled middle panel provided the birth and death dates of family members, with the front panel holding those for Henry and his wife Melissa (who died in 1915). It was festooned with a garland of roses. At the top of the pedestal were four emblems with doves and poppy leaves etched into them. Standing tall was the female figure, one breast bared, one child clinging to her dress, the other being held tightly. She is turned smiling to the child below, tousling his or her hair.

On the back panel, the reason the statue is child-centric becomes clearer. It records the short lives of two children, Henry, Jr. (three years, four months, dying in 1854), and Florence (one year, nine months, dying in 1864). The first child died before Oakwood was established, reminding us that the new rural cemeteries often provided families an opportunity to memorialize deaths previously unmarked or to erect cenotaphs for graves in other places. Overall, the monument celebrates the traditional patriarchal family held in the bosom of domesticity even as it chronicles the wretched realities of infant mortality.

Many monuments were filled with such symbolism, although few as abundantly. Garlands of ivy, and figures clasping lilies, vines, and various types of leaves, appeared on dozens of memorials. The 1888 Blocher monument in Forest Lawn Cemetery, Buffalo (NY), is

FIGURE 7.3. Charlotte Canda monument, Green-Wood Cemetery, Brooklyn, NY, 2016.

a lovely example of rigid family values creating a social tragedy.[7] The monument was the product of overbearing parents who refused to let their son supposedly ruin his life by marrying one of the family's maids. The son, Nelson Blocher, was forced instead to go to Europe for family business, and when he returned he found the maid Katherine dismissed from the family home. He sickened and died soon after.

His father designed a magnificent memorial that revolves around life-like marble figures of Nelson and his parents; they are all buried in a chamber below.

The monument casing is a truly amazing engineering marvel. Six large gray granite pilasters hold up a sixty-ton bell-shaped granite roof. The areas between the pilasters are fitted with windows showing a view of the figures in the central tableau. The mustached figure of Nelson reclines on a sofa, while his parents stand forlornly looking at their dead son. Nelson is clutching a Bible, which some stories say was his most precious possession since it had belonged to Katherine. The symbols scream loss, love, and grief to the educated nineteenth-century eye.

The tragedy of social status stopping love is integrated into the tableau by the presence of Katherine herself, at least metaphorically. Looking down from one of the pilaster walls is a fourth figure, a bare-breasted "voluptuous" angel carrying a bowl of rosewater. The figure clearly represents both an offering yet is symbolic of dangerous female attraction. Most accounts say either the maid posed for the angel or John Blocher drew her likeness from memory.

Only one of Nelson's legs is stretched straight out. The other is bent (evoking a prematurely terminated lifeline), below which flowers are carelessly piled. Flowers are everywhere: In addition to the sofa flowers, the angel holds an overflowing bowl of roses, and Nelson's mother is grasping flowers in her hands. Mr. Blocher leans on a broken column from which dangles an anchor. Outside, between the columns of the pilasters, curtained shrouds are etched over each window. A broken column, bent knee, and anchor with a broken chain all signified shortened lives, while the flowers symbolize unfailing love.[8] The sentimental symbols fit perfectly with the sorrowful Romanticism of the design.

Although the Blocher memorial is unique, similar sentimental stories in stone pervaded the reform cemeteries of the nineteenth century. As a child, one of my favorite Oakwood monuments was the Colvin family's, carved as a stone tree trunk. I loved how real the tree appeared, with its stunted branches and the veins in the bark. The design was very functional, since the names of the deceased were easy to read on the tree, yet it was highly symbolic, and just lovely. Several real trees with ivy crawling up them had grown around the stone, so the artificial memorial seemed to fit right into the natural landscape.

I admired the way the vines overlapped the small inset tablets that held the names of the people buried there. This small bit of designed disorder fascinated me, just as I found unsatisfying the more modern stones, with their deeply cut letters standing alone against an almost-empty granite backdrop. The Colvin stone intuitively suggested to me how the idea of the memorial had evolved—from something that emulated the richness and messiness of nature to a purer expression of style and aesthetics.

Although we are mostly alienated from this symbolic imagery, elements of it do appear in everyday memorials today. Much of the original meaning is lost, such as when we see an anchor and think of the sea, not of premature death or Christianity (the early Christians used the anchor as a substitute for the forbidden cross). We see a dog and presume a beloved pet was buried with their master rather than that the deceased was someone worth loving. The examples go on and on, although I think the ones that are most unintelligible to us are those related to nature. Few today know that acorns stand for potential, calla lilies for marriage, holly for foresight, and a poplar tree for sorrowful memories we have to hold.

At the same time, some meanings have persisted, such as poppies for sleep and roses for love, oak for strength and the pineapple for hospitality. Monuments erected in the twentieth century would sometimes allude to past traditions, with vines cut into one side of the front or a rose bloom above the name. The Pomeroy monument in Morningside, the cemetery adjacent to Oakwood that it manages, is a half-hourglass granite block with a sloping oval top. Etched into each shoulder of the monument are epaulets of leaves, perhaps poppies. The leaves, so prominent and exact in earlier monuments, have become almost abstractions here, serving both a decorative and symbolic purpose, harkening back to the rich symbolic language of the previous age.

So, we have a contradiction in the contemporary memorial age. On the one hand, these symbols, and ones added later such as the teddy bear, will appear over and over in everyday memorials and on laser-etched present-day memorials. Yet on the other hand, for many, walking through a nineteenth-century cemetery is like entering a foreign land. Today, even when a bronze plaque includes a vine on the side, few buyers can identify it, and fewer can articulate its symbolism. Many people chose geometric patterns instead (perhaps going back to Celtic crosses and other earlier styles) or just present the family name against a blank stone background. The loss of this language is itself symbolic of our distance from this rich past, and of the disdain modernism has had for ornamentation and ostentatiousness.

A Unique Artistic Achievement on the Way to Standardization

The Denison and Blocher monuments stand as remarkable examples of an ostentatious time. Cemetery managers certainly praised such carefully designed and ornamented family monuments, but they also wished more memorials captured the public's attention while improving the aesthetics of the cemetery landscape. Perhaps the best example of their adulation was the stunning 1891 design that Augustus Saint-Gaudens and Stanford White erected in Rock Creek Cemetery, Washington, DC, in memory of Henry Adams's wife Marian "Clover" Adams. Adams was devastated when his beloved wife committed suicide. A well-known capital writer and host, as well as grandson and great-grandson of American presidents, Adams asked his friend Saint-Gaudens, already famous for his sculptures of Abraham Lincoln, Hiawatha, and Admiral Farragut, to create his wife's memorial.

Saint-Gaudens sculpted an elegant allegorical work in which a seated, cloaked figure conveys a quiet sense of mystery and sadness. The bronze sculpture sits on a granite rock pedestal quarried in Quincy, Massachusetts, the family's longtime home. It faces a rose granite bench where Henry Adams often sat. Famed architect Stanford White, a friend of both men, designed the bench and pedestal. A

FIGURE 7.4. Adams family monument, Rock Creek Cemetery, Washington, DC, 2007.

"privacy circle" of yews surrounds the gravesite, where both Adamses are now interred. A visitor captures only glimpses of the figure before entering the circle, giving this enigmatic figure an added sense of isolation.

The overall effect is at once both unsettling and serene. Inside the yews is a quiet, separated contemplative space. Adams apparently asked Saint-Gaudens to produce a memorial that would represent the "acceptance, intellectually, of the inevitable."[9] Adams and Saint-Gaudens resisted efforts to name the figure, though the public quickly called it "Grief," a name Adams found distressing. Many tried to name the figure, he wrote, while the clergy found in it only an "expression . . . of despair, of atheism, of denial." He wondered why Americans could not see that the "interest of the figure was not its meaning, but in the response of the observer."[10] Adams did at one time say his name for it was *Peace of God.*[11]

I believe the Adams memorial is one of the most evocative in the nation, a compelling blend of art and nature, a private space in a collective place. The yews are one key to its success. Instead of creating a visual obstruction, they merge into the section, shaping and framing the internal landscape. Perhaps critically, the installation does not compete with the memorials around it—just the opposite. As you walk toward the memorial, you almost miss it, since the yews provide a natural shield that creates a private space without ostentatiously or unnecessarily interrupting the coherence of the section.

The sculpture is also a transitional piece between the very realistic figurative sculptures of the nineteenth century and the more symbolic, abstract art of the twentieth century. Saint-Gaudens was of the older generation of figurative artists, but this figure clearly is not easily named, categorized, defined—all elements that move it away from the past and point us to the future.

Saint-Gaudens and White's achievement was one of many artistic highlights of the late Victorian era cemetery. Even as European painters were experimenting with Impressionism, Lewis Comfort Tiffany was producing breathtaking stained-glass windows for many mausoleums, including one for the Smith typewriter family that is just inside the eastern entrance of Oakwood. An angel with large bright wings looks skyward from a garden captured through vibrant green leaves. "He is not Here: He is Risen" is written in glass below the figurative panels. The cloudy sky opens above the head of the angel; when the late afternoon sun pours through the glass, it brightens the entire interior of the mausoleum. These amazing windows joined famed statues by Europeans Bertel Thorvaldsen and Antonio Canova, which were copied or imitated and placed on family lots. Other well-known sculptors, such as Daniel Chester French and Harriet Frischmuth, continued to execute cemetery commissions late into their careers.

Monument to Mausoleum

Even with the artistic achievements of the age, the overall aesthetic impact of the ever larger, ever wider, ever more ostentatious memorials was negative. Amid the clutter of competing obelisks, classical columns, and boulders, wealthy lot holders constantly looked for new ways to stand out from the crowd, gain visitors' attention, and show their eminence. This effort took two almost oppositional approaches.

On the one hand, with the influence of the Arts and Crafts and "back to nature" movements, monuments using the symbolic language of nature became popular. These monuments varied from rough-hewn monuments to actual rocks being repurposed as gravestones (a hallmark today of the natural burial movement). Many of these monuments were small quartz or granite stones with a pinkish color, but a few were actual boulders left in their natural state.

Oakwood's Crouse's boulder was an extreme case. Charles Crouse wished to memorialize his father, Jacob, so he had an eighty- (or perhaps ninety-five-[12]) ton rock brought from suburban Split Rock using a capstan, with "one team of draught horses and six men . . . employed to move two-inch planks and rollers individually to slowly move the massive rock. It moved about 900 feet per day and the six mile trip to Oakwood took eight weeks." Apparently crowds gathered to watch the spectacle.[13] Eventually, the boulder stood majestically on a spacious lot closely surrounded by no other monuments. Vines grew over it, giving it an even more natural appearance.

On the other hand, after 1875, the wealthy, even some members of the middle class, turned to sophisticated artists and architects to create buildings and monuments that mirrored the massive public art being created in cities. Huge cathedral-like or chateau-like structures were built to memorialize the families of the Rockefellers, Vanderbilts, and local industrial barons. The nouveau riche filled the cemeteries with imitations. Admirers viewed them as symbols of America's greatness, icons to material and social success. Newspaper articles noted their size and expense in terms like those they used for the families' estates and country homes. Notable architects Richard Morris Hunt, James Renwick, and John Russell Pope designed mausoleums for their favorite clients. Specially crafted Tiffany stained glass graced their windows. Even the great landscape architect Frederick Law Olmsted, who disdained most cemetery work, accepted the Vanderbilts' request that he landscape the grounds surrounding their new mausoleum.

The Weiting mausoleum in the form of a Buddhist stupa at Oakwood, the Fleischman family's imitation Parthenon mausoleum in

Spring Grove Cemetery in Cincinnati, and the Gothic Woolworth chateau in Woodlawn in the Bronx left little doubt about the cost of leaving such a mark on the landscape. When typewriter industrialist Lyman Cornelius Smith decided to build a mausoleum in Oakwood, the result, according to historian Doug Keister, was "a classically elegant Beaux-Arts style" building "complete with four delicately carved Corinthian columns projecting out from the façade and a number of squared off, engaged Corinthian columns" ringing the building.[14] Add the carefully secured large-scale Tiffany window at the rear of the interior, and you have both elegance and grandeur. Smith made sure that anyone passing could not miss his name, LYMAN CORNELIUS SMITH, carved above the entrance in large letters.

Some cemeteries, such as Woodlawn, Oak Hill in Washington, DC, and Graceland in Chicago, were particularly noted for their mausoleum collections.[15] However, almost every reform cemetery had a small number of mausoleums constructed by local elites to highlight their eternal reputation. Especially in the Gilded Age, the often newly wealthy industrialists viewed the mausoleum as one of many buildings and acquisitions that solidified their social status through life and death.

The middle class were able to join in this show of status by buying a crypt in one of the new "community mausoleums" erected around the country. Firms such as Presbrey-Leland of New York City and Canada Mausoleums Limited from Toronto designed dozens of mausoleums with luxurious interiors where families could purchase a crypt just like a lot on the grounds.[16] Using imitations of a variety of architectural motifs, built mainly of granite and marble, they stood as icons to America's industrial wealth. Some companies that built them were not always as savvy or had as much integrity as one might wish, leading the Association of American Cemetery Superintendents to issue a warning regarding the "grave dangers" associated with cemeteries contracting with "an outside corporation" to build one because they too often kept a high percentage of the sales proceeds.[17] Morningside Cemetery built a community mausoleum in the early decades of the twentieth century that supposedly made more money for the builders than the cemetery. In many lawn-park cemeteries, such as Tod Homestead and Belmont Park, small private mausoleums were lined up along roadsides much like family monuments. The grandiose monuments and mausoleums increasingly overwhelmed the natural setting, leading cemetery managers to issue increasingly loud calls for the end of the "stoneyards."[18]

Standardization, Smaller Monuments, and the Rise of the Flush Marker

The last decades of the nineteenth century and the first decades of the new one presented a contradiction in memorial styles. While the wealthy bought enormous lots and built castles and chapels to demonstrate their eternal fame and the middle class raised increasingly tall obelisks and large blockish monuments, poorer Americans were buying smaller standardized monuments and markers for their two, three, or four graves. This difference was not just because they were less well off, but because the costs of death, burial, and commemoration were mounting. Many families had to choose smaller lots, memorials, and services even as they attempted to follow the traditions of their rural upbringings. Monument companies responded by offering memorials for every price, from the more elaborate to the very simple — all of them coming out of standard forms available throughout the country. Regional differences remained but were increasingly subordinated to monument company selections.

Mount Auburn and the other rural cemeteries had initiated an era where the central family monument competed with the trees as the most visible elements of the landscape. In the antebellum period, artisans reproduced these monuments in ones and twos throughout the nation, while after the Civil War monument companies produced template designs for granite monuments cut by machines. Monument dealers offered mourning families a constantly revolving set of models that were largely, save for incremental changes, the same monument.

The market for larger family monuments reflected the respect families wanted to show the dead and the victory of a consumer society where status was something one hoped to show their peers, and the monument dealers' ability to merge this sense of grief with a set of presumed actions that would show the world the family had fulfilled its obligation to the deceased. Living in a society increasingly defined by consumption, families spent money to show the highest possible respect to the dead, and also they wanted to outshine their neighbors. Even if families did not want the largest monument, they still desired a respectable one.

Among the firms that set the tone and styles for the memorial landscape was Presbrey-Leland. In an early 1950s sales book, the company claimed it had sold memorials in over 2,500 communities, with some costing over $1 million (roughly the equivalent of $18 million in 2016). They were a full-service organization, providing design, production, and placement. The catalog included four pages on celebrities who had used their services, including Broadway icon George M. Cohan, New York governor Al Smith, automotive innovator Walter Chrysler, and the architectural firm of McKim, Mead, & White.[19] Their book showed a wide selection of expensive memorials of many different design styles, including the popular Neo-Classical.

One of Oakwood's loveliest monuments is from the Presbrey-Leland Neo-Classical line: the Chapin half-circle colonnade with stairs rising up to a pedestal holding fourteen Corinthian columns. Two tablets mark the underground crypts where Henry and Marie Chapin are entombed. Presbrey-Leland noted in their description that when "the tomb is wholly underground, the esthetic is given free rein, and the designer afford full scope for his composition."[20] In one of those surprising social contradictions cemeteries represent, wedding parties and couples regularly have used the Chapin colonnade as a backdrop for photographs.

The company also offered older styles, such as the Gothic, Celtic, and Neo-Colonial. While some variations updated the older styles with simpler arches and virtually no ornamentation, many of them could easily have been placed on the grounds a half century before. The natural look, where the designer might rusticate the monument by carving the stone in uneven patches imitating a tree's bark, was also prevalent.

Some styles were quite effective in their more modernist styling without violating the boundaries of contemporary taste. After 1900, family vertical and horizontal tablet monuments were cut more squarely, giving them a more modern shape. The monuments abandoned their eighteenth-century allusions, much like new housing and furniture types did. They were often large, nicely proportioned monuments. Presbrey-Leland included the Zederbaum monument as an example of "Contemporary Design." Unlike earlier monuments with the names centered on the stone, the name is offset into the upper left corner of the monument, asymmetrically opposite a quotation from the Scriptures, and with a "band of dentils" (small blocks resembling teeth lining many building cornices) providing slight ornamentation at the top of the stone. In their words, the "nicely balanced" name and inscription are unevenly carved, with the "larger and heavier letters of the name compensating for the greater mass of the smaller characters." The stone is very attractive, but Presbrey-Leland still worried that such designs would be acceptable only "when properly controlled." Modernist designs needed to retain some elements of older forms and more traditional styles. Fully developed modern styles reflective of abstraction and expressionism would take decades before they could slip into the landscape.

If memorials were the books in the cemetery, "libraries of past lives, beliefs, and artefacts [sic]," a growing number of memorials relied solely on family rather than individual names as one strategy to produce a less cluttered monument, and a simplified visual landscape.[21] Two pages before the Zederbaum monument is the Kiernan, on which the family name is barely noticeable in the lower right-hand corner. An elongated cross is centered on the stone, with the quote "God shall wipe away all tears and death shall be no more" across the top. Stones such as this one were also not marred, from a contemporary perspective, with the multiple ornaments that the Victorians had loved. The cross is a very narrow, long line, almost imitating a dagger or sword, perpendicular to the quote and name.

Families that could not afford a big lot with a monument would continue to use upright markers right up to the present. The older styles of narrow, tall uprights would give way to lower, more stable, industrialized types such as the simple block and the slant markers. Double slant markers on a base would become quite popular as a substitute for family monuments because they could easily hold two or more names on their face. Many cemetery managers, including my dad, would place a lot of them in their cemeteries, but they were generally unloved since they were so ungainly, and they were considered monuments, so could be sold only by monument dealers, not cemeteries. Managers would push harder for flush markers; at Oakwood, my father pushed markers made of bronze, since under New York State law the cemetery could sell them.

In Catholic cemeteries particularly, but also in many other types, the simple cross would remain popular. Presbrey-Leland provides fourteen pages of choices, ranging from a simple Latin cross to the elaborate Celtic and Eastern Orthodox varieties. Some crosses were very large, such as the one for Kenneth White in Winchendon (MA) that soared thirty feet. Others would be wider so they could hold sculptures of the crucified Jesus or the Virgin Mary. Crosses could be made of wood, iron, granite, and marble. Germans especially created elaborate iron crosses, while many veterans' graves have just a simple, unadorned cross.

As the cemeteries filled with new burials and monuments, the problem was not any individual monument, but the accumulation of them on the burial sections. The tree canopy and shrubs could no longer hide the rows of hulky monuments dotted with an obelisk here and a broken column there. Critics saw "stoneyards" rather than the earlier balance of nature and culture. They railed against the standardized monuments as less lovely and more obtrusive. Since cemeteries rarely could sell monuments, depending on the state laws that governed their charters, managers were not as committed to maintaining them. While lawmakers had wanted to ensure that the sanctuaries of the dead would be untainted by commerce, managers saw revenue going to private monument dealers who had no responsibility for the long-term care or appearance of the cemetery. The result was that few cemetery managers held much love for the monument dealers who profited from selling the largest monument possible, never mind the effect on the landscape.

The negative implications of the accumulation combined with a loss of a sense of personality and individuality in the memorials. Baldwin's poignant epitaph was reduced to brief standardized epigrams, such as "Gone to heaven" or "Loved One," the bare facts of the person's life, along with a defining familial relationship, "husband," "wife," "daughter," and "son." The decline in storytelling in the cemetery changed the purpose of the memorial. The modern monument no longer narrated the life of the loved one but instead marked a space where people who already knew the person could remember them. Judged most harshly, this too often turned the cemetery into a storage space, with graves carefully and clearly organized, typed, and catalogued. With the beginning of the twentieth century, the widespread adoption of flush markers facilitated not only management's desire for easier maintenance, but also lot holders' need to limit expenses. The result was to finalize the evolution from visibly individualistic markers to the almost complete absence of the individual in the cemetery landscape.

Memorial Park "Features"

The new flush markers symbolized the reality that the culmination of these trends was simplification of the memorial landscape, just as it had been with the natural. In the memorial park concept, the answer to the incoherent, even ghastly "stoneyards" was the institutional "feature." Memorial park proponents proposed a single, well-designed, carefully chosen memorial for an entire section. This change was revolutionary for several reasons. First, the grave was privatized. Instead of large family memorials competing for the attention of the visiting public, flush bronze, granite, and marble plaques marked the graves of individuals radiating out from a collective memorial, the "feature," creating a more egalitarian space. As I've argued, the memorial parks emerged parallel to early suburbs with their fenceless front yards, standardized house styles, and more egalitarian feel (for those of the right race/ethnicity and socioeconomic class; also the case in the memorial parks).[22]

Second, the "features" distilled the social and cultural values important to contemporary middle-class white society. Previous individual and family monuments had represented these values, but now the features made them more prominent, even dominant. Christian crosses and Jewish stars were placed on some sections, while eagles (patriotism) and family groups were central on others. Other sections were crafted to draw members of popular voluntary organizations, such as the Masons and Rotary. Given that just over 4.1 million American men were Masons in 1959, many memorial parks set aside sections for them, with their key images serving as the feature.[23] Such features updated a long-standing practice where such groups purchased spaces for indigent members of the society. Eli Harvey's 1925 "Elks Rest" statue looming over such a plot in Oakwood was one of my favorite monuments in the cemetery. In the memorial parks, the lots were for purchase by individual members rather than the association. Soon, these symbols defined the memorial landscape, and thus the cemetery. Middle-class values were ever present not only in life, but also in death.

Forest Lawn Memorial Park in Glendale (CA), not surprisingly, defined the model of the memorial park. My favorite example of the successful implementation of their design is a quadrangle on the top of the hill framed by Daniel Chester French's large sculpture, *The Republic,* at one end, with John Quincy Adams Ward's *George Washington* at the other end, and a long, colorful mosaic version of John Trumbull's *The Signing of the Declaration of Independence* along the back side away from the street. In typical Forest Lawn fashion, the landscape combines two sculptures by well-known artists—French's iconic piece played a central role in the famed 1893 White City at the World's Columbian Exposition in Chicago, and Ward's statue stands in front of New York City's Federal Hall where Washington was inaugurated in 1789—with Trumbull's famous painting replicated in a different medium. The entire scene cries patriotism, but does so through an extraordinary mixture of authentic and pop art that is very unlike other memorial parks, where kitsch prevails.

Indeed, many of the memorial parks that followed Forest Lawn's success were badly planned, designed, and managed. For instance,

FIGURE 7.5. Republic, Forest Lawn Memorial Park, Glendale (CA), 2012.

in White Chapel Memory Gardens in the eastern Syracuse suburb of
DeWitt, each section has a theme, memorialized in a "feature" statue.
Plaster figures of a kneeling Christ, praying Christ, and Christ after
the Resurrection (a poor imitation of the stunning Bertel Thorvaldsen 1821 statue that Forest Lawn also uses as a feature for one of its
gardens) as well as a Mason and other symbols are centered on the

section, with flush grave markers in the grass around them. The features are artistically unimaginative and have been poorly maintained. When Oakwood assumed management of White Chapel, Jack tried to improve the entrance with a large sculpture of an eagle set in front of a flagpole and create a new section with a machine-cut bas-relief of the Last Supper, but the improvements failed to improve the dreary green and bright white plaster features and their surrounding poorly planted landscapes. From our historical perspective, a more unimaginative post–World War II suburban landscape would be hard to imagine.

Whether in Forest Lawn or White Chapel, the symbolic language of memory was dramatically simplified, yet still present. The tree stumps, ivy and plant imagery, and other icons used so effectively in the nineteenth century are absent, leaving only the values portrayed by the feature memorials. These complex older symbols have been replaced with ones only tangentially related to death. Heterosexuality, the patriarchal family, patriotism, and faith are the most typical values embedded in these suburban burial places. The simplistic three-dimensional images leave a landscape shorn of diversity, complexity, and personality.

As a result, death intentionally disappeared. The broad lawns are filled with the unseen, unrecognized dead. The traditional symbol of death, the gravestone, is invisible, flush to the ground. Instead of the moral lessons of colonial gravestones and the symbolic images of the nineteenth-century family monuments, families have privacy; no one knows where their dead lie unless they walk the grounds. Whereas in a colonial burial ground, family generations did not need to be buried together because the family felt integrated seamlessly into the community as a whole, now small nuclear families looked skyward in a larger landscape devoid of sympathy and sorrow. As I asked earlier, why would a mother come to the cemetery and look down at a plaque with her son's name when she could sit by an R.I.P. mural near her home, and have her neighbors stop by and talk with her about her loss?

Even if memorial parks were aesthetic failures, the model was widely replicated by nondenominational, Catholic, and even Jewish institutions. Forest Lawn could draw 40,000 people to a sunrise Easter service, and have multiple showings of its grandiose Crucifixion and Resurrection paintings in a specially built theater that held hundreds. And it wasn't just Forest Lawn. All across the country, the new memorial parks, memory gardens, and other variations drew urban white families who felt alienated from the older inner-city cemeteries, like Syracuse's Oakwood and Woodlawn, and newly minted white suburbanites. Too many memorial parks proved speculative ventures with too few permanent funds to care for the grounds in perpetuity, but Americans embraced the new style just as they bought houses in suburban subdivisions and shopped at new malls.

At their best, memorial parks are meticulously maintained landscapes with some remarkable art. The natural landscape is uncluttered enough that twentieth-century visitors don't feel enveloped by an atmosphere they fear, yet is engaging enough that visitors and mourners can withdraw from daily routines and contemplate the quiet, birds, and culture. Still, shedding death, stripping away individual and family identities, and having management dictate the visual and artistic landscape has a price. The visitors' focus is on finding the single grave or lot they care about, with the rest of the landscape an often undistinguishable blur. The memorial landscape no longer demands the visitor consider mortality or morality, but allows them to contemplate only immediate family memories.

And, as we enter the twenty-first century, the standardized images of the past don't necessarily speak to the next generation of potential lot holders. The racial and ethnic discrimination may be gone, but the institutional power that such discrimination represented is still very much in evidence. Not surprisingly, some people, especially young people, in our increasingly diverse society are alienated from cemeteries and memorial parks, and are searching for ways to express their grief elsewhere — with everyday memorials on the street, in their homes, and around the neighborhood.

8

COMMEMORATION
EVERYWHERE

The rise of the sleek, standardized stele family monument and the proclamation of the death of the public monument did not represent the end of memorialization as much as offer an opportunity for innovation and experimentation.[1] As I noted earlier, Maya Lin and the designers that followed her stunning design for the Vietnam Veterans Memorial in 1982 recreated our concept of the public memorial. Remarkable, moving memorials followed to the memory of the Holocaust, terrorism attacks, the civil rights movement, and many other worthy events and people. New abstract shapes were employed, like those that haunt the site of 9/11, as well as metaphoric figurative elements such as the chairs used to powerfully portray loss in Oklahoma City.

These new kinds of public monuments led to new forms of public memorialization. Today's society is far more ethnically and racially diverse than the mainstream culture of the nineteenth century, and everyday memorials are products of that diversity. They stand outside of or in opposition to the institutional controls of the cemetery, church, funeral home, and other components of the modern death industry, and as such they resist the homogenization of mourning. They are both a cry for a tolerance of diversity, and the outcome of the reality of social diversity. This diversity does not jettison the past but incorporates elements of traditions into new forms in new spaces, giving everyday memorials increased power and visibility.

People have become more comfortable expressing their grief in public. Survivors and mourners have left flowers at the front gate of Kensington Palace, painted an old bicycle white and put it on the street where their friend was killed in a car crash, embedded small rectangular memorials in the pavement outside homes in Germany where Holocaust victims had lived, created Internet cemeteries, fashioned vinyl decals that memorialized their grandmothers, and altogether reinvented the everyday memorial. They have successfully brought death back into the public dialogue.

Mourners have begun to erect public, personal, and sometimes political memorials that are sites of mourning *activity* (as in chapter 5) performed in front of intentionally designed memorial *objects*, our subject here (see table 8.1). Everyday memorials alter mourning practices by moving them to new locations, reusing old motifs in new settings producing different meanings, and attaching death to daily, public life in ways that can make some people uncomfortable. Save the innovative ghost bike, they rarely use unique new iconography in their efforts to reinvent memorials. Instead, they resituate common materials from the home, church, and cemetery to the street, yard, and other public spaces. Their efforts to make a public emotional response to death acceptable have been so successful, as we will see, that cemeteries are increasingly finding ways to abet personalization in their griefscapes.

In this return to the public, mourners draw upon imagery and practices that predate the modern way of death, finding the future of commemoration in the deep past. They reject the earlier reforms that had relocated the dead and dying, taking them from the home in favor of the hospital and funeral home. Even public war memorials had been increasingly located in inaccessible plazas, circles, and other spots. Dying, death, and memory had been placed away from our daily routines as we marginalized emotion.

Everyday memorials return mourning to the public in ways that are often visible, even intrusive to the point of discomfort. A roadside shrine juts out from the sidewalk into the street, demanding a part of the public right-of-way. A memorial vinyl decal shines from a car in a parking lot or on a highway, demanding attention. An R.I.P. mural

TABLE 8.1 Types of everyday memorials organized from personal to public

Type/*Focus*	Location	Description	Decorative motifs	Purpose	Origins
More personal					
Memorial tattoos (Individual)	Arms, legs, backs *Everywhere*	Inked represen- tations etched on bodies	Portraits, flowers, angels, religious imagery	Personal	Old prac- tice, rapid recent expansion
Internet cemeteries (Individual + Collective)	Websites *Everywhere*	Digital sites where indi- viduals can construct a memorial for a loved one	Digital imagery of candles, flowers, institutions, etc.	Personal	21st century
Memory T-shirts (Individual)	Funerals, wakes	T-shirts designed to memorialize worn by family, friends	Portraits domi- nate, personal images	Personal	21st century
Memorial vinyl decals (Individual)	Car, truck back windows *US mostly*	White vinyl decals of tradi- tional imagery placed on bumpers, back windows	Text, birth/death dates, angels, flowers, religious + symbolic + institutional imagery	Personal	Old practice, 21st- century renewal
Shrines (Individual + Collective)	Roadside, sidewalks, yards *Everywhere*	Assemblages, quickly started, varied form quite simple to very elaborate, placed at colli- sion/crash/ death	Religious imagery, candles, photographs, flowers, mementoes	Both, anti- collisions, anti- violence	Very old, recent renewal
R.I.P. murals (Individual + Collective)	Walls, building grates *Everywhere*	Painted murals of mostly young people murdered or otherwise trau- matically killed	Portraits, flowers, text, religious imagery	Advocacy, anti- police, anti- violence	1980s
Ghost bikes (Individual + Collective)	Roadside, sidewalks *Everywhere*	Old bicycle painted white placed at site of collision/crash	Flowers, notes, photographs, candles, memen- toes, portraits	Advocacy, anti- collisions	St. Louis 2003
Pavement memorials (Individual + Collective)	Roadways, sidewalks, public walls *International*	Plaques, draw- ings embedded at site of a mur- der, "disappear- ance," collision, or other trau- matic deaths	Names, text, outline portraits, hearts, symbolic imagery	Advocacy, anti- violence, anti- oppression	Late 20th century
More public					

speaks to passersby. You can't help but notice that a cashier at your local store has a memorial tattoo on her forearm as she bags your purchases. Everyday memorials' public presence is a critical element of their power. Avoiding them is difficult because they pop up as you turn around the corner, walk through your neighborhood, or drive your car—as you live your life.

However, all types don't inhabit the same space. Some everyday memorials are more public than others. None are truly private, although a memorial tattoo could be placed where few will see it. Others have not reached the public's consciousness. Not everyone is aware of ghost bikes, memorial vinyl decals, and especially Internet cemeteries, which remain out of view for most, as people only go to those sites either purposefully or by accident as they roam the web. Some memorials are intensely, and quite intentionally, public, like some roadside shrines and ghost bikes, which have a political or advocacy purpose.

Overall, the components of everyday memorials tend to reinforce their public visibility, whether through the bright white paint of a ghost bike, a smiling face on a memory T-shirt, or a pile of roses and

FIGURE 8.1. Memorial vinyl decal, Los Angeles, CA, 2008.

FIGURE 8.2. R.I.P. mural to Ray Jackson, Buffalo, NY, 2015 (courtesy Bradshaw Hovey).

lit candles at a roadside shrine, all looking for your attention. The bright flowers, Gothic script, and the deceased's looming portrait in an R.I.P. mural serve the same purpose, as do the reflective surfaces of vinyl decals. The newer online memorial sites have flashy home pages. All of these elements are intended to ensure that one notices, one stops, one remembers, and one acts in response to the death.

Locating Memorials in the Public Realm

Earlier, I noted that many everyday memorials are reminders of the structural inequities of our society and the traumatic deaths that result. A surprising number of the notable nineteenth-century monuments discussed in the last chapter also reflect the historical role of traumatic death in society: Clover Adams committed suicide, the Denisons experienced the loss of their babies, and Laura Baldwin died of a sudden, inexplicable illness. Today's traumatic deaths — due to gun violence, the opioid epidemic, rising numbers of suicides, seniors falling, and other intentional and unintentional injuries — are likely to be remembered not just with more evocative monuments in a cemetery but also immediately in public spaces.

For instance, the R.I.P. murals are panel drawings on the side of a building or on the front pull-down metal doors many businesspeople use to protect their stores. The building space dictates the size and shape of the panel. Some cover wide spans of large buildings; others fit neatly onto small areas. For instance, a mural to two young men who died in 1993 is located on the wall facing the basketball courts where two of their friends initiated an annual tournament in their honor.[2]

The sites where the R.I.P. murals might be painted are near where a person died, especially if the death was very public, such as in a confrontation with a police officer, or in some visible space where the community could continue to "see" the person and remember them. For instance, in Buffalo, the street artist "Risk" used the side of an old stand-alone garage at the side of an early twentieth-century house as a canvas. The whole side of the garage facing an empty lot is covered with the R.I.P. mural to Ray Jackson, "Voice of PUSH" (People United for Sustainable Housing), a local community leader. A black angel sadly peers out of the fluffy white clouds next to a large red heart partially covered with a banner showing Ray Jackson and his dates of birth and death (1952–2010), with a small teardrop falling from the clouds. The combination of traditional imagery (the angel) with a street twist (the teardrop of paint) and a culturally appropriate figure (the black angel) is typical of R.I.P. murals.

Likewise, even though it originates in a very different social context, that is, the largely white bicycle community of St. Louis and other major American cities, the design of the ghost bikes is crucial to their worldwide acceptance and cross-culture effectiveness. The white paint evokes the invisible—that is, the dead. Since the bicycles are older, sometimes even damaged, the ghost bikes are purposeful reminders of roadway deaths across cities and suburbs. Piling flowers at the foot of the bike, or adding them to a bike basket, adds color and texture to its stark visage. In Hawaii, the bike for Zachary Major Manago was placed in a grassy area near the site of his death, covered with vibrantly colored flowers contrasting with the bright white paint. Photographs of Zachary alone and with family and friends were slipped between the spokes of the wheels.[3] In contrast, in Mexico, mourners attached the ghost bike for Carlos Rivera Rosas to a light

FIGURE 8.3. Ghost bike, Brookline, MA, 2014.

post, roughly twenty feet in the air; it was spectral white against the ink black sky.[4]

Many roadside shrines disappear in the darkness of night unless their candles are lit or streetlights shine upon them, but ghost bikes typically are painted purposively with reflective white paint. One evening as I was going to dinner with a high school friend near Boston, I suddenly saw a ghost bike glowing under the stark light of a streetlamp, in the middle of a block, in front of a parking lot. Deflated balloons lay across its crossbar, while white flowers were looped around the handlebars. It had a front basket filled with notes and offerings. The space was not desolate, but in the chill of a fall New England night, the bike shone bright in its isolation.

Constructing Memories in Public Spaces

The surprise encounter with the roadside shrine or other public everyday memorial speaks to their power, acceptance, and spread. The sudden appearance of a new memorial can be startling. Walking down Sunset Boulevard near my house, I came upon a skateboard taped to a light post surrounded with flowers. A note said angrily, "Here's your fucking skateboard." (Some kids had demanded it from a family's son and brother, then left it behind after fatally stabbing him.) Like several others, I was stopped in my tracks, a few blocks from my home, at the sudden appearance of violent death, and the awful emotional consequences it creates. On a white piece of cardboard taped above the skateboard, several people had signed their names with R.I.P. and the dead man's name. More than fifty candles had burned out throughout the night at the bottom of the light post. Flowers had been laid at the bottom of the pole, too, and more were stuffed into the tape holding the skateboard. Someone had sprayed *Rest in Peace* in blue in front of the shrine on the sidewalk. The skateboard was a cry of pain, but also a cry for peace in the face of violence.

Other everyday memorials straddle the private and public worlds in somewhat uncomfortable ways. Memorial vinyl decals are situated in a liminal space because of the emotional attachment many people have to their car or truck. While people have been putting decals and bumper stickers on the backs of their cars and trucks for decades, the memorial decals have become popular in a very short time, certainly due to their simplicity as a heartfelt statement of memory.[5] Similarly, the business in memory T-shirts—often portraits of smiling young men sometimes posed in a menacing stance and holding a gun—has boomed in some cities. The shirts are worn at the wake, funeral, and memorial service, with some families making new ones for each service, and again for each birthday.[6] Likewise, what does one say when the barista hands over your coffee, and a memorial tattoo suddenly appears as the shirtsleeve pulls up? Seeing this very personal memorial to a friend, combat buddy, or grandmother feels almost as if one has caught sight of something they should not see. Still, the tattoo, T-shirt, and decal are all there in public sight.

Yet we don't expect them to be there. We anticipate bumper stickers proclaiming the success of a child, the love of a sports team, a commitment to a radio station, even some political statements, but suddenly we are confronted with a decal describing the life of a grandmother or child with the stark dates of birth and death and an often iconic image like a soldier's boots, an angel, or a dove. Similarly, T-shirts are supposed to be funny, stupid, and personal, not reminders of the homicide or opioid epidemics. Yet they are everywhere. Once I was walking down a street in Tanzania and a young African man walked by wearing a T-shirt memorializing a family reunion in Pennsylvania. And, living in LA, I see tattoos all the time, everywhere, but only a few that suggest a person is in mourning or is haunted by the death of someone meaningful enough that they felt the need to embody their memory on their arm.

Even when everyday memorials are where we would imagine them to be, they still might surprise us. The virtual cemetery mimics the physical cemetery in that it "relocates the deceased to a place that is accessible but separate from the spaces usually occupied by the living."[7] Perhaps this distancing explains why relatively few people know about Internet cemeteries. The presence of death in the digital space has been widely discussed, but discovering your first Internet cemetery or "visiting" your first Facebook memorial page still seems surprising.

The everyday memorials serve as beacons of the traumatic society and as stops on the passage between life and memory. They serve as public beacons warning of traumatic deaths, while also allowing mourners a place to meet, greet, and talk about their friend that is outside the institutions of death. In this way the everyday memorials draw on older death practices, such as the Mexican descansos. Descansos could be simple crosses placed at the site of the death or the place where mourners rested the casket on the walk to the cemetery. In some cases, mourners have built small shrines or *nichos* (small freestanding enclosures) at the spot.[8] When asked why they continue to mark the site where a loved one died with a descanso, responses included: "It is the place where the victim's soul departed from the body"; "It is a marker to remind us where a loved one was lost"; and "It is a mark of an interrupted journey in the road of life."[9] R.I.P. murals, roadside shrines, and ghost bikes often are located at similar places where souls were lost, a loved one left us, and a life journey was interrupted.

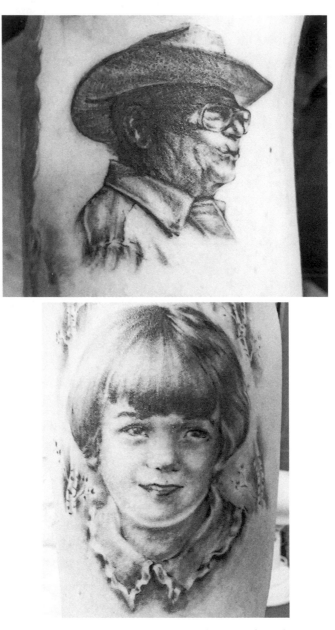

FIGURE 8.4A AND 8.4B. Memorial tattoos of grandmother and grandfather, Los Angeles, CA, 2017. (Courtesy of Shizhy Saldamando.)

FIGURE 8.5. Roadside memorial, Buenos Aires, Argentina, 2012.

Designing Everyday Memorials

In their designs, everyday memorials incorporate the innovative characteristics of the new large public memorials while sustaining tradition motifs and icons. Literally millions of Americans first understood that they could mourn in public either at the Vietnam Veterans
Memorial, the AIDS Memorial Quilt, or the interactive memorials
that followed. These memorials asked, even perhaps demanded, that
visitors strip away that distance we have been taught between us and
grief, us and death. They offered the opportunity to cry, to talk, and
to leave behind a trace of the person we loved. The material left became part of the canvas to create a new style of public remembrance.
While everyday memorials' materials, the iconography, the sentimentality all drew upon the premodern practices of the nineteenth century, they established new traditions for people who had little or no
connection to that past.

Indeed, everyday memorials are not simply imitations of the
mourning practices at the Wall or the Oklahoma City memorial. As
with the majestic new 9/11 memorial in New York City, each of these

large public monuments awe us with their representative metaphors for a dreadful loss. Even though they are more approachable than earlier more formal, less interactive spaces, they are still majestic in their styling and size compared to the average everyday memorial. Further, the National Park Service and other organizing entities ensure that offerings are picked up and catalogued at these sites; these national sites are neat, almost tidy, representations of our loss.

In contrast, at the everyday memorials ephemeral informality reigns, and it defines the experience. They are spontaneous, makeshift, heartfelt, often messy representations of deeply felt emotions. This informality expresses itself in multiple ways in the design of everyday memorials. The two most prominent are the materials chosen, which are often borrowed from the deceased's closet or gifted by mourners, and the structure, which typically keeps the deceased firmly at the center of the memorial but varies across types in other ways. For instance, at the extensive memorial for a 2004 nightclub fire in Buenos Aires that took 194 mostly teen and young adult lives, the immediate impression is of peeling plastic, layers of memories, and a lack of a clear order.[10] A cross sits in front of the main shrine, with a Jewish star on one side, and a Muslim star and crescent on the other. Dozens of pairs of sneakers brought by the families hang from a rope at the entrance—and other pairs are located throughout the shrine.

An informal order between the layers does eventually emerge. The main shrine site is a shed entitled "El Santuario De Nuestros Angeles Del Rock 30–12–04 Nunca Mas Cromanon." In it are dozens and dozens of smaller shrines to the individuals killed. The overall shrine is tiered: first the sneakers, then the religious/ethnic symbols, followed by photographs hung on a line, and finally, under the roof, the detailed shrines to the individuals. The combination of sorrow and anger—driven even further by revelations of the club's negligence—is palpable. Yet the structure evokes the ancient saint shrines of Latin culture, which are also often tiered in this way. Indeed, the structure is not so rigid as to constrain people from displaying the personalized memories so central to an everyday memorial.

A roadside shrine and ghost bike are almost always immediately recognizable. The shape and contents are distinctive yet almost universal. A photograph, tall flower, bike, or significant memento sits at the center of a cascading assemblage of candles, flowers, notes, and other offerings. The bright colors of the flowers typically draw attention, as well, in the twilight, as does the flickering of candles.

The informal elements help us define the deceased by their love of sports, a band, friendships, family events, and just stuff the person did. The sites mix the traditional with the individual and personal in ways that echo decades or centuries of mourning, yet with a new DIY informality. When friends and family set up a card table outside the home of five-year-old Samantha Runnion after she was abducted and killed, it was covered with candles, photographs, and flowers. A small stuffed lamb and a ceramic angel were placed amid the other items.[11] The lamb and angel have been symbols of childhood since at least the nineteenth century, and still can be found on many children's cemetery graves. Older teen shrines are more likely to have photographs and mementoes, perhaps symbols of a teenage rebellion.

Since memory T-shirts and memorial vinyl decals are designed and completed by professionals, they are less informal. You will rarely see a haphazardly placed item or a mismatch of crosses and beer cans. Many times a single element—a rose, a portrait, or a soldier's boots—dominates the scene on the T-shirt or car window. These everyday memorials can be very complex, but they often have space constraints. So, keeping them simple makes their message clearer and more powerful.

R.I.P. murals and memorial tattoos sit somewhere in between the informality of the roadside shrine and ghost bike and the structured layout of the decal and T-shirt. They are often made by artists, so are carefully structured, but are intended to authentically represent a contemporary teen, so include transgressive elements. A portrait of a young man shot by police or an unknown assailant brings that person immediately to mind for family and neighbors.

For instance, a number of Baltimore R.I.P. memorials are very simple.[12] Instead of a portrait with surrounding text, these murals just have an R.I.P. painted above or beside a domed or rectangular tablet tombstone. The tombstone is then filled in with the deceased's real or street name, finished with some very sad tag lines — "Get It or Die Trying," "Soldier from the Cradle to the Grave," and "Death before Dishonor." While these murals are similar to memorial T-shirts in their simplicity, and also mirror the iconography of the vinyl decals, which rarely have room for more than a single image, the tag lines of violent death and the liquor bottles that friends will artfully arrange in front of them shift the representation from the sentimental to the street.

On the murals or T-shirts, other icons and images might be painted around the central one. A set of praying hands, an angel, a cross, and other traditional iconography will surround the name or the portrait. These styles of memorials are especially likely to include more text than just the name and basic information — everything from the simple inscriptions one finds on modern gravestones ("Forever in Our Hearts") to elaborate poems that tell the story of the deceased or the tale of the violence that ended his or her life.[13]

In many cases, more than one type of everyday memorial will be incorporated into a family's mourning. Many people at a shrine will be wearing a memory T-shirt, and some might host a memorial tattoo from a previous death. They might also have heard about a remembrance ride or memorial service through Facebook or other social media. Many murals have a shrine in front of them on the sidewalk or roadside. In Baltimore, "R.I.P. Ricky" was written on the side of a brick building, which was fronted with an elaborately designed assemblage of liquor bottles spelling out "Ricky." Of course, the most visible examples of this have occurred in relationship to the series of tragic police shootings in Baltimore, New York City, and elsewhere. After Freddie Gray's death in April 2015, a quickly painted R.I.P. mural became a place for people (often wearing memory T-shirts) to gather and mourn his death and advocate for justice from the city. A roadside shrine quickly appeared here, as well as at the site of his death.

Memorial tattoos epitomize the psychological aid everyday memorials play within mourning. Psychologist Susan Samuel characterizes a memorial tattoo as "a concrete symbolization of an abiding presence of the lost person, which helps in the process of ongoing identification and internalization."[14] The images on the people she studied reflected some specific personal value or item related to the dead person. For instance, one memorialized his grandfather by having a picture of an anchor put on his arm with the years of birth and death. This image reminded him of his grandfather's own anchor tattoo.[15] Perhaps not surprisingly, psychologist Shannon M. Bates notes, the tattoo shop she frequents reported a person arriving daily for a memorial tattoo, as illustrated by the memorial tattoo portraits in figure 8.4.[16]

The cultural regularity of memorial tattoos, representative of the heightened public consciousness of everyday memorials, is indicated by the stories regarding San Antonio Spurs forward Kawhi Leonard in the 2014 NBA playoffs. This shy young man played brilliantly and became a media darling. Announcers talked about his rough neighborhood, his devoted parents, the tragedy of his dad's murder in front of his car wash, and his ability to overcome the odds to become a superstar athlete. In those descriptions, commentators often came back repeatedly to the tattoo tribute to his father on Leonard's arm: a "tombstone with an 'R.I.P. Dad' inscription with angel's wings sprouting from each side."[17] Leonard has many more tattoos, but this one is typical of many people's in that it forcefully and simply portrays his loss and sorrow. Leonard's tattoo allows him to carry the memory of his father with him everywhere, all the time. It also makes him a living everyday memorial in a postmodern world.

Outside the Cemetery Gates

While informality is the primary characteristic defining everyday memorials, their complicated relationship with institutional memorials like those in a cemetery is almost as important to their design. While some elements of traditional memorial design, such as crosses and coffins, are regularly present in everyday memorials, others, such as mementoes that cemeteries regularly ban, are also critical parts of the design. The result is that the everyday memorials resituate traditions into the public sphere, but also reshape the meaning and control of the images by making them part of a DIY creation.

DIY memorials are rooted in our social belief that anyone can make meaningful objects.[18] The pervasive acceptance of the roadside shrine is probably most indicative of this belief. The shrines come in many varieties, from a single cross with a small bunch of flowers to elaborate assemblages with many flowers, candles, and mementoes. I have seen shrines that were simply a group of tall glass candles, often with the Virgin Mary stenciled on the glass, and notes marked on the glass in black.

A surprising number of everyday memorials are reminiscent of a grave. Near where I live in Los Angeles, after a young person died, the family carved a cross into a tree in the parkway, the little space between the sidewalk and the street, in front of their building. They fashioned a flower garden descending from the cross, protected by a tiny fence, and they carefully tend it. Every holiday, it has new flowers and mementoes, often with a childhood theme. In an area where graffiti and vandalism are common, no one has ever defaced this space. In some small way, the cemetery has come to the street, and even the vandals recognize it.

A cross in a shrine or mural is almost always the centerpiece. All the other elements are positioned around it, usually in a descending order of density and height. Candles are often clustered around the cross in the center, with flowerpots and other, more permanent features (for instance, photographs in frames) close by. Away from the center, bundles of flowers are more casually placed, along with perhaps a stuffed toy. DIY designers seem to unconsciously create hierarchies, giving prominence to specific items. Even at a very large shrine, such as in Paris at Place de la République after the heartbreaking shootings there in 2015, the lion sculpture at the center of the square served as an organizing feature, with candles, flowers, and other items circling it.

The bike serves as the centerpiece of the ghost bike, often initially appearing as if it stands alone on the roadside.[19] Yet people typically surround it with a small shrine, candles radiating out to the sidewalk, photographs and notes interwoven in the spokes, and bunches of flowers surrounding the bike. The result is a DIY sculpture with the luminous white demanding one's attention. One reason the ghost bike has been adopted internationally so rapidly—beyond the coherence of the international bicycling community—is that it is not an overt religious symbol, instead literally representing the people killed.

On the web, the design and appearance of Internet cemeteries is probably the closest that everyday memorials come to looking like cemeteries. The earliest online memorials were personal projects: World Wide Cemetery, Virtual Memorial Garden (US), and MuchLoved were all founded by people who sought a place to remember their loved ones or themselves on the Internet. Not finding one, they created their own. While they were radically reimagining mourning as a digital experience, they often borrowed their imagery from common conceptions of cemeteries and included familiar language in their titles and sections. MuchLoved is divided into "gardens," much like a physical memorial park. While the names they use, including "Celestial Garden," "Wildlife Garden," and "Fairytale Kingdom," would be unusual in a physical burial ground, their imagery of wildlife, wildflowers, water, floral gardens, and the like would fit right in. Along similar lines, the Virtual Memorial Garden (UK) has an image on its home page that mimics the entrance of an older cemetery: an iron rod gate holds a semicircle with the name, and is framed by vaguely Gothic posts and backed by a canopy of deciduous trees. Three buttons are below the gate: information, memorials, and remember. Some sites have photographs that recall burial sections; their naming techniques draw from cemetery ones, and the ways that visitors can interact with the memorials mimic how people would act in a physical cemetery.

All the everyday memorial spaces challenge the restrictions of the physical cemeteries. For instance, when someone does not want to post a photograph of the deceased in Fairytale Kingdom, the site posts images of a teddy bear, a petal heart, a butterfly, or balloons instead. These are icons of mementoes that cemeteries restrict or prohibit since they don't reinforce the memorial aesthetic and can interfere with the grounds maintenance. Outside the cemetery gates, though, mementoes play an important part in the design of everyday memorials.

Short-Term Commercial Solution?

While everyday memorials have successful reintegrated death into public life, their long-term impacts are still uncertain. The roadside shrine beneath the electric pole on Sunset Boulevard remained for two weeks, then disappeared. Ghost bikes come, and ghost bikes go when city cleanup crews decide they are nuisances. Even the memorial tattoos and the vinyl decals last only as long as the person lives or the family owns the car or truck. I hope that some everyday memorials can sustain themselves, such as the grave-like shrine near my home with the cross cut into the tree, but if the family should move, the apartment building be sold, or the tree die, the memorial will be at risk.

Internet cemeteries seem to offer a more stable circumstance, but websites come and go as fast as cars these days. Early simplicity has already given way to more elaborate, visually compelling pages. Moreover, the entrance of larger, more expensive, sometimes very elaborate, and certainly more mainstream consumer companies, such as Legacy.com, has altered the virtual cemetery landscape, diminishing or stripping away the imagery of the cemetery and leaving a sensibility similar to the greeting card industry. While the WWC retains a background photograph of a veterans' section with its rows of equally sized markers set amid a leafy green canopy, at Legacy.com, a deck goes out into a slowly rippling blue lake overshadowed by beautiful mountains. A sunset fades off to the right, and to the left is a large box titled "Where Life Stories Live On," combined with a search box.

We know a great deal about digital mourning, but less about how Internet cemeteries are used as online memorials, and whether users sustain their interest in the memorials they virtually erect.[20] Do people sustain their interest in these sites, or are they just part of an immediate response, like the temporary everyday memorials? In an unscientific exploration of MuchLoved, I looked at ninety-six memorials; a sampling of MuchLoved's Village Garden, which was dominated by memorials to people over sixty; and Enchanted Forest, where the memorials were for a greater diversity of age groups, though almost two-thirds of the memorials were for people under twenty-four. MuchLoved presents its memorials in rows of four, so I randomized my selection by looking down the last of the four columns in both gardens. The memorials were almost evenly male and female, with most of them over age fifty.

I had cynically imagined that the site would attract people in the immediate sorrow of their loss, and that the vast majority would not come back again. Instead, I found mixed evidence. Forty-five percent of the sites had no activity after the first three years, with roughly 15 percent having no tributes, one or no photographs, and no life stories, such as a eulogy or family reminiscence. While fewer than 10 percent were willing to pay to light a virtual candle, almost one-quarter (23 percent) had tributes five or more years after the death, and almost half had photographs that were posted more than three years after the death. My conclusion is that the memorials served as both an immediate need for some families, and an important continuing place of memories and mourning for a smaller, yet significant, number of others.

These findings strike me as generalizable to many everyday memorials. Just as families and friends put an enormous amount of effort into these memorials, while knowing they might be taken away by the city at any time, a smaller number of survivors are very committed to ensuring the continuation of the memorial. I think back to the Nemis memorial near my Los Angeles home. The company taking care of that electric pole pulled their memorial down again and again, yet the family continued for years to return and replace it. I am also reminded of the stories of "shrine keepers," who after 9/11 maintained memorials even as the media declared that society needed to move on from the tragedy.[21]

Mourning does not happen in some neat and orderly fashion, and for some people MuchLoved, a roadside shrine, an R.I.P. mural, and a cemetery grave can each serve a similar, complementary purpose of providing a space where grief is allowed. For many people and communities, an everyday memorial will quickly become a visual nuisance. In our diverse society, though, many others will see a carefully maintained shrine, such as the one near me with a cross carved into a tree, as part of the neighborhood's landscape. Instead of demanding its disappearance, they will tolerate, even support, its maintenance.

We don't know how many people complement a visit to the cemetery with one to the R.I.P. mural or take flowers to the grave and click to buy flowers at the Internet cemetery. Combing through MuchLoved, I found a few photographs of other types of everyday memorials and cemetery memorials, but at least in their use of illustrations, the Internet mourners displayed the person, not the gravesite or the social media link.

Mainstreaming Everyday Memorials

The immediacy of the shrine, bike, mural, and T-shirt has had another impact; they have become public symbols of death. I have lived in Los Angeles since the 1990s, and during that time, roadside shrines have become an accepted part of the city's life. I have seen dozens of them. They have included the famous, such as Ronald Reagan, whose remains were in a Santa Monica funeral home for a short time prior to being moved to the nation's capital and eventual burial elsewhere in Southern California. The funeral home's lawn literally was covered in floral tributes. Yet they also include the little known. Two years after the Reagan memorial, I saw a heartbreaking shrine to a small child killed in the Antelope Valley, far from the congested streets of the big city. Her little teddy bear sat by itself next to the wooden plaque with her name and dates drawn on it. Many shrines have honored Latinos or African Americans, but pretty much every community has adopted the practice, especially when a high school or other youth is killed by or in a car.

As the practice has become more common, the *Los Angeles Times* and other media outlets have used photographs of shrines as emblems of tragedy. In 2014, a teenager was killed when he struck his head on a bridge while riding on the upper deck of a bus. Two bundles of flowers were placed in his memory outside his school in Manhattan Beach, a small suburb of Los Angeles. The story was accompanied by a large photograph shot from a ground angle of the flowers propped up on a flagpole. The bundles seem lonely, yet the iconic power of the shrine is illustrative.[22]

An image of a much more elaborate shrine was printed in 2013, when five teens were killed in a car crash in Burbank, in the San Fernando Valley. Dozens of candles, many with saints' figures on them, burned in front of two large white cardboard posters on which many people had left notes of remembrance and condolences. Flowers in pots and in plastic lay throughout the shrine, along with mementoes and photographs in plastic frames. The newspaper's photograph captured two students, their heads down, a hand covering one's eyes, their arms draped around each other.[23] The photograph reminds us that the shrine serves a dual purpose: as a caution to passersby that once again a car crash has taken a life, and as a space where people can mourn, long before the funeral can be conducted, the grave has been closed, and the monument placed.

The photo archive Getty Images holds more than 200 shrine and other images from the *Los Angeles Times* alone.[24] The collection exemplifies each reason why these new public memorials are such powerful conveyors of mourning and message. They range from the famous, such as Michael Jackson; to the official, such as five Oakland police officers killed in the line of duty; to the almost unknown, a thirteen-year-old killed by a drunk driver. Portraits fill many frames, such as a photograph that included a large flyer photo of a killed school principal (covered with mourning messages) with a couple of his young students comforting each other. Others show mourners in the process of constructing the shrine by leaving flowers, gathering notes, or staging a small scooter on the stairs near a dead toddler's home. Most photographs show people mourning in front of a shrine. Small children kneel, light candles, and wave good-bye, while adults add flowers, stand and contemplate, talk among themselves, hold their children, weep, and pray.

A couple of the images show a newscaster positioned near the shrine, reinforcing it as an emblem of grief accepted and recognized by a wide media audience. Many photographs have people assuming traditional mourning poses and positions. They kneel or stand with their hands held in prayer, sit on the ground in groups as if in pews, or hug and hold each other for comfort and support. While cemetery and church memorials are in locations that reflect centuries of tradition, these photographs find shrines at sea, on the sidewalk, in front yards of apartment buildings and houses, on the beach, at memorial plaques, on stairs, along driveways, and in the street. Recently, I was walking along beautiful Echo Park Lake and came across a shrine to a young man who apparently had died in the park. The randomness of the location combined with the power of the mourning messages help everyday memorials integrate death into contemporary life.

Public Emotion amid Private Grief

The potency of the everyday memorials is not lodged in any one component of their architecture. Instead, their emotional effect comes from the combination of the elements into an often messy, evocative, personal, dramatic, even melodramatic piece. The memorials play an important role in families' and friends' performance of mourning. The acts of building a shrine, decorating a ghost bike, affixing the decal, painting the mural, or getting the tattoo are ways that people both work through their grief and create something that allows others to interact with them about it.

The act itself is important. The cemetery long has been the place for a performance of grief, but especially over the past three or four centuries the landscape was crafted to either encourage grieving or privatize it. Now some cemetery managers are trying to allow families to bring more personality back into their grounds and onto their gravestones.

9

A PAINTER'S EASEL

Cemetery memorials are the opposite of everyday memorials. They are more permanent, embody conservative values, and are located in landscapes that only hesitantly integrate innovation. Yet cemetery memorial landscapes do change. Cemetery managers spent much of the period from the 1880s until the present simplifying memorial landscapes. They spent decades convincing lot holders to eliminate elements, such as footstones, fences, clustered shrubs, dense tree canopies, and finally family monuments, that cluttered the landscape and created massive inequities. Finally, they succeeded in creating a sleek, serene memorial park landscape with flush markers and institutional monuments amid a backdrop of lawns and prettified nature. They successfully designed the institutional monuments to express a handful of traditional values, while the individual and family memorials contained just the barest of information about the deceased.

In many ways, these efforts reflected the society's medicalizing of death, avoidance of mourning, and isolation of the dying. However, they also were a rejection of the traditional imagery of death that had made colonial graveyards as well as the nineteenth-century reform cemeteries vital cultural places visited not only by mourners but also by a much wider group of visitors. By following the dictates of modernism without actually adopting modernist design, cemetery operators failed to see that they were giving up something important in their efforts to more effectively maintain a more coherent landscape of targeted values and norms.

What they gave up was the individuality and personality that made Laura Baldwin's poignant marker in Oakwood or the tragic teenager killed on her birthday after being dragged down a city street by her carriage Charlotte Canda's elaborate monument in Green-Wood so compelling to visitors.[1] They forsook the graphic skills and melancholy willow and urns of the eighteenth century and the glorious stained glass of Tiffany and mysterious figure of Saint-Gaudens in their efforts to better control their grounds and provide what landscape architects, naturalists, and other cultural commentators thought was the supreme aspiration, a cohesive memorial and natural landscape.

You can walk through most memorial parks and conventional cemeteries today and see that same landscape being replicated time and again. However, even as the simplified memorial landscape was becoming the norm, a contrary trend was emerging. Reluctantly, cemetery managers were allowing lot holders to erect personalized and individualized monuments with pictorial etchings. Indeed, "personalized headstones have proliferated since the 1970s and . . . few contemporary cemeteries do not have examples of them."[2]

Why is this so? First, new technologies have made it easier to etch images and portraits on monuments, something that appeals to many lot holders. Second, cemeteries and monument dealers are less dogmatically controlling the landscape given the rise of cremation rates. Third, the same demographic and cultural diversity that is driving the acceptance of everyday memorials and the introduction of a wider variety of holiday celebrations into the cemetery is propelling managers to accept changes in memorial design. However, the change is sporadic since many cemeteries, especially well-endowed ones with a strong connection to a more conservative aesthetic, are less likely to allow the new style of headstones and more likely to be reinforcing their traditional components by building new mausoleums and columbaria.

These changes are exemplified in two trends shaping the memorial culture of cemeteries. First, since the 1950s, cemeteries have mostly ended their racial, ethnic, and social discriminatory practices. While the few instances discussed above represent continuing ethnic, racial, and identity biases, most cemetery operators have seen the business wisdom of accepting society's demographic diversity. As a result, they allow Blacks, Latinos, Asians, and others to express their cultural values on their memorials, potentially altering the cemetery as a space. In the traditional cemetery, a visibly emotional African American funeral would end much the same way as a constrained white Episcopalian one, with a bronze flush marker set at the top of a grave disappearing into the grassy surroundings. Now families can leave behind a more personalized memorial that speaks for them. This shift makes visible that which was invisible, whether a memorial carved with a bus bound for heaven, as the song has it, or a beautiful sculpture of two women intertwined in homage to their lesbian relationship.

Second, new carving techniques have introduced informality into memorial design. As a result, stones can be more expressive, be culturally specific, and combine sacred and profane elements. The exuberance of everyday memorials has slipped over the cemetery fence to redecorate the graveyard, even in color. Again, immigrant, ethnic, and LGBTQ cultures are using this new freedom to memorialize in ways my father would have found disturbing, even as he oversaw the transition to the more pictorial headstone. Many of the new markers will draw their imagery from cemetery traditions, while others will introduce pictorial slang, such as a pink triangle for a deceased gay serviceman, into the cemetery landscape.[3]

Southern California culture is heavily influenced by large Latino, African American, and Asian populations. Institutions here have long accepted that traditional practices need to adapt to changing social conditions. Even Forest Lawn Memorial Park, as we saw, long has allowed Christmas ornaments and decorations, presumably part of Hubert Eaton's efforts to make the cemetery a happier place. Farther east, social traditions are less diverse and less open to informality, but change is still in the air. After the Red Sox finally won a World Series, celebratory T-shirts were tucked over many gravestones all around New England. Even though they weren't replaced when management

FIGURE 9.1. Mizener family monument, Oakwood Cemetery, Syracuse, NY, 2005.

required they be taken down, they symbolized a new openness. The adoption of etched gravestone images and an easing of what families can leave on graves is not evenly spread, but I believe that the forces behind these trends will be difficult for all but the wealthiest and most traditional cemeteries to deny.

From Ceramic Photographs to Golf Scenes on Monuments

The number of unmarked graves throughout history must reach into the millions. The financial ability to have a gravestone, and to have that gravestone survive wars, urban development, weather, even theft, shrinks the number much further. And we know that for some populations, the chance that the grave survived, much less the gravestone, was far less likely. Native Americans had a rich diversity of mourning and burial cultures, which white society rarely has honored. Chinese workers on the rail lines of the West, slaves throughout the Americas, seamen of all ethnicities, and many other primarily poor and minority peoples have had their graves built over, disturbed, unacknowledged, even purposefully destroyed.

In recent years, though, historians, archivists, genealogists, and others have begun to rediscover this past. In 2013, history student Sandra Arnold was seeking to create what is now known as the National Burial Database of Enslaved Americans, overseen by the Periwinkle Institute. The database is intended to record sites of slave burials, of which, Arnold said, "it's almost like that they are kind of vanishing from the American consciousness." Some have been saved previously, but usually only when their disturbance has gotten media attention, such as when a slave graveyard was found near New York City's City Hall in 1991.

The recognition that such graveyards are meaningful is relatively new. Lisa Ann Sanders, a South Carolina preservationist, helped save a slave graveyard because she "thought it was awfully sad that people can get thrown away."[4] While we are a long way from recognizing as a society that all burial grounds are equally valuable, we do have a greater sense that they all have meaning.

I was always proud that Oakwood had never, as far as I can find, refused burial to African Americans—unlike some prominent Midwestern cemeteries, which had refused minorities or had buried them only along the margins of the cemetery. Instead, at Oakwood they were present, yet they were not visible. Their gravestones rarely spoke to their racial identity. More likely they were similar to other monuments and markers, with basic information and a brief inscription. While their graves were not disturbed or their markers vandalized, they still were forced or cajoled to accept invisibility in the larger landscape.

The process of individualizing monuments by adding pictorial scenes to them started in the 1950s, and the technology improved decade after decade so that portraits got more realistic, nature scenes more diverse, and finally informal, personalized elements could be clearly etched. The industry moved from hand carvers to machine carvers with artificial diamonds to laser-etching machines relying on Computer-Aided Design (CAD) programs. The shift resulted in more detailed, sharper, less machinelike, and more realistic scenes.[5] Monuments in the new style often transfer the diverse elements of everyday memorials back into the cemetery. Flowers, portraits, children's toys, and other components of many everyday memorials are included in pictorial headstones. Teddy bears, speedboats, even sports equipment are also appearing on the fronts of monuments, just as they populate roadside shrines, R.I.P. murals, and memorial tattoos. The monuments return us metaphorically to the nineteenth century, while stretching propriety with informal, personalized, materialist images.

Yet the new headstones also embrace old traditions from within the cemetery. Leaving behind the modernist moment that stretched from the 1920s to the 1980s, they return to the symbolic natural scenes that were so prevalent in nineteenth-century cemeteries. The tree stumps that signified a shortened life, the elk that represented a fraternal organization, the carved vines, flowers, and other natural elements are now being combined in natural scenes etched onto monuments. Indeed, in my travels through dozens of cemeteries, the natural scene competes with portraits as the most prevalent and popular motifs on etched stones.

The return of the portrait to the monument is symbolic. Of course, the first cemetery portraits were the sculpted busts and figures. In America, from Ball Hughes's striking monument of pioneering scientist Nathaniel Bowditch (1844, recast 1880) to Dan Ostermiller's whimsical bronze bear astride painter William Holbrook Beard's monument (2002), stone and bronze portraits have long been part of the memorial impulse in the cemetery.[6] As well, ceramic photographs were a popular component of the individual headstone, especially in many immigrant burial places. These small photographs were attached to the gravestone, so they were allowed in the increasingly regulated cemetery landscape. They are a poignant record of people's individual lives as well as the changes in a community. In the small Jewish cemeteries that my father cared for, many of the photographs showed women in traditional garb from the old country, while others showed men in business suits with yarmulkes or bowler hats.

The portraits allowed marginalized communities to become more visible than on the standard stone. This new visibility included the scarfed women of the Jewish congregation, and the African American women in Evergreen Cemetery in East Los Angeles. On one tall, upright flecked gray granite stone, two ceramic photographs depict the Reverend Thomas Lee Griffiths, pastor of the oldest Baptist church in Los Angeles, and the new building he oversaw, completed debt-free in 1924.[7] Nearby, the Tom couple's stones with their ceramic photographs had oranges (a sign of good fortune) atop the individual upright granite monuments and flowers around them the day I visited. Proud African Americans joined Chinese and other ethnicities in representing themselves and their people.

Along with machine-carved rosettes and other simplified images, the photographs represented a continuation of memorial decoration within the constraints, cost, and regulation placed on the monument as a narrative. Sculptured monuments were far out of the reach of most families, so adding individuality through a photograph or, later, an etched pictorial scene allowed people to create a kind of personalized narrative.

One issue with the early pictorial stones is that they often duplicate others in the same cemetery, and the scenes they depict are ordinary. As monument companies developed more sophisticated machine-carving capabilities in the later twentieth century, many families bought monuments depicting nature scenes. In a Northern California cemetery, I came across two small ones with roughly hewn sides, and a polished plate on their front holding the same nature scene, only reversed by the color of each stone. One monument was deeper gray granite, so the highlights were the snow-covered ground, leafless trees, and small deer standing to the sides. The other was lighter gray granite on which the deer and small evergreen bushes were less distinct, and the backdrop line of fir trees created a strong black line across the middle of the stone. On both stones, large trees bordered the scene, framing the tableau for the viewer. The scene is clearly mechanically cut, without any of the artistry of earlier seventeenth-century carvers or nineteenth-century sculptors.

While nature scenes have remained a constant throughout, the content of such stones began to evolve as early as the 1970s. In Morningside Cemetery (which merged into Oakwood in the 1960s), in

FIGURE 9.2. Chrisfield family monument, Morningside Cemetery, Syracuse, NY, 2010.

Syracuse, the Chrisfield family erected a monument around 1975, when Percy Chrisfield died, that depicts a golfer as he tees off, with a few trees and shrubs lining the fairway. The power of the scene lies in its informality, not in its artistry. The design used a minimal number of cuts to convey a sense of topography, and a few more to produce the figure. However, the presence of a sports scene on a cemetery monument brought the American obsession with leisure, long viewed as inappropriate for an eternal setting, into this sacred space. Bicyclists still cannot pedal the roads of the cemetery, but a golfer can look out over his fairway shot for eternity.

In the 1990s, the digital revolution that brought us social media and Internet cemeteries began to affect monument makers as well. The use of computers allowed firms to cut stone much more precisely, even delicately. While many of the early programs were used to cut large blocks of stone for skyscrapers and other buildings, CAD programs combined with improved laser technology to revolutionize monument etching. The history of one firm, Cochran's, suggests the rapid influence the new technology had on the monument industry.[8] Founded in 1976, the company began selling a CAD program for monumental drafting and stencil cutting in 1987. According to

Sherm and Diane Cochran, the company's founders, they introduced laser etching in 1995: "Laser-etchings are as detailed and exquisite as hand-etchings, but can be produced faster and more efficiently." That change meant that companies could cut costs on stones that would have been too expensive for most consumers. Rather rapidly, the new technology permitted families to provide a monument dealer with a photograph or drawing that could be duplicated on a black granite monument.

Painting the Gravestone with Etched Images

In a small cemetery in Etna, New Hampshire, the Thornton monument portrays a country home tucked in among the trees.[9] The stone's details are sharp, realistic, and believable. Below the house is a pond, in which the house is mirrored. A gazebo sits adjacent to the pond, while a dock for swimming or boating juts out into it. A single tall birch tree towers over the family garage and is distinct from the shrubs or smaller trees that provide the backdrop. A cluster of spruces is forefront left, setting the visual stage much as similar natural features created the scale for mid-nineteenth-century picturesque landscape paintings. The rough black granite of the original stone creates a dark sky, while a deeply cut section just above the tree line suggests the sunset. The name prominently fills a part of the sky, while a street address in much smaller type provides a caption. The first time I saw it, I just stopped. A street address on a tombstone was a first for me in decades of roaming through cemeteries.

Beyond my surprise, though, the stone was a fascinating artifact. Etchings like the one in Etna retain the symbolic language of the Victorians while updating the imagery for a more individualized era. Many stones have what appear to be stock images of homes, landscapes, and other elements of an idealized American domestic life, as well as personalized and angelic portraits. All these images reflect a continuing fascination with domestic life and the centrality of the home in the myth of the American dream. Mourners seem to connect images of nature with memory, death, and morality. They draw

FIGURE 9.3. Thornton family monument, Hanover Center Cemetery, Hanover, NH, 2005.

upon centuries of imagery that have helped shape our culture, and its relationship to nature, the wilderness, and wild animals.

The scenes in these stones remind me of nineteenth-century cemetery operators who tried to portray their cemeteries as pastoral scenes, as in the illustrations etched on the first map of Woodland Cemetery, roughly six years before my great-great-grandfather became sexton. Here, the cemetery's entrance, gateway, and lodge are shown together (although not in the actual sequence or topography), all of which sends a message of civilization and nature safely coexisting. To the left, a small boy strolls off the page balancing books on his head, followed by his dog. To the right, two other children, accompanied by their mother, head to the lodge. The bright green of the scene sharply contrasts with the pale beige of the lodge, reminding viewers of the power of nature. Is Mom on her way to make arrangements for a funeral in this bucolic scene?

A similarly pastoral stone in the same cemetery has trees to the left and right of a pond or stream filled with reeds, a boat pulled up onshore just beside a dock. Even as the cemetery landscape around the stone is manicured and the elements of nature carefully controlled, this stone and others include elements of a wilder nature. Does the road that travels along the left side of the image allude to life's never-ending journey, or is it the real road near the family's home? Either way, the image is suggestive of the power nature holds for mourners.

But in contemporary memorials like the Etna stone, the scene is not religious, sacred, or a template for resurrection. Instead, I saw dozens of domestic scenes in the Upper Connecticut Valley region. Technology allowed the families, like those who paint R.I.P. murals or ink memorial tattoos on arms and backs, to establish a story of their lives. Nature is not just symbolic nor simply valued, as one might infer from the two nature scenes above. This scene is domestic, with nature playing a supporting role in a family's narrative.

Similarly, in Greenwood Memorial Park outside San Diego, one Hawaiian family created a narrative for itself, using an etched portrait. One wide monument of black granite is shaped into three panels, with the central one taller than the others. While the side panels are the same rectangular shape, the middle section rises up unevenly with a life-sized etched portrait of a young couple, a deceased husband and his living wife, as "Soul Mates." The portrait shows him in what looks like a formal zoot suit, while she wears a long formal dress slit to her knee. They look very happy—at their wedding? His wide, beautiful smile is bright white against the black stone.

While the portrait creates a powerful narrative of a happy couple saddened by the early death of a husband, the stone further brings the influence of everyday memorials into the cemetery. Recognizing the restrictions on offerings at graves, the monument designers put small mailboxes into each upper corner of the stone. Survivors can use these boxes to leave mementoes for the deceased at holidays and on birthdays. The memorial boxes evade the regulations. Finally, on the reverse of the stone, notes from the couple's children about their deceased father are etched into one half, while the other remains blank, presumably awaiting etchings to the mother's memory. One daughter's note ends with a small heart filled with eight other smaller hearts. In a sense, this stone takes the small ceramic photograph, blows it up to life size, and surrounds it with the notes and mementoes one would find at a roadside shrine.

The etchings personalize monuments in ways standard symbols never could. They commemorate specific life events and family memories. For instance, in 1995, the Parker family in Vermont experienced a horrible event. The father and his six-year-old son were killed in a car accident, leaving the mom and another son. The son's gravestone aspires to depict nice moments in the family's life. The center of the stone shows the family fishing in a small rowboat on a tinted blue pond. The deceased boy's brother fishes from one end of the boat, he at the other, while Mom and Dad steer from the center. This scene is surrounded by images of domestic family activities. On the left, the family picks fruit from a tree. On the right, rays of sunshine fall on a recreational vehicle, its tarp extended, with Dad standing in the doorway of the vehicle. On the far side of the pond is a pink-and-green-hued mountain scene, above which lie the names, dates of birth and death, and other information. In a somewhat disjointed exaggeration, a set of oversized Rollerblades is in the top left of the stone, opposite the sun's rays shining down on the family's vacation spot. "Precious Memories" is the text at the center bottom, just inside the frame of the pond on which sits the family boat.

The Rollerblades represent a child's happy activity even if they don't fit well with the design of the stone. At the same time, they break down the bucolic frame with an image of recreational informality. The Rollerblades give the stone a childlike personality that the family portraits alone would not convey. Similar etched stones include railroad engines, buses, fire engines, and footballs.[10] Some people wonder who would etch a symbol of leisure activity onto a gravestone intended as a sacred space for all of eternity. One professional monument dealer, when asked about popular symbols on stones, noted, "There's a move among baby boomers to what I call surfboard monuments—monuments with more color and design."[11] Maybe the informality is simply a better surfboard, but perhaps the better question is, who would not choose them in an age when towns are defined by national franchises and people regularly wear clothing that advertises a business? Putting Rollerblades on the stone is one way to say this stone belongs to this child, and allows him to retain his individuality in the homogeneity of the cemetery.

The efforts to instill the monuments with individuality contrasts sharply with the replication of themes and triteness in the etched scenes. The proliferation of nature scenes may result from families' love of hiking and hunting, but they may also represent a safe image of bucolic and sacred space. How we portray ourselves is more personalized, but we don't seem able to escape the traditional motifs and their connection to our mass culture. While I continue to find the new expressiveness a positive shift, I hope that we will not simply turn the new etched stones into another cultural product rather than an individualized statement.

One striking element of the Parker gravestone is its use of color. Since the introduction of the color television in the 1950s, and its widespread adoption in the 1970s, depictions of American culture have become ever more intensely bright. Black-and-white images are less acceptable in the era of colorful visual media. Engraver Randy Wesley views color as adding a "major conflict" to the design. He finds color distracting, and argues that it "defeats the integrity of the stone itself." He also worries that the color will not last.[12]

However, in Woodlands Cemetery, one family stone has two green-leafed deciduous trees framing a farm scene with a red barn, a large garden patch, and a white house with a red chimney. A brown and white dog and a black and white cat are situated next to a brown fence that frames the forefront of the scene, dominated by the green of the trees, fields, and surrounding mountains. In White Chapel Memory Gardens, the memorial park Oakwood manages, a bright orange basketball in one corner signifies the twenty-nine-year-old deceased's love for Syracuse University basketball, while the other side has a slightly less bright football in honor of the Chicago Bears. A profile of Walter Payton, one of the Bears great stars, in uniform is near the football. Above, on each side of the family name, are color ceramic photographs, one of Mom and the two boys, the other of the deceased son.

While many of the nature scenes seem to be company templates, images like Rollerblades, houses, and buses seem more likely to be the choice of the families. In one magazine for monument dealers, an author calls for professionals to guide families to retain a high-quality design.[13] She wrote, "When a memorialist can't or doesn't guide them, the result can be noise, not music." An etching artist she interviewed notes, "Clients naturally find it difficult to leave out any of the disparate items they consider important in a loved one's life." The experts try to remind clients that the blank, black space (the negative space) frames the messages they want to convey, so filling the stone can actually obscure a message or create conflicts. Customers apparently often want to violate that rule, but as Randy Wesley stated, "the more black you leave, the more contrast you get," and that allows the sentiment to be clear and emotionally effective.[14]

In the Sloane family of cemeteries, etched monuments are making uneven inroads. Woodlawn in the Bronx is a good example. Famous for its collection of mausoleums and remarkable statuary commencing after the Civil War, recently it has started a summer jazz concert series in honor of "jazz corner." The corner started when Duke Ellington passed away in 1974. He had purchased the family lot when his folks died, apparently because cabaret singer Florence Mills was interred nearby. He erected a very traditional monument with two tall, slender crosses. When Miles Davis died in 1991, he wanted to be near Duke, so his family erected an etched black gravestone with a trumpet facedown (rather than upright, as he notably played it) and an etched line of musical notes along the bottom of the stone face.

Over the next decade, Lionel Hampton, Max Roach, and a group of other jazz greats joined jazz corner. Their gravestones reinforced the differences between styles. Hampton's gravestone is a simple gray granite stele with the family name and the short epitaph "flying home" carved on the front. Roach's is shiny black granite with his name and a longer epitaph, "your hands shimmering on the legs of rain," carved in front. Jean-Baptiste Illinois Jacquet has a black eight-foot-high stone with two laser-etched portraits, each with him holding his tenor saxophone, a very thin etched Christian cross interwoven with another saxophone, all fronted with a flat black granite stone in the shape of a grand piano. The corner shouts the hybridity of contemporary memorial styles.

Just down the road from Davis, the Cuban "queen of salsa" Celia Cruz has a traditional mausoleum but designed so "her fans could look in" and see a revolving set of photographs, the Cuban flag, and other mementoes of her life.[15] If you go, you might take a moment to notice her neighbors, my mom and dad. The family erected a small gray granite bench etched with the Sloane family name as a monument to them. My dad believed in cemetery benches, since they provided mourners and visitors a place to sit and contemplate the enormity of life, death, and memory. Take a seat, look into the neighboring mausoleum, then walk the short hill up to jazz corner; the trip is worth it. Before you leave to see Miles, say hi to Jack and Rose for me.

Maintaining the Traditional while Moving into the Future

In Mount Auburn or other large, well-funded cemeteries that sustain their reputation partly by retaining their nineteenth-century glories, you will find no or just a few black laser-etched stones. The landscapes are more restrained, aesthetically polite, even archaic. Yet their seeming nostalgic stance hides their efforts to modernize their operations and present contemporary faces to the public.

In 2015, I toured Green-Wood Cemetery in Brooklyn with its longtime president, Richard Moylan. Moylan is from the old school, having started at Green-Wood in lawn maintenance in the 1970s. As we drove and walked around the property, he related how Green-Wood was modernizing its maintenance practices, adopting new sales techniques, and offering new cremation and crypt options while retaining its overall aesthetic (although etched stones had begun appearing in some burial sections). Green-Wood was one of the first rural reform cemeteries in the United States, a grand old lady that went through hard times in the middle of the twentieth century but through good management recovered to become a fashionable tourist destination. Green-Wood had long had the reputation of being the final home of New York's wealthy elite, such as famed Brooklyn pastor Henry Ward Beecher and journalist and politician Horace Greeley.

Green-Wood had recently completed a mausoleum and a columbarium, each of which is a step away from the past in that they are more modernist in their design. Each of them clearly speaks to the contradictions of trying to sustain a nineteenth-century aesthetic even as New York cemeteries welcome a very diverse population and celebrate modernist and contemporary architecture.

Hillside Mausoleum is five stories tall, with over 2,300 casket spaces and almost 2,900 cremation niches. Two glass windows across its entire front complement a water feature that cascades down the inside. Indeed, the mausoleum is a modern building inside, a kind of faux hotel accented by the water feature and padded chairs scattered around each floor for mourners to sit on while consoling each other. Wood paneling effectively softens the granite crypt faces.

Set into the hillside, the mausoleum opens onto the top of the hill from its fifth floor. You step out into a nineteenth-century burial section whose monuments and natural setting contrast with the large modern building. Two small pyramids emerge from the concrete deck leading out of the building, at least alluding to the vertical pedestal monuments and obelisks on the grass. The view from the interior upper floors is very bucolic, looking out over several older sections scattered with a diverse set of family and individual monuments. Given Green-Wood's age, the charming mature deciduous trees provide exactly the setting the cemetery's nineteenth-century founders aspired to in their design and plantings. Of course, the building shifts the scene once you are outside because of its size, massed front, and alternative aesthetic. Still, the mausoleum works well by not overwhelming the surroundings.

I was even more impressed by the Tranquility Gardens' columbarium complex that is tucked in between the cemetery's iconic main entrance gate, designed by famed nineteenth-century New York architect Richard Upjohn, and their spectacular 1911 chapel by the New York firm of Warren & Wetmore, most famous for their design of Grand Central Terminal in Midtown Manhattan. The new complex, which holds over 9,000 interior and exterior cremation niches, could have clashed horribly. Instead, the buildings have a gentle low-rise horizontal presence centered around a glass obelisk and a reflecting pool crossed by pavers. The buildings are designed to draw together the gate and the chapel as well as provide a quiet sense of contemplation just one hundred yards from a busy Brooklyn street.[16] Small patches of bamboo frame the space, while small potted trees and tall pots with forsythia are scattered strategically in front of the buildings. As a whole, the complex is very calming.

The surprising element for me was the smoke from the offerings of Chinese families after cremation services, made to ensure that their loved ones were safely on their way into the afterlife. While Green-Wood, like Oakwood, was never racially segregated, the presence of the fire pits suggested the influence of an ethnically diverse clientele. Other cemeteries across the nation, like Forest Lawn Memorial Park in Glendale, have felt this influence as well. At Green-Wood, the new complex had been planned so that multiple families could be concluding their services with small fires. The act would not have been permissible in many traditional cemeteries decades ago. The ethnic and racial expressions of informal and personalized sentiments on etched gravestones and the Chinese offerings are ways that the traditional cemetery is adapting.

A remarkable example of a cemetery highlighting diversity is Patricia Cronin's *Memorial to a Marriage* (2002), an expressive monument in Woodlawn Cemetery. When my brother Steven worked there, he showed me the two-ton horizontal marble sculpture, which shone brightly in the cold fall sunshine. Two women are depicted lying in bed, naked to the waist and in each other's arms. Their feet sneak out from under the gorgeously carved bedsheets.[17]

The memorial was both remarkably conservative and radical. The style evoked nineteenth-century sculpture, with its exquisite marble folds reminding me of the draping on Daniel Chester French's angel's gown in the sculpture for Martin Millmore in Forest Hill Cemetery near Boston. Yet Cronin's memorial is a radical social and artistic statement. Socially, it memorialized her own life relationship with Deborah Kass. Although partners for many years, they could not legally marry until 2002, a decade after the sculpture was placed in

Woodlawn. So the sculpture represented a rejection of social and legal barriers to gay and lesbian rights. As Cronin has said, "Aristotle said that the artist looks out and sees the world incomplete and tries to finish it. I think the piece, because it's so emotional and can get under people's skin about death and loss, there is a really type of aggressive aspect to it." She thus reminds us that the cemetery is a place for the living as well as the dead, a place where social statements have been made for generations. Few places are more patriarchal or heteronormative than cemeteries, where sculptures of wives and their children abound yet so many girls and women have been memorialized only through their roles as daughters and mothers.

Still, the sculpture was not simply a rejection of social norms; it also represented both a move away from the aesthetic of modernist simplicity with a reaffirmation of the pictorial and representational, and a feminist artistic statement. Cronin has called the memorial an "anti-monument" since, unlike so many previous towering vertical monuments, she purposively laid it horizontally. Just as Maya Lin feminized the national mall with the horizontal Vietnam Veterans Memorial, Cronin shifted the gaze from the obelisk to the tablet. The simple depiction of the two women lying in their bed in each other's arms, luxuriating in their relationship, draws us to the piece, holding our attention but also challenging us to recognize the love it embodies. The form is traditional, yet here becomes subversive, drawing upon Gustave Courbet's nineteenth-century controversial painting "The Sleepers" of two embracing nude women that Cronin cites as an influence. The difference from the often-chaste monuments of the past, perhaps symbolized best by the monument to Heloise and Abelard in Père Lachaise, is stark and purposeful. The willingness of Woodlawn to accept Cronin's potentially controversial piece is a statement about the cemetery's potentially renewed function as a place of memories and art for all of society.

Similarly, a grave in the Congressional Cemetery in Washington, DC, suggests that difference can be sculpted into simpler, traditional memorials. Founded in 1807, the cemetery holds the memorials of Civil War photographer Mathew Brady; Taza, the son of famed

American Indian leader Cochise; architect Robert Mills; and vice presidents, congressmen and -women, generals, and other leaders.[18] And yet, "Tucked away at the intersection of two walking paths [is] a cluster of headstones that [share] a unique quality—all of them openly [acknowledge] the sexual orientation of the grave's resident." The cluster began with the interment of Leonard Matlovich. Matlovich died of HIV/AIDS in 1988 after becoming in 1975 the first serving military personnel to openly state his sexual orientation.[19]

Matlovich's gravestone draws inspiration from Oscar Wilde's and Gertrude Stein/Alice B. Toklas's gravesites in Père Lachaise in Paris. He felt gays and lesbians should have memorial sites of their own.[20] The gravestone consists of a standard, small granite raised tablet monument fronted by a grave-sized granite slab with Matlovich's name engraved at the foot. The tablet monument is etched with two pink stars, like those gays and lesbians had to wear in Nazi Germany, under which is etched "Never Again" (with birth date) and "Never Forget" (with death date). Below the stars is this text:

A Gay Vietnam Veteran

When I was in the military
They gave me a medal for killing two men
And a discharge for loving one

The memorial became more than a site for military men and women protesting the treatment of gays and lesbians in the military. One prominent discharged veteran was married here. Others also wanted to be buried nearby. Several gay and lesbian former military personnel are interred in surrounding lots. Some hope the individual and family lots are only the beginning. There are plans for a National LGBT Veterans Memorial not far from Matlovich's grave.[21] Of course, the best irony of Matlovich's choice is that he apparently purposefully chose his lot down the row from the notorious homosexual baiter and possible closeted gay man, FBI director J. Edgar Hoover, and his longtime associate director, heir, and possible lover Clyde Tolson.

The efforts to raise the visibility of gays and lesbians within the cemetery is representative of the shift from the cemetery as a place of collective burial defined by institutional memorials reflecting a small set of accepted values to a resurgence of individuality. Whether the pink stars in Washington, DC, the football at White Chapel, the bus at Oakwood, the zoot suit in San Diego, or any of the other stones that display African American, Latino, Vietnamese, Chinese, or any other visible ethnicity, they signify a new era of acceptance and pride. Similarly, the burnt offerings in Green-Wood and the new Dia de los Muertos at Forest Lawn in Glendale suggest a new recognition by cemetery managers that they need to always keep adapting to changing clienteles and times.

A New Age of Commemoration

As these examples suggest, the grassroots memorials and private memorials are expressions of Americans' struggle with state and private institutions for control of memory. People are engaged in creating memorials and shaping their meaning and their place within the culture. Using items from daily life that also represent symbolic relationships—photographs, flowers, decorative items, and candles—Americans are claiming a role in the culture's landscape of memory. Their statements are public, even when they occur in a private cemetery. Their role is individual, even when played out on a public monument. The people's memorials contest the state's or an institution's right to mandate a vision of the past, the visual emptiness of the roadside, and the standardization of the memorial park landscape. They embody a contentious and creative force in American culture.

This force has affected cemeteries in many ways, as we have seen. Perhaps the most remarkable change, though, has been to the acts that join together everything we have discussed so far: mourning and remembering. How will we mourn in the future? Will we be sitting at home looking at a computer, standing next to a gravestone, or doing a little of both? Just to one side of Leonard Matlovich's gravestone is a small, barely discernible rectangular card. The card holds a squiggly square known as a QR code.[22] If you have the right app on your smartphone, you can point it at the QR code, and a story about Matlovich will appear. Such codes may already be an outdated technology, but their presence here and throughout the Congressional Cemetery suggests that cemetery managers are trying to cope with another challenge to the conventional view of the cemetery. In a digital age, we should not be surprised that grief has moved to the Internet, and digital images are offering new venues for mourning.

THE FUTURE OF DEATH

We live in a time when the older traditions surrounding death, mourning, and commemoration are not being sustained. Yet we have not transitioned to a new world. We are instead engaged in a cultural performance of mourning and memory where a diversity of beliefs, activities, and traditions coexist. These performances reveal "a fabric of space and time defined by a complex realm of social practices— a conjuncture of accident, desire, and habit."[1] When a group of teen- agers construct a roadside shrine or a grandmother travels to her son's grave in a cemetery, they are similar acts that symbolize that new hy- bridity. The two activities are differently situated—one on the streets, the other in an enclosed space; one informal (even possibly illegal), the other in an institutional setting. Yet each performance is "con- nective tissue" binding those individuals to each other, and to their communities. The grandmother continues a long convention of the cemetery as a secret space, as a place of contemplation and somber remembrance. The teenagers use similar components of mourning— flowers, photographs, mementoes—but situate themselves in a space of "imagination" and "transition" that stitches "the fabric of space" back together by bringing the dead into the land of the living.[2]

In concluding, I want to think about the future that performances like these hold for mourning and memory. The three elements around which change is happening are the *role of the body, places of mourning*, and *ways of commemoration*. Keeping in mind that we are not experi- encing a linear shift from one style of mourning to another, such as what happens in the move from the premodern to the modern way of death, we need multiple scenarios to understand what is happening, and what might happen in the future.

The Role of the Body

During the twentieth century, the body gradually receded from many, if not most, funerals. Two shifts propelled this disappearance. First, many families stopped holding traditional religious funerals, turning instead to memorial services, where the body was much less likely to be present. Zygmunt Bauman argued that we medicalized the body, and thus death—meaning our relationship to it dramatically shifted, and our need for its presence diminished.[3] Second, the rapid acceptance of cremation in the last decades of the century meant that even more services were held without the body. When the deceased plays a prominent role, such as with Rachel Scott's funeral after the Columbine shooting when teenage mourners wrote notes of love and sadness on her casket, the focus is on loss, not—as we are increasingly seeing—a celebration of the life.[4]

Three scenarios for future developments seem likely regarding the role of the body in mourning and commemoration. Cremation has been accepted by a majority of Americans, as well as in many other societies around the world, especially in Asia and Europe. While the differences in cremation rates vary substantially from state to state, throughout the United States the rate is increasing everywhere, and remarkably rapidly. As a result, the body will continue to disappear. Some ethnic and religious groups will continue to honor the body as a key element in the funeral service, but the vast majority of corpses will be cremated.

Yet in the second scenario, if the natural burial movement can convince more people that cremation is an unsustainable technological practice, they may move the body back into a more prominent position within death rituals. Natural burial re-engages family and friends in preparing the body for the funeral and restores its centrality in the burial service. Families digging graves after washing the body harkens back to premodern practices, and may mean that the deceased can once again "speak" to mourners in a way that was impossible under the modern way of death.

However, concerns about cremation may be alleviated by bio-cremation or promession, both of which entail more environmentally friendly methods using less energy and emitting fewer toxic emissions than conventional crematories. Such technologies could blunt the impact of the natural death movement's critique, and buttress the spread and acceptance of cremation. However, they have their own public relations issues, with bio-cremation sending remains down the drain and promession freeze-drying bodies, much like a meal for the astronauts.

A third scenario views the body quite differently. A small group of reformers reject both the body as part of the death ritual and cremation (by fire or alkaline hydrolysis), arguing for even more rigorous scientific and environmental solutions, such as "human composting." The name induces shivers, but the concept is not that far removed from the natural death movement or from the mass graves that existed in Europe for centuries. While I believe this scenario has many obstacles to success, is it really that different from the conservation natural burial grounds, where bodies are used to fertilize space that will eventually be used for recreation?

I do believe that a return to whole body funerals in a religious institution with an open casket is very unlikely. People have accepted the role of technology, the emphasis on the life not the death, and the distance of the living from the dead. Natural burial proponents may be able to shrink the distance and personalize the experience, but a return to the formality and institutionalization of the funeral seems unlikely in most populations.

Places of Mourning

While the changing role of the body in death rituals is perhaps the most fundamental shift from traditional practices, the resituating of mourning from the religious institution, funeral home, and cemetery to the street is a monumental reintegration of death into the land of the living. Yet this move is again not a simple change from one place to another. Select cemetery managers have made real efforts to reconceptualize their properties to make them more accessible and attractive to the public, so at least two scenarios result here.

In the first scenario, the adoption of everyday memorials in public mourning will continue to increase. Just as the purposes for which mourners use roadside shrines have expanded from car crashes to homicides, even deaths from chronic disease, the ways in which people use the spectrum of everyday memorials could easily develop further. During the awful summer months of 2015, when police officers seemed to shoot an unarmed black man every week, R.I.P. murals were prominently displayed in communities where they had previously been unlikely. In the same vein, but in a very different context, the availability of vinyl decals on the Internet has clearly brought them to the attention of many demographics. Just as the fast diffusion of the ghost bike memorials occurred because of the international interconnectedness of the bicycling community, seeing a vinyl decal or R.I.P. mural or memorial tattoo leads others to adopt the practice. If you doubt that, remember the worldwide attention Princess Diana's enormous roadside memorial outside Kensington Palace received, and how quickly others adopted that practice for other celebrities and ordinary people.

If everyday memorials are adopted more extensively, the role of commemoration in mourning may become more ephemeral. Everyday memorials are generally not intended to be permanent, nor are public authorities likely to allow them to become so. Transportation and police agencies have pushed back against the adoption of roadside shrines, ghost bikes, and some R.I.P. murals as distracting or offensive. The contestation over uses of public space will continue, but so far all everyday memorials are at risk of demolition or vandalism. Of course, vinyl decals and memorial tattoos live as long as the car and the body last—longer than the other kinds of memorials, but assuredly not permanent.

The outliers among the everyday memorials could be the pavement memorials and the Internet cemeteries. Pavement memorials could be destroyed by road construction, vandalism, and other acts of demolition, but they are also embedded in the concrete or other sidewalk material, giving them greater permanence. Online memorials are the most difficult to predict. At one level, the Internet is a rapidly changing, very ephemeral space. At the same time, the World Wide Cemetery and Facebook have sustained themselves for a generation, and show no signs of disappearing. The question remains, do they serve a "permanent" function in which people continue to visit them, or are they, like the other everyday memorials, more of an ephemeral place where people can assuage their immediate sorrow but rarely return?

The concerns about the ephemerality could be addressed by innovative efforts such as Columbia University's DeathLab project. They are promoting a reconsideration of the memorial as a landscape and an architectural space, planning to integrate new mourning sites within the urban fabric of New York City.[5] Essentially, they are attempting to produce a brick-and-mortar public mourning space with a minimalist aesthetic. The design team hopes that their Constellation Park will honor the dead "in short-term shrines" that have been woven into civic life, providing "semi-private intimate experiences and spaces" that allow the bereaved to contemplate death and life within the public realm. While their initial design to place the park underneath a bridge seems far-fetched, the idea of integrating everyday memorials (shrines) with more permanent public spaces is an intriguing concept.

The second scenario suggests a DeathLab innovation where the cemetery recreates itself as a significant mourning space. Given that cemetery managers have been complaining about declining visitations since the 1930s, and also given, again, the rise of cremation, the cemetery's re-emergence as a primary place of mourning may seem unlikely. Still, as we have seen, select cemetery managers have attempted to make their grounds more accessible and attractive for a diverse group of users, including younger people.

Cemeteries have a number of potential avenues to resurrect interest. As repositories of sculpture, art, and natural oases in increasingly dense cities, they are positioned to offer themselves as places for contemplation, education, and recreation. Many nineteenth-century cemeteries are located in inner-city neighborhoods that are undergoing gentrification or at least are getting improved city services for diverse populations. Since their grounds are large and convenient, if they can find the appropriate ways to reach out to surrounding populations, they could attract new interest. Given the contemporary interest in historical tourism, including to places classified as "dark tourism" because of their association with death, cemeteries should be able to exploit the treasures of their grounds (as many of them are already beginning to do).[6] Cemeteries could also exploit contemporary interests in vernacular architecture and DIY culture by expanding nascent workshops and tours to move beyond the individual histories of famous people to the nature and art of commemoration.

The most significant obstacle to this scenario is once again the continuing adoption of cremation, which could drain cemetery finances, forcing them to curtail these efforts and leave them with a deteriorating physical plant: an ancient ruin rather than a plush garden. Only rare cemeteries have sufficient endowments to withstand a dramatic drop in operational income. Most live year to year. If cremation rates continue to soar, they will be selling many fewer lots, and those that they do sell will bring in less money. Natural burial sections might help, since these currently are being sold at premium prices, but will that market grow to provide sufficient income to offset the lost income?

Ways of Commemoration

Perhaps the most powerful example of the current cultural hybridity occurs in commemoration. Internet sites are apparently doing a good business selling jewelry made from cremation remains, while memorial artists are imaginatively subverting traditional motifs even within the cemetery gates. Outside the cemetery, everyday memorials provide a range of modes of expression, while inside the gates, many have embraced etching technologies that allow personalization and individuality to return to the gravestone. Thus, several scenarios seem possible.

In one, the natural burial option, commemoration is diminished, is collectivized, or disappears. Natural burial advocates are conflicted about commemoration. Ken West argues that while memorialization is going to be incorporated into many burial sites, prohibiting memorials "has many advantages."[7] Such a sentiment would have appalled my father, and pretty much every other cemetery manager. Yet, if the cemetery is going to become a habitat rather than a cultural artifact, removing the memorials is a critical first step.

Even so, as we saw, the complete disappearance of memorials seems unlikely. Still, wooden and native stone markers would meld into the tall native grasses, gradually sink into the soft soil, and merge with the landscape in ways that pyramid mausoleums and thirty-foot obelisks could never do. Yet convincing families to subordinate their individual identity to the collective ecological principles will be difficult.

More likely is the scenario in which ways of commemoration continue to expand, both inside and outside the cemetery. Everyday memorials have reached a comfortable level of acceptance. Internet trolls are less likely to scorn them, and when they do, defenders seem quick to respond. Communities and governments are also more accepting, if often with gradually clarifying constraints. The informality associated with many types of everyday memorials raises less resistance as new generations view them more as standard practice. They have become embedded in many neighborhoods, cities, and towns.

Even inside the cemetery gates, more informal gravestones and digital practices seem to be gathering greater acceptance. The change is slow, with cemetery managers apparently fearful of other lot holders' reactions as much as anything. Still, the QR code on Leonard Matlovich's gravestone is no longer as unusual as it once was, as cemeteries use QRs to tell visitors about prominent historical figures, and families embed them on gravestones to tell personal stories. These efforts, alongside the artistry of black etched gravestones with portraits, angels, trucks, speedboats, and other consumerist images, are appearing more regularly nationwide. Personally, I think these changes are a positive trend. Just as with the wonderful carved gravestones of the eighteenth and nineteenth centuries, these return individuality and emotion to the cemetery. I am sure that someone thought the first willow-and-urn motif in the eighteenth century was objectionable as well, but those became normalized, and speedboats might be, too.

Still, cemeteries could lose this moment of cultural hybridity out of a reluctance to embrace change. People could continue to fear cemeteries or dismiss them as environmental hazards and archaic cultural spaces. Merely bringing people in for movies and special events will not, generally, be sufficient. Somehow the cemetery needs to reassert its place as a vibrant cultural institution; reaching out beyond current practices is probably crucial.

A third scenario is an offshoot of the second one. Here, the Internet, virtual reality, holograms, and other digital gizmos yet to be invented produce virtual memories that simply overwhelm any effort to sustain a place for memorials in society. Forecasting is dodgy at best anyway, but predicting the future of digital media seems especially dangerous. While new means of commemoration and memorialization might appear, a reaction demanding "reality" might also result. Just as writers using old-fashioned typewriters are lauded among millennials, who can predict how far digital media can aggravate as well as entrance us? Still, the potential for digital media to create a virtual reality where we can speak with the deceased, relive important moments in their lives, recall special events, and in a sense bring them back to life presents a dynamic alternative to the static cemetery.

Future of Death

With all these competing scenarios, what is the future of death? I think the best way is to imagine the future as the past and the present. Much of what I have discussed returns us to a premodern approach to death. The family washing the body, digging the grave, making the memorial, and erecting the roadside shrine, ghost bike, or other commemoration all restore the individuality and participation of earlier

days: before the institutions were born or matured, before professionals replaced family members, prior to the modern way of death.
These activities adapt past practices to contemporary circumstances
driven by concerns for our environment, our fragmented society, and
our loss of autonomy. Even as we harken back to the premodern, we
use digital technologies to personalize graves, provide solace through
social media, adapt the physical cemetery to create a virtual one, and
develop new disposition practices.

I tell my students that whenever someone tells you they are thinking of the future, you can usually identify how they are returning to the past or extrapolating from the present. The same is true
of the future of death. Few ideas are truly new, even though I have
chronicled many innovations. The ones that really offer new ideas,
such as human composting or the under-the-bridge memorial sites of
DeathLab, test the resolve of people by challenging the very precepts
of how society manages the dead. Should we compost our dead, or is
that the next step toward a *Matrix*-styled world? Should we reinvent
the cemetery as a cold, minimalist art space? Or will these innovative
ideas allow us to break with both past and present, managing the dead
in new ways that are more environmentally sound, without losing our
basic humanity and creativity? My brother Larry has been working
on a project using Elmwood Cemetery in Detroit as the hub of such
a network through which cemeteries could adapt by changing their
institutional structures, creating networks that share expenses and in-
comes in ways that allow community-based organizations to retain
their roles in a very rapidly evolving culture.[8] Using the cemeteries'
rich history and bountiful nature as topics to attract the public to the
institution may provide one means of extending the lives of endan-
gered institutions.

Tensions and Opportunities

These reflections reveal four tensions that have emerged from my ex-
plorations in the past, present, and future of memory and mourning:
the juxtaposition of ephemeral and permanent, remembering and

forgetting, physical and virtual, and individual and collective. They are not aligned against each other, with ephemeral, forgetting, virtual, and collective posed against permanent, remembering, physical, and individual. That sort of division would miss the nuances of how we are struggling with mourning and commemoration now. The natural burial movement wants a physical collective space where we forget the individual memory in favor of the collective good. Everyday memorials honor the individual with a physical or virtual memorial that aims to remember the deceased, but only ephemerally. Virtual cemeteries offer permanence to families hoping to remember individuals in sites that appear as collective memorials, much like the physical cemeteries they emulate. Virtual social media sites offer the illusion of permanence, a focus on the individual, and the hope of remembrance.

The tangled routes of mourning and memory suggest that as the modern way of death loses adherents, people are searching for alternatives that match their needs. They want choice and change, but as I have shown, they rarely want the new to be entirely separate from the old. People cling to the iconic and graphic symbols that humans have used for centuries, even millennia, to represent love, loss, and sorrow. The natural burial movement is instructive. Even when survivors choose grounds with no memorials save trees, they pick trees that have personal or symbolic meaning. And, more times, survivors choose natural burial grounds where they can erect some sort of physical memorial or add a name to a collective one. As my father said, he wanted "my name on something to show that I was here." We live in a time of dramatic change, yet we bring along elements of our traditions and rituals to comfort us.

SELECTED READINGS

Sociologists, historians, psychologists, and other scholars have published a large literature on the topic of death and dying. I have drawn liberally from the works of Tony Walter and Zygmunt Bauman. I have also gone back to the standard studies of the funeral by Gary Laderman and of cremation by Stephen Prothero. Ultimately, this book is about urban dynamics, leading me to consult Margaret Crawford, John Chase, and John Kaliski's *Everyday Urbanism*, as well as a number of contextual studies, including Dell Upton's fabulous study of civil rights movement memorials, *What Can and Can't Be Said* (2015), and Marita Sturken's two books, *Tangled Memories: The Vietnam War, the AIDS Epidemic, and the Politics of Remembering* (1997) and *Tourists of History: Memory, Kitsch, and Consumerism from Oklahoma City to Ground Zero* (2007). Thomas Lynch's books, especially *The Undertaking: Life Studies from the Dismal Trade* (1997), Ken Worpole's *Last Landscapes: The Architecture of the Cemetery in the West* (2003), and Keith Eggener's *Cemeteries* in the Norton/Library of Congress Visual Sourcebooks in Architecture, Design & Engineering series have been very helpful in thinking about traditions and rituals.

One important gap in traditional cemetery studies is good empirical studies on consumers—the mourners. We are fortunate that Doris Francis, Leonie Kellaher, and Georgina Neophytou (2005) and Philip Bachelor (2004) have produced pioneering works for London and Australia, but we need a good study for the United States. We also lack good studies on ethnic and racial mourning commemoration differences, especially the consequences of many cemeteries' discrimination against non-Caucasians. While articles have appeared considering the many issues tied to this concern, we need a good study that builds on the volume edited by Richard E. Meyer (1993).

The literature on the alternatives to the conventional cemetery is quite varied in its depth. On woodland burial grounds, Douglas Davies and Hannah Rumble, *Natural Burial: Traditional-Secular Spiritualities and Funeral Innovation* (2012), is a good start, but the most accessible discussion is Andy Clayton, Trish Green, Jenny Hockey, and Mark Powell, *Natural Burial: Landscape, Practice and Experience* (2015). For the international implications of the English movement, see a fascinating study by Sébastien Penmellen Boret, in *Death and Dying in Contemporary Japan*, edited by Hikaru Suzuki (2013), on the story of "tree burials" in Japan.

The literature on grassroots memorials is much more extensive. A small sample would include Martha Cooper and Joseph Sciorra, *R.I.P. Memorial Wall Art* (1994); Holly Everett, *Roadside Crosses in Contemporary Memorial Culture* (2002); Jack Santino, ed., *Spontaneous Shrines and the Public Memorialization of Death* (2006); Erika Doss, *Memorial Mania* (2010); and Peter Jan Magry and Cristina Sânchez-Carretero, eds., *Grassroots Memorials: The Politics of Memorializing Traumatic Death* (2011). Very little has been published about vinyl memorials and memorial tattoos. Even R.I.P. murals suffer from a lack of research. Cooper and Sciorra provided us with an outstanding original work, but we need to know more about places other than New York City, and see how far these types of memorials have diffused from their origins.

The mourning literature is simply enormous and growing at what seems like a daily pace. I have found works by Peter N. Stearns especially helpful. An edited book by Carla J. Sofka, Illene Noppe Cupit, and Kathleen R. Gilbert, *Dying, Death, and Grief in an Online Universe* (2012), has a good start to understanding chat rooms and other components.

ACKNOWLEDGMENTS

Even as, in the twenty years since the publication of my first book on cemeteries, my research interests have expanded to include other topics, I have remained interested in the cemetery, and its importance to American culture. This book is the result of my continuing fascination. I wish that I had written it before 2000, when my father was still alive, not only so he could have read it, but also so he could have contributed more to it. I would have benefited as well from talks with my mother, who passed away about five years after my dad. While I couldn't talk with them, I have spent hours thinking about them as I have written this book.

I have consulted my siblings Greg, Larry, Chris, and Steve (and their spouses Joan, Lesley, and Beth) about many issues related to the book. I thank them for their patience and support. Other family members, especially Carl Stollenmeyer, Karen Klomp, and Jeanne Manche, provided key family information. Carl has been working on the family's genealogy, and I learned a lot from him, and hopefully added a bit to his understanding of the Sloanes (or is it Sloans?).

No scholar could possibly produce a book without the help of colleagues and friends. Over the thirty years I have been writing about cemeteries, the list of supporters has grown far too long to list here, but I do have to mention Annmarie Adams, Todd Gish, Greg Hise, the late Barbara Rotundo, David Schuyler, Marita Sturken, and Dell Upton. I have also benefited from the rapidly expanding scholarship on cemeteries and death, especially that of Gary Collison, Joseph

Edgette, Keith Eggener, Doris Francis, Sylvia Grider, Gary Laderman, Stephen Prothero, Julie Rugg, and Brian Young. A number of students have helped out in various ways—reading and research—over the years, and I thank all of them, especially Erica Fine, Eli Glazier, Bryce Lowery, and Brettany Shannon. The administrative staff at USC Price, especially Constance Rodgers and John Sonego, has been remarkably helpful, as have my faculty colleagues, especially Dean Jack Knott, Raphael Bostic, Liz Falletta, Elizabeth Graddy, Martin Krieger, Rodney Ramacharan, and Lisa Schweitzer.

I have benefited from several presentations of this work. Lisa Schweitzer kindly offered her seminar for a conversation, and Martin Krieger his doctoral research class. Mattias Frihammar and Helaine Silverman organized a very helpful conference on the heritage of death in Stockholm that allowed me to experiment with ideas regarding commemoration, and Karla Rothstein and Christina Staudt invited me to present an overview of the argument at their stimulating symposium on death and disposition in the metropolis at Columbia University. Planning colleagues offered thoughtful comments after a talk at the Association of Collegiate Schools of Planning in Houston. And USC colleagues Rochelle Steiner and Scott Fisher graciously invited me to present my everyday memorials findings in the Emerging Cities Seminar. I also thank the two anonymous reviews for saving me from some egregious errors and pushing me to reshape key elements of the book. Of course, I remain fully responsible for any errors that remain.

This book was intended to be quite different in its first conceptualization. I thank George Thompson for getting me going. I am very grateful to Eli Pulsinelli for the time and care she took in editing an early version of this manuscript, through which she taught me a lot about my bad habits as a writer. Hopefully this version is better.

I very fortunately met Tim Mennel in 2011. Since then, he has been incredibly supportive of my work. This, our second book together, has, like the earlier one, been enhanced by his involvement, and made possible by his vision. I would like to thank him, Rachel Kelly, Ashley Pierce, Marianne Tatom, and the other staff at the University of Chi-

FIGURE B1. The author with Jack and Rosemary Sloane, dedication of the Oakwood Centennial Monument, 1959.

cago Press for their flexibility, rigorous approach to publishing, and generosity of spirit.

Finally, writing is a remarkably hard process for me. It takes hours of ruminating and cogitating, which often may appear to those around me more like sitting around doing nothing except playing with my wonderful dogs Jetta and Bella. My late wife, Beverlie, watched over this process for just over thirty years, and she often understood it better than I. I miss her patience, commitment, confidence, and love.

Many friends stepped in after she died. They not only kept me sane but also supported me when I finally began writing again. I cannot thank them enough, or have room to list all of them. One friend, my new wife, Anne Bray, especially aided me in getting the manuscript finished. I thank her for her incisive questions and infectious laugh that made the product, especially the illustrations, better, and the process much more fun.

NOTES

Introduction

1   As infectious and contagious diseases have given way to heart disease and cancer as the primary killers in our society, the chances of a young person, or even a middle-aged person, dying have dropped dramatically. In the century after 1900, the death rate (not age adjusted) dropped from 17.2 per 1,000 to 8.7 even as our population grew by over 300 percent. Department of Health and Human Services (www.dhhs.gov), National Center for Health Statistics, Centers for Disease Control and Prevention (www.cdc.gov); *National Vital Statistics Reports*. Accessed at http://www.infoplease.com/ipa/A0005131.html#ixzz 3UZWMaqIl.

2   Peter N. Stearns, "American Death," in Stearns, ed., *American Behavioral History* (New York: NYU Press, 2005), 143–54.

3   Tony Walter, *The Revival of Death* (London: Routledge, 1994).

4   The most famous attack on the cost of death is Jessica Mitford's *The American Way of Death* (New York: Vintage Books, 1963, revised 1998); for a recent discussion of funerals, Gary Laderman, *Rest in Peace: A Cultural History of Death and the Funeral Home in Twentieth-Century America* (New York: Oxford University Press, 2003).

5   For a discussion of earlier critiques, see David Charles Sloane, *The Last Great Necessity: Cemeteries in American History* (Baltimore: Johns Hopkins University Press, 1991). The current book is partly a sequel to my earlier one.

6   Holly Johnson, "The Cost of Funerals, Death, and Dying," at https://blog.per sonalcapital.com/retirement-planning/cost-of-funerals-death-and-dying/. The National Funeral Directors Association (NFDA) originally compiled the cost statistics in 2013.

7   Beverlie Conant Sloane and I discussed one example of these changes, in *Medicine Moves to the Mall* (Baltimore: Johns Hopkins University Press, 2003).

8   Some exceptions to the avoidance of cemeteries as a topic include Thomas Bender, *Toward an Urban Vision: Ideas and Institutions in Nineteenth-Century America* (Baltimore: Johns Hopkins University Press, 1982); James Stevens

Curl, *Death and Architecture: An Introduction to Funerary and Commemorative Buildings in the Western European Tradition, with Some Consideration of Their Settings* (Stroud: Sutton Publishing, 2002; original edition published 1980); Blanche Linden-Ward, *Silent City on a Hill: Landscapes of Memory and Boston's Mount Auburn Cemetery* (Columbus: Ohio State University Press, 1989); Kenneth T. Jackson and Camilo Jose Vergara, *Silent Cities: The Evolution of the American Cemetery* (New York: Princeton Architectural Press, 1989); Barbara Rotundo, "Mount Auburn Cemetery: A Proper Boston Institution," *Harvard Library Bulletin* 22 (1974): 268–79; and Dell Upton, *Another City: Urban Life and Urban Spaces in the New American Republic* (New Haven, CT: Yale University Press, 2008).

9   Elisabeth Kübler-Ross, *On Death and Dying* (New York: Scribner, 1969).

10   Joan Didion, *The Year of Magical Thinking* (New York: Vintage, 2005), 27.

11   Philippe Ariès, *Western Attitudes Toward Death: From the Middle Ages to the Present* (Baltimore: Johns Hopkins University Press, 1974), 85.

12   Philippe Ariès, *The Hour of Our Death* (New York: Alfred A. Knopf, 1981), 578.

13   Christy Heitger-Ewing, "The 8 Worst Things You Can Say to Someone Who Is Grieving," *Huffington Post*, September 25, 2014, accessed at http://www.huffing tonpost.com/christy-heitgerewing/the-eight-worst-things-yo_b_5868492 .html.

14   For a different time line on changing dying and death, see Vibeke Poulsen Graven, Louise Lund, and Michael Hviid Jacobsen, "A Revival of Death? Death, Dying and Bereavement in Contemporary Society," in M. H. Jacobsen, ed., *Deconstructing Death: Changing Cultures of Death, Dying Bereavement and Care in the Nordic Countries* (Odense: University Press of Southern Denmark, 2013), 27–54. They allude to the work of Walter, *The Revival of Death*.

15   James Stevens Curl, *The Victorian Celebration of Death* (London: History Press, 2001); and Blanche Linden-Ward, "Strange but Genteel Pleasure Grounds: Tourist and Leisure Uses of Nineteenth Century Rural Cemeteries," *Cemeteries and Gravemarkers: Voices of American Culture* (Ann Arbor, MI: UMI Research Press, 1989), 293–328.

16   Mitford, *The American Way of Death*.

17   Quoted from James Jacobs, "The Dying of Death," *Fortnightly Review* New Series 72: 264–69, in Walter, *The Revival of Death*, 1.

18   American Society of Planning Officials, *Planning Service Advisory #97: Funeral Homes* (Chicago: ASPO, 1957), 2. By the twenty-first century, the funeral industry as a whole grossed above $20 billion per year. POV, "Economics of the Funeral Industry" (June 24, 2013), at http://www.pbs.org/pov/homegoings/eco nomics-of-the-funeral-industry/.

19   Jacobs, "The Dying of Death," 264–69.

20   Sloane, *The Last Great Necessity*, 180–81.

21   Walter, *The Revival of Death*, 2.

22   Peter Rhee, MPH, Bellal Joseph, Viraj Pandit, Hassan Aziz, Gary Vercruysse, Narong Kulvatunyou, and Randall S. Friese, "Increasing Trauma Deaths in the United States," *Annals of Surgery* 260, no. 1 (2014): 13–21.

23   NFDA (2014).

24   Susan Letzer Cole, *The Absent One: Mourning Ritual, Tragedy, and the Perfor-*

mance of Ambivalence (University Park: Pennsylvania State University, 1985), 171.

25 The percentages quoted in this paragraph and the next are from Gallup, "Religion," accessed at http://www.gallup.com/poll/1690/religion.aspx.

26 Ariès, *Western Attitudes Toward Death*, 1. Kübler Ross quoted at Sutori: "The History of the Hospice," www.sutori.com.

27 Ibid., 85–89.

28 Zygmunt Bauman, *Mortality, Immortality & Other Life Strategies* (Stanford, CA: Stanford University Press, 1992), 150.

29 Walter, *The Revival of Death*, 22–23.

30 Kenneth Patrick, *Journeying to the End of Life: Discovering the Ancient Hospice Way of Companioning the Dying* (Bloomington, IN: Amber House, 2010), 194–95.

31 Riley E. Dunlap and Angela G. Mertig, eds., *American Environmentalism: The U.S. Environmental Movement, 1970–1990* (New York: Taylor & Francis, 1992).

32 Leopold, quoted by Jane Caputi, "Feeding Green Fire," *Journal for the Study of Religion, Nature and Culture* 5, no. 4 (2011), 413.

33 Rachel Carson, *Silent Spring* (Boston: Houghton Mifflin, 1962).

34 Lin's design was, and remains, a subject of great interest to scholars and the public alike; see, for example, Marita Sturken, *Tangled Memories: The Vietnam War, the AIDS Epidemic, and the Politics of Remembering* (Berkeley: University of California Press, 1997); Karal Ann Marling and Robert Silberman, "The Statue Near the Wall: The Vietnam Veterans Memorial and the Art of Remembering," *Smithsonian Studies in American Art* 1, no. 1 (1987): 4–29; and Kristin Ann Hass, *Carried to the Wall: American Memory and the Vietnam Veterans Memorial* (Berkeley: University of California Press, 1998).

35 Hass, *Carried to the Wall*.

36 John Chase, Margaret Crawford, and John Kaliski, *Everyday Urbanism* (New York: Monacelli Press, 1999); on extending the memorial impulse, see Ericka Doss, *Memorial Mania: Public Feeling in America* (Chicago: University of Chicago Press, 2010).

37 Alyson Shontell, "Flashback: This Is What the First Ever Website Looked Like," *Business Insider* (June 29, 2011), http://www.businessinsider.com/flashback-this-is-what-the-first-website-ever-looked-like-2011-6.

38 The early site is available at https://web.archive.org/web/19961218230339/http://www.cemetery.org/.

39 Walter, *The Revival of Death*, 189.

40 Jack Sloane, "Why I Became a Cemeterian," handwritten notes, from family papers held by Chris Sloane, n.d. His thoughts were drafted for publication in a cemetery journal.

41 The 2001 National Survey of Veterans is available at Census.gov, sections 8–4 to 8–8. Other research supports this hybridity; see Richard A. Kalish, "Cemetery Visits," *Death Studies* 10, no. 1 (1986): 55–58; and James A. Thorson, Bruce J. Horacek, and Gail Kara, "A Replication of Kalish's Study of Cemetery Visits," *Death Studies* 11, no. 3: 177–82.

42 Thomas Lynch, "Socko Finish," *New York Times*, July 12, 1998, http://www.thomaslynch.com/1/234/new_york_times.asp?artID=16484, accessed July 14, 2010.

Chapter One

1   H. P. Smith, *History of Oakwood Cemetery* (Syracuse, 1871), 36.

2   Upton, "The Urban Cemetery and Urban Community: The Origins of the New Orleans Cemetery," *Perspectives in Vernacular Architecture* 7 (1997), 131–45.

3   Ibid.

4   Hilary Ballon, ed., *The Greatest Grid: The Master Plan of Manhattan, 1811–2011* (New York: Museum of the City of New York and Columbia University Press, 2012).

5   Peter Johnson, "The Changing Face of the Modern Cemetery: Loudon's Design for Life and Death," *berfrois* (June 12, 2012), http://www.berfrois.com /2012/06/foucault-and-the-cemetery/.

6   Ibid.

7   Brian Young, *Respectable Burial: Montreal's Mount Royal Cemetery* (Montreal: McGill-Queen's University Press, 2003), 6.

8   Gridley, "The Planting of Rural Cemeteries," *Magazine of Horticulture* 26 (May 1860): 200–203.

9   Simon Schama, *Landscape and Memory* (New York: Alfred Knopf, 1995), 578.

10   E. W. Leavenworth, *The History and Incorporation, Rules and Regulations of Oakwood Cemetery, at Syracuse, N.Y., Together with the Dedication Odes and Addresses, with Other Papers*, 2nd ed. (Syracuse, 1859), 23–24. See Sloane, *The Last Great Necessity.*

11   Smith, *History of Oakwood*, 12–13.

12   Ibid., 12–13.

13   Ibid., 19.

14   The best description of the public's fascination with the rural cemeteries remains Blanche Linden-Ward, "Strange but Genteel Pleasure Grounds: Tourist and Leisure Uses of Nineteenth-Century Cemeteries," in *Cemeteries and Gravemarkers, Voices of American Culture*, ed. Richard E. Meyer (Logan: Utah State University Press, 1992), 293–328.

15   Smith, *History of Oakwood*, 13.

16   David Schuyler, *Apostle of Taste: Andrew Jackson Downing, 1815–1852* (Baltimore: Johns Hopkins University Press, 1996).

17   Julia Rogers, *Among Green Trees: A Guide to Pleasant and Profitable Acquaintance with Familiar Trees* (Chicago: A. W. Mumford, 1902), 73.

18   Fanny Copley Seavey, "The Cemetery as a Work of Art," presented to the Tenth Annual AACS Conference, 1896; available at http://www.iccfa.com/reading /1887–1899/cemetery-work-art. Simonds quote; Young, *Respectable Burial*, 111.

19   Howard Evarts Weed, *Modern Park Cemeteries* (Chicago: R. J. Haight, 1912), 72.

20   Please note the switch in spellings from "Sloan" to "Sloane." The family has several stories why the "e" was added, including one of anti-Irish/German feelings tied to World War I, but I cannot find any sources. I do believe that my grandfather Fred seems to have made the change, even adding the "e" to his aunt's name on her gravestone.

21   Bellett Lawson, "Is Flower Planting Desirable in the Modern Cemetery?,"

AACS Proceedings of the 7th Annual Convention, August 1893, available at http://www.iccfa.com/reading/1887–1899/flower-planting-desirable-modern -cemetery.

22 Schama, *Landscape and Memory*, 573.

23 Ibid.

24 *The Cemetery Handbook: A Manual of Useful Information on Cemetery Development & Management* (Chicago: Allied Arts Publishing Co., 1910s?), 321.

25 Virginia Scott Jenkins, *The Lawn: A History of an American Obsession* (Washington, DC: Smithsonian Institution Press, 1994), 4.

26 G. J. Klupar, *Modern Cemetery Management* (Chicago: Catholic Cemeteries of the Archdiocese of Chicago, 1962), 212–14, with the quote on 223.

27 Drew Gilpin Faust, *This Republic of Suffering: Death and the American Civil War* (New York: Vintage Books, 2008).

28 Jessica Mitford, *The American Way of Death Revisited* (New York: Vintage Books, 1998), 46.

29 Thomas B. Meehan, "Suitable Trees and Shrubs for a Modern Cemetery," *AACS Proceedings of the 8th Annual Convention*, September 1894, available at http://www.iccfa.com/reading/1887–1899/suitable-trees-and-shrubs-modern -cemetery.

30 John C. Plumb, Woodlawn Cemetery, New York City, "Landscape Planting in Cemeteries," *4th Annual Convention, NYACS*, 1932, 15.

Chapter Two

1 Quote from *The Legacy: A Memorial Ecosystems Newsletter* 1 (March–October 1998), accessed as a cached document from the Internet, April 16, 2014.

2 Green Burial Council, http://www.greenburialcouncil.org/.

3 Tad Friend, "Shroud of Marin," *The New Yorker* (August 29, 2005), 56.

4 *The Legacy.*

5 Michael P. Johnson, "Environmental Impacts of Sprawl: Survey of the Literature and Proposed Research Agenda," *Environment and Planning A* 33, no. 4 (2001): 717–35.

6 Frederick Law Olmsted, "Parks at Home and Abroad" (1861), quoted in Sloane, *The Last Great Necessity*, 90.

7 Andy Clayton, Trish Green, Jenny Hockey, and Mark Powell, *Natural Burial: Landscape, Practice and Experience* (London: Routledge, 2015), 26.

8 Andy Clayton, Trish Green, Jenny Hockey, and Mark Powell, "From Cabbages to Cadavers: Natural Burial Down on the Farm," in A. Maddrell and J. D. Sidaway, eds., *Deathscapes: Spaces for Death, Dying, Mourning and Remembrance* (Farnham, Surrey: Ashgate, 2010), 119–38.

9 Josefine Speyer and Stephani Wienrich, eds., *The Natural Death Handbook* (London, 2003); also see Association of Natural Burial Grounds, http://www .naturaldeath.org.uk/index.php?page=the-anbg.

10 Andrew Clayton and Katie Dixon, "Woodland Burial: Memorial Arboretum versus Natural Native Woodland?," *Mortality* 12, no. 3 (2007): 240–60.

11 Ibid.

12 An example of the international influence is the concept of "tree burial" in

Japan; see Sébastien Penmellen Boret, "An Anthropological Study of a Japanese Tree Burial: Environment, Kinship, and Death," in H. Suzuki, ed., *Death and Dying in Contemporary Japan* (London: Routledge, 2013), 177–201.

13   The distinction could be even more rigorous, dividing the new burial places by those associated with conventional cemeteries and those that are not, but I am trusting that the cemetery managers creating new separate cemeteries under the Green Burial Council guidelines are developing not only a new aesthetic, but also a new ritual separate and different from those they would practice in the conventional cemetery.

14   Mitford, *The American Way of Death Revisited*. I am simplifying the story. In actuality, a number of writers had expressed concerns about the cost and impact of the costs of the modern cemetery at least since the 1930s; for more, see Sloane, *The Last Great Necessity*.

15   Mitford, *The American Way of Death Revisited*, 46.

16   Information accessed at http://www.glendalenaturepreserve.org/.

17   Quoted in Jenkins, *The Lawn*, 155.

18   Jenkins, *The Lawn*, 142.

19   Cristina Milesi, Christopher D. Elvidge, John B. Dietz, Benjamin T. Tuttle, and Ramakrishna R. Namani, "Mapping and Modeling the Biogeochemical Cycling of Turf Grasses in the U.S.," *Environmental Management* 36, no. 3 (2005): 426–35.

20   Jenkins, *The Lawn*, 156. The chemicals reinforced the new control of the landscape represented by the development of the memorial park lawnscape.

21   Ahmet S. Üçisik and Philip Rushbrook, World Health Organization, Regional Office for Europe, *Impact of Cemeteries on the Environment and Health* (Copenhagen, 1998).

22   Richard Mabey, *Weeds: In Defense of Nature's Most Unloved Plants* (New York: HarperCollins, 2010), 70.

23   William Cockerham, "Cemeteries Suitable for Bird Watching," *New York Times*, April 8, 2001, http://www.nytimes.com/2001/04/08/nyregion/cemeteries-suitable-for-bird-watching.html, alludes to rural cemeteries as a preferred place.

24   Mitford's *The American Way of Death*, 112. For the reversal, see Neptune Society in her index.

25   National Funeral Directors Association, "Consumer Preference for Cremation Expected to Surpass Burial in 2015," http://nfda.org/news-a-events/all-press-releases/4046-consumer-preference-for-cremation-expected-to-surpass-burial-in-2015.html.

26   Cremation Association of North American (CANA), "Industry Statistical Information," http://www.cremationassociation.org/?page=industrystatistics.

27   For more information, see Sloane, *Last Great Necessity*, 128–58; and Stephen Prothero, *Purified by Fire: A History of Cremation in America* (Berkeley: University of California Press, 2001).

28   Ken West, *A Guide to Natural Burial* (London: Shaw & Sons, 2010), 1.

29   Montse Marti and José L. Domingo, "Toxic Emissions from Crematories: A Review," *Environment International* 32 (2010): 131–37.

30   UNEP, *Global Mercury Assessment 2013* (Geneva: UNEP Chemicals Branch, 2013).

31   Marian Shoard, *The Theft of the Countryside* (London: Temple Smith, 1980), accessed through Marian Shoard's personal website at http://www.marion shoard.co.uk/Documents/Books/The-Theft-Of-The-Countryside/The-Theft -Of-The-Countryside-Introduction.pdf. Also see Richard Mabey's *The Common Ground* (London: Arrow, 1981); and Paul Kingsnorth, *Real England: The Battle Against the Bland* (London: Granata UK, 2009).

32   Global Ideas Bank, "Nature Reserve Burial in the States," archived at https:// web.archive.org/web/20100709195907/http://www.globalideasbank.org/LA /LA-23.HTML.

33   West, *Guide to Natural Burial*, 131–34.

34   Sébastien Penmellen Boret, *Japanese Tree-Burial: Ecology, Kinship, and the Culture of Death* (New York: Routledge, 2014), 7.

35   Christopher Coutts, Carlton Basmajian, and Timothy Chapin, "Projecting Landscapes of Death," *Landscape and Urban Planning* 102, no. 4 (2011): 254–61.

36   Boret, *Japanese Tree-Burial*, 11–12.

37   Ibid., 7–9.

38   Ibid., 10.

39   Lily Wong, "No Place, New Places: Death and Its Rituals in Urban Asia," *Urban Studies* 49, no. 2 (2012), 415–33.

40   Wong, "No Place, New Places," 426.

41   Mirjam Klaassen and Peter Groote have written several articles on natural burial grounds in the Netherlands. The description here is taken from Klaassen's book, *Final Places Geographies of Death and Remembrance in the Netherlands* (Amsterdam: Rozenberg Publishers, 2011), 95–116. She acknowledges Groote at the start, and especially at the opening of the chapter on Bergerbos.

42   Ibid., 105–7.

43   Catrin Einhorn, "A Project to Turn Corpses into Compost," *New York Times*, April 13, 2015, http://www.nytimes.com/2015/04/14/science/a-project-to-turn -corpses-into-compost.html.

44   The process is described on the promotional websites at http://biocremation info.com/ and http://www.resomation.com/.

45   Sara Marsden, "Aquamation or Resomation: A 'Green' Alternative to the Traditional Funeral," US Funerals Online (2014), http://www.us-funerals.com /funeral-articles/aquamation-or-resomation-a-green-alternative-to-the-tradi tional-funeral.html#.WCpNYOErIUF; "Alkaline Hydrolysis Laws in Your State," NOLO (2016), http://www.nolo.com/legal-encyclopedia/alkaline-hyd rolysis-laws-your-state; and Renee Murray, "Alkaline Hydrolysis for Human Remains," Security National Life (2014), http://www.snlabetterway.com/alka line-hydrolysis-for-human-remains/#.WCpQCuErIUG.

46   Spencer Hunt, "State Halts Liquid Cremation," *Columbus State Dispatch*, March 23, 2011, http://www.dispatch.com/content/stories/local/2011/03/23 /state-halts-liquid-cremation.html.

47   Quoted in a story in the UK's *Daily Mail*, "Ohio Health Chiefs Order Funeral

Boss Told to Stop the Liquid Cremation of Bodies," March 23, 2011, http://www.dailymail.co.uk/news/article-1369349/Funeral-boss-told-stop-liquid-cremations-bodies.html.

48 New Hampshire Public Radio, "Liquid Cremation Process May Soon Be Legal in N.H. Again," April 3, 2013, http://nhpr.org/post/liquid-cremation-process-may-soon-be-legal-nh-again.

49 Karla Maria Rothstein, "Reconfiguring Urban Spaces of Disposal, Sanctuary, and Remembrance," in Christina Staudt and J. Harold Ellens, eds., *Our Changing Journey to the End: Reshaping Death, Dying, Grief in America* (Santa Barbara, CA: Praeger, 2014), 60–61.

50 Einhorn, "A Project to Turn Corpses into Compost."

51 The description is taken from the Urban Death Project website, "Process," at http://www.urbandeathproject.org/#process.

52 Ibid.

53 Einhorn, "A Project to Turn Corpses into Compost." The quote that follows in this paragraph is from the same source.

54 Ibid.

55. Jae Rhimm Lee, "My Mushroom Burial Suit," TED Talks, www.ted.com.

Chapter Three

1 William Currie, quoted in Stephen Prothero, *Purified by Fire: A History of Cremation in America* (Berkeley: University of California Press, 2001), 120.

2 See Clark Kerr, *The Uses of the University* (Cambridge, MA: Harvard University Press, 1963), 220. Kerr claims only eighty organizations have survived over the past 500 years, seventy-five of them universities.

3 West, *A Guide to Natural Burial*, 131–38.

4 Glen Forest Natural Burial Cemetery Rules, 2014, http://www.miamitownship.net/cemetery_glen.html.

5 Pine Forest Memorial Gardens, accessed in 2014, at https://pineforestmemorial.com/.

6 White Haven Memorial Park, accessed in 2014, at http://www.whitehavenmemorialpark.com/cemetery-nature-recreation-pittsford-ny.html.

7 Hillside Memorial Park, accessed in 2014, at http://www.hillsidememorial.org/.

8 Ibid.

9 For information on green burials, see http://www.joshuatreememorialpark.com/green-burial/index.php.

10 The information in the following paragraphs comes from personal observation, and Susan Loving, "Creating a Natural Resting Place," *ICFM Magazine*, March 2005, http://www.iccfa.com/reading/2000–2009/creating-natural-resting-place.

11 For a description, see http://www.cavehillcemetery.com/sales/lots/scattering_garden/index.php.

12 Information on the cremation options at Forest Lawn Cemetery in Buffalo is available at https://www.forest-lawn.com/faq.

13 Anna Hiatt, "Traditional American Funerals Are Dead—But Not Buried,"

Aljazeera America, March 12, 2015, http://america.aljazeera.com/articles/2015/3/12/traditional-us-funerals-are-dead-but-not-buried.html.

14 Genevieve Roberts, "'Green Scheme' Will Harness Energy from Crematorium to Heat Swimming Pool," *Independent* (February 7, 2011), http://www.independent.co.uk/environment/green-living/green-scheme-will-harness-energy-from-crematorium-to-heat-swimming-pool-2206355.html.

Chapter Four

1 Doris Francis, Leonie Kellaher, and Georgina Neophytou, *The Secret Cemetery* (Oxford and New York: Berg, 2005),

2 Susan Letzer Cole, *The Absent One: Mourning Ritual, Tragedy, and the Performance of Ambivalence* (University Park: Pennsylvania State University, 1985), 5–6.

3 Ibid.

4 Stanley B. Burns with Elizabeth A. Burns, *Sleeping Beauty II: Grief, Bereavement and the Family in Memorial Photography* (New York: Burns Archive Press, 2002), 81.

5 Peter N. Stearns, *Revolutions in Sorrow: American Experiences of Death in Global Perspective (New York: Paradigm Publishers, 2007)*, 98.

6 Peter N. Stearns, "American Death," in Stearns, ed., *American Behavioral History* (New York: NYU Press, 2005), 145.

7 Brian Young, *Respectable Burial: Montreal's Mount Royal Cemetery* (Montreal: McGill-Queen's University Press, 2003), 45.

8 Stearns, *Revolutions in Sorrow*, 80.

9 Richard A. Kalish, "Cemetery Visits," *Death Studies* 10, no. 1 (1986): 55–58, and James A. Thorson, Bruce J. Horacek, and Gail Kara, "A Replication of Kalish's Study of Cemetery Visits," *Death Studies* 11, no. 3 (1987): 177–82.

10 Francis, Kellaher, and Neophytou, *The Secret Cemetery*, 26.

11 Ibid., 3.

12 Ibid., 25.

13 Philip Bachelor, *Sorrow & Solace: The Social World of the Cemetery* (Amityville, NY: Baywood Publishing, 2004). The quotes below appear on 170.

14 W. Lloyd Warner, *The Living and the Dead* (New Haven, CT: Yale University Press, 1959), 285.

15 Carolyn Ellis, "Grave Tending: With Mom at the Cemetery," *Forum Qualitative Sozialforschung/Forum: Qualitative Social Research* 4, no. 2 (2003): 28, accessed at http://www.qualitative-research.net/index.php/fqs/article/view/701/1520.

16 Charles Benisch, "Co-Operation with Allied Industries," *Proceedings of the Seventh Annual Convention of the New York State Association of Cemeteries* (July 15–17, 1935), 75.

17 Elizabeth Mathias, "The Italian-American Funeral: Persistence Through Change," *Western Folklore* 33, no. 1 (January 1974): 35–50.

18 Paul C. Rosenblatt and Beverly R. Wallace, *African American Grief* (New York: Routledge, 2005), 134.

19 Gwynedd Cannan, "Name: Unearthing Our Past," *News and Blogs, Voices from*

the *Trinity Community*, 2004, https://www.trinitywallstreet.org/blogs/news /unearthing-our-past.

20   James Carroll, *Felix Longoria's Wake: Bereavement, Racism, and the Rise of Mexican American Activism* (Austin: University of Texas Press, 2003).

21   Angelika Krüger-Kahloula, "On the Wrong Side of the Fence: Racial Segrega- tion in American Cemeteries," in Geneviève Fabre and Robert O'Meally, eds., *History and Memory in African-American Culture* (New York, 1994), 130–49.

22   Fred P. Graham, "Blacks Get Equal Rights Even in Death," *New York Times*, August 30, 1970, http://www.nytimes.com/1970/08/30/archives/blacks-get -equal-rights-even-in-death.html?_r=0.

23   Helen A. Regis, "Blackness and the Politics of Memory in the New Orleans Second Line," *American Ethnologist* 28, no. 4 (2001): 752–77.

24   Regina M. Marchi, *Day of the Dead in the USA* (New Brunswick, NJ: Rutgers University Press, 2009), 12.

25   Frederick Lau, "Serenading the Ancestors: Chinese Qingming Festival in Honolulu," *Yearbook for Traditional Music* 36 (2004): 131.

26   Marchi, *Day of the Dead in the USA*, 11–15.

27   Ibid., 47–48.

28   Ibid., quotes from 43; dates of cemeteries' festivities, 153–54, footnote 19.

29   Warner, *The Living and the Dead*, 266. I first saw the quote in James M. Mayo, *War Memorials as Political Landscape: The American Experience and Beyond* (New York: Praeger, 1988), 32 (Mayo mistakenly cites another historian by the name of Warner).

30   David Blight, *Race and Reunion: The Civil War in American Memory* (Cam- bridge, MA: Harvard University Press), 70.

31   Michael Kammen, *Mystic Chords of Memory: The Transformation of Tradition in American Culture* (New York: Vintage Books, 1991), 103.

32   James Stevens Curl, *Death and Architecture: An Introduction to Funerary and Commemorative Buildings in the Western European Tradition, with Some Con- sideration of Their Settings* (Stroud: Sutton Publishing, 2002; original edition published 1980), 317–18.

33   John Bodnar, *Remaking America: Public Memory, Commemoration, and Pa- triotism in the Twentieth Century* (Princeton, NJ: Princeton University Press, 1992), 80.

Chapter Five

1   David Sloane, *The Last Great Necessity: Cemeteries in American History* (Balti- more: Johns Hopkins University Press, 1991), 159–90.

2   Paul Sheedy, "Easter Sunrise Services to be Heard from KHJ," *Los Angeles Times* (April 4, 1926), B7.

3   Walter, *The Revival of Death*.

4   Jean Camp and Y. T. Chien, "The Internet as Public Space: Concepts, Issues, in Public Policy," *ACM SIGCAS Computers and Society Newsletter* 30, no. 3 (Janu- ary 2000).

5   Rhee et al., "Increasing Trauma Deaths in the United States."

6   The 2015 numbers come from German Lopez and Sarah Frostenson, "How the

Opioid Epidemic Became the Worst Drug Crisis Ever," Vox, March 29, 2017, http://www.vox.com/science-and-health/2017/3/23/14987892/opioid-heroin -epidemic-charts. Also see Centers for Disease Control and Prevention, "Ten Leading Causes of Injury Deaths by Age Group," accessed September 2016 at http://www.cdc.gov/injury/images/lc-charts/leading_causes_of_injury_deat hs_violence_2014_1040w760h.gif.

7   Viviana Zelizer, *Pricing the Priceless Child: The Changing Social Value of Children* (Princeton, NJ: Princeton University Press, 1994).

8   Julie Alev Dilmac, "The New Forms of Mourning: Loss and the Exhibition of Death on the Internet," *OMEGA* (2016): 3.

9   Holly Everett, *Roadside Crosses in Contemporary Memorial Culture* (Denton: University of North Texas, 2002); and Jonathan Lohman, "A Memorial Wall in Philadelphia," in J. Santino, ed., *Spontaneous Shrines and the Public Memorialization of Death* (New York: Palgrave Macmillan, 2006), 177–214.

10   Tony Walter, "The Mourning After Hillsborough," *Sociological Review* 39, no. 3 (1991): 599–625.

11   For multiple examples of how newspapers use such photographs, visit a page that shows examples from the *Los Angeles Times* at http://www.gettyimages .com/photos/los-angeles-times-makeshift-memorials?excludenudity=true& family=editorial&page=4&phrase=los%20angeles%20times%20makeshift% 20memorials&sort=best#license.

12   Jane Gross, "Seeking Solace with Final Gestures," *New York Times*, July 25, 1999, WK3.

13   Sarah Coombs, "Death Wears a T-Shirt—Listening to Young Talk About Death," *Mortality* 19, no. 3 (2014): 299.

14   Gross, "Seeking Solace with Final Gestures."

15   Jennifer Mena, "Store Opens Doors to Grief," *Los Angeles Times*, July 2, 2003, B6, photograph on B1; Alessandra Stanley, "In Slain Girl's Hometown, an Invisible Fear Lurks," *New York Times*, July 19, 2002, A1, A14; Dan Barry and Paul von Zielbauer, "Day of Public Grieving and Private Inquiry in Deadly Nightclub Fire," *New York Times*, February 24, 2003, A14; and Diane Puchin, "Too Many Are Unaware, Too Many Don't Care," *Los Angeles Times*, February 20, 2003, D1.

16   A contemporary discussion of Greek shrines is available at http://gogreece .about.com/library/weekly/aa011501a.htm.

17   Alberto Barrera, "Mexican-American Crosses in Starr County," in Joe S. Graham, ed., *Hecho en Tejas* (Denton: University of North Texas Press, 1991), 278– 92; Everett, *Roadside Crosses*, 38–80.

18   Robert Frank, *The Americans* (New York: Steidl, 1959), "Crosses on Scene of Highway Accident, U.S. 91, Idaho."

19   Kenneth E. Foote, *Shadowed Ground: America's Landscape of Violence and Tragedy* (Austin: University of Texas Press, 1997), 170.

20   Jennifer Clark and Majella Franzmann, "Authority from Grief, Presence and Place in the Making of Roadside Memorials," *Death Studies* 30 (2006): 579–99.

21   Dean Olsen, "Roadside Memorials Gain Popularity," *Peoria Journal Star* (September 10, 1998), emphasis added.

22   Everett, *Roadside Crosses*, 93.

23 Lohman, "A Memorial Wall in Philadelphia," 197.

24 Ibid., 199.

25 Ibid., 199–203; the quote below is from 201.

26 Carla J. Soka, Illene Noppe Cupit, and Kathleen R. Gilbert, "Thanatechnology as a Conduit for Living, Dying, and Grieving in Contemporary Society," in their edited volume *Dying, Death, and Grief in an Online Universe* (New York: Springer Publishing Company, 2012), 3.

27 Cendra Lynn and Antje Rath, "GriefNet: Creating and Maintaining an Internet Bereavement Community," in Sofka, Cupit, and Gilbert, *Dying Death, and Grief*, 87–102. Elizabeth Drescher, "Pixels Perpetual Shine: The Mediation of Illness, Dying, and Death in the Digital Age," *Crosscurrents* (2012): 204–18.

28 Brandwatch, "47 Facebook Statistics for 2016," accessed at https://www.brand watch.com/blog/47-facebook-statistics-2016/.

29 Max Kelly's comments were posted by Kathy H. Chan, "Memories of Friends Departed Endure on Facebook," October 28, 2009, https://www.facebook.com /notes/facebook/memories-of-friends-departed-endure-on-facebook/163091 042130.

30 Brandon Ambrosino, "Facebook Is a Growing and Unstoppable Digital Graveyard," BBC (March 14, 2016), http://www.bbc.com/future/story/20160313-the -unstoppable-rise-of-the-facebook-dead.

31 Rebecca Kern, Abbe E. Forman, and Gisela Gil-Egui, "R.I.P. Remain in Perpetuity. Facebook Memorial Pages," *Telematics and Informatics* 30 (2013): 2–10.

32 Ibid., 9.

33 Jaleed Kaleem, "Death on Facebook Now Common as 'Dead Profiles' Create Vast Virtual Cemetery," *Huffington Post,* January 16, 2012, accessed at http:// www.huffingtonpost.com/2012/12/07/death-facebook-dead-profiles_n_22453 97.html.

34 Kimberly Hieftje, "The Role of Social Networking Sites in Memorialization of College Students," in Sofka, Cupit, and Gilbert, *Dying Death, and Grief*; quotes are on 38–39.

35 Warren St. John, "Web Sites Set Up to Celebrate Life Recall Lives Lost," *New York Times,* April 27, 2006, A1, A19; the quote that follows is on A19.

36 Irene Stengs, "Public Practices of Commemorative Mourning: Ritualized Space. Politicized Space, Mediated Space (Three Cases from the Netherlands)," in P. Post and A. L. Molendijk, eds., *Holy Ground: Reinventing Ritual Space in Modern Western Culture* (Leuven: Peeters, 2010), 119–43.

37 Lohman, "A Memorial Wall in Philadelphia," 194.

38 Anonymous, A Rish Family, "Memorial Decals," August 5, 2009.

39 MVP, The Chronicle of the Horse, "Memorial Stickers on Cars," September 2, 2013.

40 Claudia Rankine, "The Condition of Black Life Is One of Mourning," *New York Times Magazine,* June 22, 2015), accessed at https://www.nytimes.com/2015/06 /22/magazine/the-condition-of-black-life-is-one-of-mourning.html?_r=0.

41 The quotes were gathered at the *Hinterland Gazette* website for a story, "Freddie Gray Memorial Mural Spawns Twitter Hate," at http://hinterlandgazette.com /2015/05/freddie-gray-memorial-mural-baltimore.html.

42 Jason Gay, "Five Bicycles in Kalamazoo," *Wall Street Journal,* June 14, 2016,

accessed September 17, 2016, at http://www.wsj.com/articles/five-bicycles-in
-kalamazoo-1465945453.

43 Foote, *Shadowed Ground*, 171. See also George E. Dickinson and Health C.
Hoffman, "Roadside Memorial Policies in the United States," *Mortality* 15,
no. 2 (2010): 154–67.

44 A few scholars have examined the dangers associated with roadside shrines,
and generally have found no relation between shrines and distracted drivers.
Examining the effect of a roadside shrine at an intersection, Richard Tay found
that "the number of red light violations was reduced by 16.7% in the 6 weeks
after" installation, while two comparable sites "experienced an increase of
16.8%." His research, however, also has found that roadside shrines, which
some proponents view as enhancing safety, had no positive effect either. Richard Tay, "Drivers' Perceptions and Reactions to Roadside Memorials," *Accident Analysis and Prevention* 41 (2009): 663–69; Richard Tay, A. Churchill,
and A. G. de Barros, "Effects of Roadside Memorials on Traffic Flow," *Accident
Analysis and Prevention* 43 (2011): 483–86.

45 Jennifer Clark and Majella Franzmann, "Authority from Grief, Presence and
Place in the Making of Roadside Memorials," *Death Studies* 30 (2006): 579–99.

46 "Bicycles Chained to Public Property," website of the New York City government, http://www1.nyc.gov/nyc-resources/service/1191/bicycle-chained-to
-public-property.

47 Kern, Forman, and Gil-Agui, "R.I.P.," 10.

48 Pin Sym Foong and Denisa Kera, "Applying Reflective Design to Digital
Memorials," International Workshop on Social Interaction and Mundane
Technologies 2008, http://mundanetechnologies.com/goings-on/workshop
/cambridge/papers/FoongKera.pdf, accessed July 18, 2010.

49 Adrian Chen, "Why People Troll Dead Kids on Facebook," Gawker, December 15, 2011, http://gawker.com/5868503/why-people-troll-dead-kids-on-face
book.

50 Whitney Phillips, "LOLing at Tragedy: Facebook Trolls, Memorial Pages, and
Resistance to Grief Online," *First Monday* 16, no. 12 (2011), http://journals.uic
.edu/ojs/index.php/fm/article/view/3168/3115.

51 Chronicle of the Horse, "Memorial Stickers on Cars," September 2, 2013,
http://www.chronofhorse.com/forum/showthread.php?414175-Memorial
-stickers-on-cars&s=322da394d081b23b47708a3ab3467610.

Chapter Six

1 Cemetery friends' organizations are understudied; the material for this discussion comes mainly from ephemeral material gathered at cemeteries and
websites. On Laurel Hill, see https://thelaurelhillcemetery.org/.

2 For further information on the organization, and their events, see Laurel Hill
Cemetery at https://thelaurelhillcemetery.org/about/mission.

3 For information on the Friends of Grove Street Cemetery, see http://www
.grovestreetcemetery.org/grove_street_cemetery_bulletin_newsletter.htm.

4 For example, see the friends' organization's activities at Mount Auburn Cemetery, http://mountauburn.org/the-friends-of-mount-auburn-cemetery/.

5   The group's home website is at http://www.gravestonestudies.org/.

6   Benjamin Weiser, "Expert Charged in Sale of Tiffany Glass Stolen from Tomb,"
      New York Times, May 19, 1999, http://www.nytimes.com/1999/05/19/nyregion
      /expert-charged-in-sale-of-tiffany-glass-stolen-from-tomb.html, accessed
      June 22, 2010.

7   Joshua Berlinger and Rob Frehse, "Jewish Cemetery Vandalized in New York,
      Third Case in Recent Weeks," *CNN*, March 3, 2017, http://www.cnn.com/2017
      /03/03/us/jewish-cemetery-vandalized-headstones-new-york/.

8   *Syracuse Post-Standard*, September 2, 1961; in "News and Clippings, 1960s–
      2000s, Shades of Oakwood," at http://www.shadesofoakwood.com/pages
      /newsclip/clip1960-00.html, accessed November 12, 2010.

9   David Eck, "Two Teen Boys Arrested in Cemetery Vandalism," *Cincinnati En-
      quirer*, July 17, 2002, http://www.enquirer.com/editions/2002/07/17/loc_two
      _teen_boys.html, accessed August 4, 2010.

10   Minda Powers-Douglas, *Cemetery Walk: A Journey into the Art, History and
      Society of the Cemetery and Beyond* (Bloomington, IN: AuthorHouse, 2005),
      236.

11   Jane Jacobs, *Death and Life of Great American Cities* (New York: Vintage, 1961),
      109.

12   Information on Oakland Cemetery is available at http://www.oaklandcemetery
      .com/.

13   Richard E. Meyer, "Images of Logging Contemporary Pacific Northwest
      Gravemarkers," in R. E. Meyer, ed., *Cemeteries and Gravemarkers* (Logan:
      Utah State University Press, 1992), 3.

14   "Cherubs & Angels of Mount Auburn," January 22, 2017, http://mountauburn
      .org/2017/cherubs-angels-of-mount-auburn-6/.

15   The tours are described in Woodlawn Conservancy, *Fall at Woodlawn*, 2015,
      accessed at https://issuu.com/woodlawnconservancy/docs/wc_fall15_issuu.

16   A brief description of the event is posted on Facebook at https://www.face
      book.com/events/417178545013538/.

17   Jessica Inman, "Looking for a Fright on Halloween? Don't Go On a Cemetery
      Tour," October 27, 2015, http://www.orlandosentinel.com/business/tourism
      /os-cemetery-tours-not-meant-to-spook-20151022-story.html.

18   For information on the Mount Hope tour, see http://www.fomh.org/Events
      /SpecialTours/.

19   Bachelor, *Sorrow & Solace*, 2.

20   Joseph Wood, "Vietnamese American Place Making in Northern Virginia,"
      Geographical Review 87, no. 1 (January 1997): 63–64.

21   Barbara Rubin, Robert Carlton, and Arnold Rubin, *Forest Lawn* (Santa
      Monica, CA: Westside Publications, 1979).

22   Frederick Law Olmsted, "Public Parks and the Enlargement of Towns," in
      Charles E. Beveridge and Carolyn F. Hoffman, eds., *The Papers of Frederick
      Law Olmsted: Writings on Public Parks, Parkways, and Park Systems, Supple-
      mentary Series Volume 1* (Baltimore: Johns Hopkins University Press, 1997),
      185.

23   The run is described at http://www.active.com/atlanta-ga/running/distance
      -running-races/run-like-hell-5k-run-like-heck-1k-2016.

24   The comments that follow were written within the stream at Reddit started

by a question about the appropriateness of running in a cemetery, at https://www.reddit.com/r/running/comments/24abb2/is_it_disrespectful_to_run_through_a_cemetery/.

25   Tanja M. Laden, "'Revolutions 2' at Forest Lawn Celebrates Classic Music Industry Art," *LA Weekly,* March 3, 2015, http://www.laweekly.com/music/revolutions-2-at-forest-lawn-museum-celebrates-classic-music-industry-art-5413161.

26   Alison Meier, "An Installation Weaves Through a Brooklyn Cemetery Chapel," *Hypoallergenic,* October 12, 2016, at http://hyperallergic.com/329294/aaron-asis-installation-greenwood-cemetery/.

27   Dani Katz, "Hollywood Forever Movies Sell Out Every Weekend Because Douches Don't Go," *LA Weekly,* July 25, 2005, accessed at http://www.laweekly.com/arts/hollywood-forever-cemetery-movies-sell-out-every-weekend-because-douches-dont-go-video-5800562.

28   The film and band names come from the Cinespia website at http://cinespia.org/, while the date of construction comes from Pauline O'Connor, "7 of LA's Most Magnificent Examples of Masonic Architecture" (2014), on Curbed LA, http://la.curbed.com/archives/2014/10/7_of_las_most_magnificent_examples_of_masonic_architecture.php.

29   Ron Russell, "The *Cemetary* [sic] Kid," New Times Los Angeles (2000), http://www.hollywood-underground.com/hfarticle1.htm.

30   On Forever Lifestories, see http://www.hollywoodforever.com/stories.

31   Sarah A. Webster, "Funeral Software Brings Startup to Life: FuneralOne Founder, Creator of Several Sites, Revolutionized Industry with Video Tributes," *Chicago Tribune,* September 15, 2008.

32   Find a Grave is available at https://www.findagrave.com/; Legacy is available at http://www.legacy.com/.

33   Mount Calvary Cemetery, "Grief Support," http://www.mountcalvarycemetery.com/_mgxroot/page_10837.php.

Chapter Seven

1   Perianne Boring, "Death of the Death Care Industry and Eternal Life Online," *Forbes,* April 25, 2014, https://www.forbes.com/sites/perianneboring/2014/04/25/the-death-of-the-death-care-industry-and-eternal-life-online/#419f54e41c1a.

2   Lewis Mumford, *The Culture of Cities* (New York: Harcourt, Brace, and Company, 1938), 438. Also see Andrew Shanken, "Planning Memory: Living Memorials in the United States during World War II," *Art Bulletin* 84, no. 1 (2002): 130–47.

3   James E. Young, "The Counter-Monument: Memory Against Itself in Germany Today," *Critical Inquiry* 18, no. 2 (1992): 267–96.

4   Richard F. Veit and Mark Nonestied, *New Jersey Cemeteries and Tombstones: History in the Landscape* (New Brunswick, NJ: Rivergate Books, an imprint of Rutgers University Press, 2008), 40.

5   Ernest L. Abel, "Changes in Gender Discrimination after Death: Evidence from a Cemetery," *Omega* 58, no. 2 (2008–2009): 150.

6   Bob Drinkwater, "Marble for the Multitudes: Industrialization of the Monu-

ment Trade in Western New England, c. 1790–1850," *Markers* 30 (2002): 116–41.

7   Richard O. Reisem, "The Forest, The Lawn, and The Creatures That Live There," in Reisem, ed., *Forest Lawn Cemetery: Buffalo History Preserve* (Buffalo: Forest Lawn Heritage Foundation, 1996), 106; and Douglas Keister, *Stories in Stone: A Field Guide to Cemetery Symbolism and Iconography* (Layton, UT: Gibbs Smith Publishes, 2004), 244–47.

8   See the Cemetery Club, "Gravestone Symbolism," for a complete list of symbols, at http://www.thecemeteryclub.com/symbols.html.

9   Paul J. Hamill, "Living and Dying in History: Death in *The Education of Henry Adams*," *Soundings* 60, no. 2 (Summer 1977): 153.

10   Henry Adams, *The Education of Henry Adams* (30), chapter 21 ("Twenty Years After").

11   Cynthia Mills, "The 'Adams Memorial' and Its Doubles," *American Art* 14/2 (2000): 5–6.

12   Keister, *Stories in Stone*, 248–29.

13   Information gathered from the Shades of Oakwood, "History of Oakwood," http://www.shadesofoakwood.com/pages/oakhistory.html.

14   Keister's quote can be found at "Cornelius Smith Mausoleum," Mausoleum .com, accessed at http://www.mausoleums.com/portfolio/cornelius-smith -mausoleum/.

15   Mausoleums are discussed in Edward Bergman, *Woodlawn Remembers: Cemetery of American History* (Utica, NY, 1989); John Vinci, "Graceland: The Nineteenth-Century Garden Cemetery," *Chicago History* 6, no. 2 (1977): 86–98; and Keister, *Going Out in Style*.

16   Dorothy J. Smith, "Taking Care of Business: Canadian Community Mausoleums and the Commercialization of Death, 1912–1936," *Markers* 31 (2015): 31–51.

17   Report of the Committee on Community Mausoleums, American Cemetery Superintendents, *Cemetery Handbook*, 396–97.

18   Committee for the Annual Conference, *Park and Cemetery and Landscape Gardening* 18, no. 5 (1908): 370.

19   Presbrey-Leland, *Commemoriation: The Book of Presbrey-Leland Memorials* (no publishing information, ca. 1950). The list of "celebrities" is on xvi–xix, Zerbau on 59, Kirnan on 56, and the crosses on 62–77.

20   Ibid., 111.

21   Ken Worpole, *Last Landscapes: The Architecture of the Cemetery in the West* (London: Reaktion Books, 2003), 104.

22   Please see the chapter "The Ideal Cemetery: The Memorial Park," in my *The Last Great Necessity*, 159–90.

23   Masonic Service Association of North America, "Masonic Membership Statistics, 2014," http://www.msana.com/msastats.asp.

Chapter Eight

1   Lewis Mumford, *The Culture of Cities* (New York: Harcourt, Brace, and Company, 1938), 438; and Ericka Doss, *Memorial Mania: Public Feeling in America* (Chicago: University of Chicago Press, 2010).

2   Martha Cooper and Joseph Sciorra, *R.I.P. Memorial Wall Art* (New York: Henry Holt and Company, 1994), 32.

3   Colin Waki, "Our Friend Zach," on his blog Dresearch Photography, http://www.colinwaki.com/?p=1130.

4   "Carlos Rivera Rosas," http://ghostbikes.org/culiac%C3%A1n/carlos-rivera-rosas.

5   Allison Engel, "In the Rear Window, Tributes to the Dead," *New York Times*, December 11, 2005, http://www.nytimes.com/2005/12/11/fashion/sundaystyles/in-the-rear-window-tributes-to-the-dead.html.

6   Robert Andres Powell, "Fitting Tribute: As the Murder Rate in Miami's Liberty City Climbs, Memorial T-Shirts — Part Tombstone, Part Fashion Statement — Proliferate," *Mother Jones* (May–June 2007), accessed September 20, 2016, at http://go.galegroup.com.libproxy1.usc.edu/ps/i.do?p=AONE&u=usocal_main&id=GALE|A162789851&v=2.1&it=r&sid=summon&userGroup=usocal_main; and Sonja Sharp, "Remembering the Dead with T-Shirt Memorials: T-Shirt Tributes Have Become a Mainstay of Wakes and Funerals, and Demand for Them Rises in the Warmer Months," *Wall Street Journal* (August 17, 2015), accessed September 20, 2016, at http://search.proquest.com.libproxy1.usc.edu/docview/1704276989?pq-origsite=summon&accountid=14749.

7   Tim Hutchings, "Wiring Death: Dying, Remembering and Grieving on the Internet," in Douglas J. Davies, ed., *Emotion, Identity and Death: Mortality across Disciplines* (Farnham, UK: Ashgate, 2012), 51; quoted in Martin Gibbs, James Meese, Michael Arnold, Bjorn Nansen, and Marcus Carter, "#Funeral and Instagram: Death, Social Media, and Platform Vernacular," *Information, Communication & Society* 18, no. 3 (2015): 256.

8   Rebecca Kennerly, "Getting Messy: In the Field and at the Crossroads with Roadside Shrines," *Text and Performance Quarterly* 22, no. 4 (2002): 243.

9   Barrera, "Mexican-American Roadside Crosses in Starr County," 279; quoted in Kennerly, "Getting Messy," 243.

10   For a brief description of the fire, see Kristin McCleary, "Inflaming the Fears of Theatergoers: How Fires Shape the Public Sphere in Buenos Aires, 1880–1910," in Greg Bankoff, Uwe Lübken, and Jordan Sand, eds., *Flammable Cities: Urban Conflagration and the Making of the Modern World* (Madison: University of Wisconsin Press, 2012), 254–72.

11   Christine Hanley and Greg Krikorian, "FBI Says Slain Girl's Abductor Sent Message: 'Come Find Me,'" *Los Angeles Times,* July 18, 2002, 1, 26, with photographs of the shrine table by Mark Boster.

12   Peter Barry, "R.I.P. Baltimore," located on the "Social Documentary" site, at http://socialdocumentary.net/exhibit/Peter_Barry/301.

13   Cooper and Sciorra, *R.I.P. Memorial Wall Art*, 23, 25, 27, 28, and 30–31.

14   Susan A. Samuel, "An Examination of the Psychological Role of Tattoos in Mourning," doctoral thesis, Chicago School of Professional Psychology (2009), 2.

15   Ibid., 18–20.

16   Shannon M. Bates, "Embodying the Soul's Pain: A Study of Memorial Tattoos and the Grieving Process," master's thesis, Institute for Interpersonal Psychology (2009), 1.

17   Ben Bolch, "Spurs Kawhi Leonard has Prevailed in Tough Times," *Los Angeles Times,* June 12, 2014, C7.

18   Emily Talen, "Do-It-Yourself Urbanism," *Journal of Planning History* 14, no. 2 (2015): 135–48.

19   Steve Lopez, "Uptick in Bicyclist Deaths Keeps Ghost Bike Volunteers Busy," *Los Angeles Times,* February 22, 2014, http://articles.latimes.com/2014/feb/22 /local/la-me-0223-lopez-ghost-20140223.

20   Pamela Roberts, "The Living and the Dead: Community in the Virtual Cemetery," *Omega* 49, no. 1 (2001): 57–76; and Christopher Moreman, ed., *Digital Death: Mortality and Beyond in the Online Age* (New York: Praeger, 2014).

21   Steve Zeitlin, "Oh Did You See the Ashes Come Thickly Falling Down? Poems Posted in the Wake of September 11," in Jack Santino, ed., *Spontaneous Shrines and the Public Memorialization of Death* (New York: Palgrave Macmillan, 2006), 106.

22   "Student Mourned," *Los Angeles Times,* July 15, 2014, AA4. The photograph is by Jabin Botsford.

23   "This Week in Pictures," *Los Angeles Times,* September 30–October 6, 2013, http://framework.latimes.com/2013/10/04/the-week-in-pictures-151/#/1.

24   I searched Getty Images for "Los Angeles Times Makeshift Memorials" at http://www.gettyimages.com/photos/los-angeles-times-makeshift-memorials ?excludenudity=true&family=editorial&page=4&phrase=los%20angeles%20 times%20makeshift%20memorials&sort=best#license.

Chapter Nine

1   David Charles Sloane, *The Last Great Necessity: Cemeteries in American History* (Baltimore: Johns Hopkins University Press, 1991), 77–78.

2   Albert H. Hamscher, "Pictorial Headstones: Business, Culture, and the Expression of Individuality in the Contemporary Cemetery," *Markers* 23 (2006): 9.

3   For one of the earliest discussions of such pictorial monuments, see Richard E. Meyer, "Images of Logging Contemporary Pacific Northwest Gravemarkers," in R. E. Meyer, ed., *Cemeteries and Gravemarkers* (Logan: Utah State University Press, 1992), 61–86.

4   Sarah Maslin Nir, "Slave Forgotten Burial Sites, Marked Online," *New York Times,* March 18, 2013, http://cityroom.blogs.nytimes.com/2013/03/18/a-mis sion-to-find-and-preserve-forgotten-slave-graveyards/?_r=0.

5   Hamscher, "Pictorial Headstones," 13–18.

6   Allison Meier, "A Guide to the 19th Century Artists Graves of New York City," Hyperallergic, June 25, 2015, http://hyperallergic.com/208363/a-guide-to-the -19th-century-artist-graves-of-new-york-city/.

7   Paul Revere Williams Project, "Second Baptist Church, Los Angeles," http:// www.paulrwilliamsproject.org/gallery/1920s-churches/.

8   The Cochran's Inc. material comes from a personal interview conducted by the author, July 2005, and their website, https://www.cochrans-monuments .com/. Also see Hamscher, "Pictorial Headstones," 6–35; C. D. Abby Collier, "Tradition, Modernity, and Postmodernism in Symbolism of Death," *Sociological Quarterly* 44 (2003): 727–49; Rollo K. Newson, "Motorcycles and Major-

ettes: Grave Markers for Youth in Central Texas," in Francis Edward Abernathy, ed., *Corners of Texas* (Denton, TX, 1993), 246–66; and Meyer, "Images of Logging on Contemporary Pacific Northwest Gravemarkers," 61–85.

9   Examples of laser-etched monuments can be found in Lucinda Bunnen and Virginia Warren Smith, *Scoring in Heaven: Gravestones and Cemetery Art of the American Sunbelt States* (New York: An Aperture Book, 1991).

10   Ibid.

11   Lee Jansen, "Retailor Roundup: Popular Symbols Range from Classic Crosses and Roses to Golf Carts and Log Cabins," *Stone in America* 115, no. 5 (2002): 35.

12   Connie Evener, "Etching: Symphonies in Stone," *Stone in America* 116, no. 3 (2003): 9.

13   Ibid.

14   Ibid.

15   The jazz corner is described on Woodlawn's website. David Gonzalez, "Keeping the Flame Burning for a Beloved Queen of Salsa," *New York Times*, October 26, 2009, http://www.nytimes.com/2009/10/27/nyregion/27cruz.html.

16   Green-Wood Cemetery Tranquility Gardens and Chapel/Crematorium, Archtober, October 29, 2014, http://www.archtober.org/2014/building/green-wood -cemetery-tranquility-gardens-and-chapel-crematorium/.

17   Jan Garden Castro, "Making the Personal Monumental: A Conversation with Patricia Cronin," *Sculpture* 22, no. 1 (2003), http://www.sculpture.org/docu ments/scmag03/janfeb03/cronin/cronin.shtml, accessed July 15, 2010.

18   On the Congressional Cemetery's history, see Abby Arthur Johnson and Ronald Maberry Johnson, *In the Shadow of the United States Capitol: Congressional Cemetery and the Memory of the Nation* (Washington, DC: New Academia Publishing, 2012).

19   The Matlovich story is briefly told in Francine D'Amico, "Sex/uality and Military Service," in Craig A. Rimmerman, Kenneth D. Wald, and Clyde Wilcox, eds., *The Politics of Gay Rights* (Chicago: University of Chicago Press, 2000), 251.

20   The stone is visible on many websites, but the Leonard Matlovich website has a nice description at http://www.leonardmatlovich.com/home.html.

21   Pablo Maurer, "At Congressional Cemetery, A Solemn Tribute to Gay Servicemen," http://dcist.com/2012/08/congressional_cemetery_piece.php. The national memorial is discussed at http://www.nlgbtvm.org/Home_Page.html.

22   The QR panel is shown at the Leonard Matlovich website, at http://www .leonardmatlovich.com/storyofhisstone.html.

Epilogue

1   Martina Bellisario and Donato Paolo Mancini, "Wall of Love Commemorates Paris Attacks," *New York Times*, February 11, 2016, http://www.nytimes.com /interactive/2016/02/11/arts/design/paris-wall-of-love.html?ref=arts.

2   Ibid.

3   Bauman, *Morality*, 147–52.

4   "Rachel Joy Scott," http://racheljoyscott.tumblr.com/.

5   The quotes below, and a further description of their work, are available at http://www.deathlab.org/.

6   On the concept of dark tourism, and its relationship to cemeteries and commemoration, see Philip R. Stone, "A Dark Tourism Spectrum: Toward a Typology of Death and Macabre Tourist Sites, Attractions, and Exhibitions," *Tourism* 54, no. 2 (2006): 145–60.

7   West, *A Guide to Natural Burial*, 132.

8   For more information, please go to http://www.elmwoodhistoriccemetery .org/.

INDEX